D0231028

The Riddles of Wipers

An Appreciation of *The Wipers Times*,
A Journal of the Trenches

John Ivelaw-Chapman

Pen & Sword
MILITARY

First published in Great Britain in 1997 by Leo Cooper
Reprinted by Pen & Sword Military in 2005

Published in this format in 2010 by

Pen & Sword Military
an imprint of
Pen & Sword Books Ltd
47 Church Street
Barnsley
South Yorkshire
S70 2AS

Copyright © John Ivelaw-Chapman 2010

ISBN 978-1-84884-191-8

The right of John Ivelaw-Chapman to be identified as Author of this Work
has been asserted by him in accordance with the Copyright, Designs and
Patents Act 1988.

A CIP catalogue record for this book is available from the British Library.

All rights reserved. No part of this book may be reproduced or
transmitted in any form or by any means, electronic or mechanical
including photocopying, recording or by any information storage and
retrieval system, without permission from the Publisher in writing.

Typeset in 11.5pt Ehrhardt by
Mac Style, Beverley, E. Yorkshire

Printed and bound in the UK by CPI

Pen & Sword Books Ltd incorporates the imprints of Pen & Sword
Aviation, Pen & Sword Maritime, Pen & Sword Military, Wharncliffe
Local History, Pen and Sword Select, Pen and Sword Military Classics and
Leo Cooper.

For a complete list of Pen & Sword titles please contact
PEN & SWORD BOOKS LIMITED
47 Church Street, Barnsley, South Yorkshire, S70 2AS, England
E-mail: enquiries@pen-and-sword.co.uk
Website: www.pen-and-sword.co.uk

LIBRARIES NI	
C700264288	
RONDO	25/02/2010
070.4499404144	£ 9.20
BESSBR	

Contents

Dedication

Their average life expectancy on the Western Front was six weeks; they had little military training and less experience. They were unquestionably loyal and unthinkingly gallant and they laughed in the face of the most appalling circumstances. Without their wit and wisdom there would have been no *Wipers Times* and probably no victory. It is to the British Infantry Subalterns of the Great War that this book is respectfully dedicated.

Acknowledgements

I am indebted to the following people for their assistance in writing *The Riddles of Wipers:*

John Terraine for his Foreword.

My sister Adrianne for enthusiasm and the loan of books.

Patrick Beaver for permission to use some of his diligent research into the *Wipers Times.*

Tonie and Valmai Holt for permission to reproduce items from their book

The Best of 'Fragments from France'.

Jack and John Disbrey of Aston Clinton who know most of what there is to know about the battles of the Western Front

Nico and Brian, two understanding and respectful archaeologists of The Salient who provided, free of charge, photographs of the excavation of the Hellfire Corner dugout.

Tim d'Arch-Smith for permission to quote from Gilbert Frankau and for the loan of a priceless original *New Church Times.*

The Imperial War Museum.

Toc H, Wendover and Poperinghe.

'Black Dog' for careful correction and wise counsel.

Frank for enthusiasm and Friday afternoons.

My wife Julie for understanding and support.

Foreword

John Terraine

'If I should die' wrote Rupert Brooke in 1914 'think only this of me,
There is some corner of a foreign field
That is forever England.'

If, by 'England', the poet is permitted to mean all those who came 'from
the uttermost ends of the earth' in the ranks of the British Empire's
mass recruitment, then that 'corner of a foreign field' has to be the Ypres
Salient. Seen from above, the British war cemeteries are sprinkled over the
Salient like bridal confetti. It contains the largest of them all – Tyne Cot,
with 11,871 graves and 34,000 names of men 'missing' with no known grave,
inscribed on marble panels at the back. A quarter of a million British dead
lie in the Ypres Salient.

But Rupert Brooke knew nothing of them. He never even saw the Salient
or the ruined spires of Ypres. His whole brief war, his long-cherished dream
('all my life I have wanted to go on a military expedition to Constantinople')
was spent in the Middle East, and he died early in 1915, on a Greek island,
of blood poisoning.

Those who did experience the Salient in its terrible glory found it hard to
forget – or forgive. Stretcher-bearer Frank Dunham made his first
acquaintance with it in the chill and darkness of a winter night in November
1916. Many years later he wrote its epitaph in the incomparable tight-lipped
language of that Army. When he and his comrades passed through the
dismal portals of the old Menin Gate, picking their way through the shell-
holes, the corpses and the wreckage of the Menin Road of evil repute, Frank
Dunham tells us:

'It didn't leave a good inpression'

It didn't leave one on Norman Gladden either; he was in the Salient in 1917 and he says,

'I was filled with an almost tangible expectancy of evil'.

My own first visit to Ypres and 'the corner of a foreign field' was not until 1958; the Flemish name, Ieper, was just beginning to assert its supremacy. French was still commonly spoken, and the town was still very much a reconstructed shrine. I learned the gradients of the almost imperceptible 'ridges' which supply the rim of the saucer with Ypres in the middle, on a bicycle. The new Menin Road, of course, bore no trace of shell-holes or corpses, and like many others I marvelled at the trim, prosperous-looking Belgian farms and green fields, looking quite innocent of any knowledge of war. Every time I returned to Ypres I had a sense of homecoming.

The Wipers Times, whose 'riddles' John Ivelaw-Chapman seeks to read, is an essential part of the shrine literature. His preoccupation with 'less researched aspects of the First World War', he tells us, 'stemmed originally from the extraordinary musical, 'Oh! What A Lovely War!'; the soldiers' own songs, featured in it suggest a running chorus in the same mood and speaking the same language as the contributors to *The Wipers Times*. Other inspirations for John Ivelaw-Chapman are Robert Graves, Gilbert Frankau and the indefatigable Wipers Times editor, Colonel FJ Roberts (Sherwood Foresters).

It would be Roberts who decided to print 'To My Chum' which John Ivelaw-Chapman calls 'one of the strongest poems from *The Wipers Times*. Two verses will serve well to conclude this foreword:

What times we've had, both good and bad,
We've shared what shelter could be had,
The same crump-hole when the whizz-bangs shrieked,
The same old billet that always leaked,
And now - you've 'stopped one'...

Well, old lad, here's peace to you,
And for me, well, there's my job to do,
For you and the others who lie at rest,
Assured may be that we'll do our best,
In vengeance.

It is an unfashionable sentiment, but the authentic voice of its generation. Ivelaw-Chapman is impressed by its 'unrelenting sadness' and asks 'Where is the Victory? Where is the Glory?' The Victory, of course, was the scarcely remembered Fourth Battle of Ypres (September 28-29, 1918). The Glory was the endurance, the devoted patience of the men who hung on in the Salient for four years until that glad day came. *The Wipers Times* shows us a good deal of how they did it.

John Terraine
November, 1996

Introduction

Wednesday 18th February, 1993; Hornsey Auctions, 7.30pm, Lot 122. We don't send out catalogues at Hornsey. The auctioneer's list is spewed out from a word processor and incorporates the usual unthinking errors; so when the young lad shouted, 'Showing here' and held up a battered blue volume entitled *The Wipers Times*, I had to decide in an instant if that indeed was the name of the book, or was Wipers a misprint for Whippers or Pipers? As auc-tioneer, I could hardly shout from the rostrum, 'Is there an apostrophe before the "s" ?' I was aware that the book might have some connection with the Belgian town of Ypres whose barely pronounce-able name British soldiers of the First World War bastardized to 'Wipers'; and if that was the case, I was interested.

My preoccupation with less-researched aspects of the First World War stemmed originally from the extraordinary musical, 'Oh What a Lovely War.' I recall the scene in which a party of newly arrived and untrained Irish soldiers are at one moment shouting their patriotic determina-tion to give the Boche a good hiding and at the next are blown to pieces by their own artillery. I remember the plaintive cry of the Sergeant as the friendly shells rain down; 'Stop, cease firing, we're on your side ...' but his cries are lost in the thunder of the guns. I remember the stern unsenti-mental women with white feathers cajoling mere boys to volunteer for the front, and I remember the songs, the wonderful, sad, witty songs with which the poor bloody infantry kept up their spirits and vented their cynical spleen.

'What do we want with eggs and ham, when we've got plum and apple jam?'

'One staff officer jumped right over the other staff officer's back.'

The burial chorus, 'The bells of hell go ding-a-ling-a-ling for you but not for me.'

And the madman's lullaby, 'Hush, here comes a whizz-bang.'

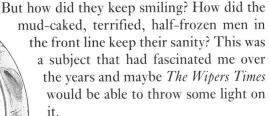

But how did they keep smiling? How did the mud-caked, terrified, half-frozen men in the front line keep their sanity? This was a subject that had fascinated me over the years and maybe *The Wipers Times* would be able to throw some light on it.

'Fifteen pounds then, thank you, Sir', I said in the same direction as the last bid was supposed to have come from, dropped the hammer and wrote down my own name in the buyer column. 'Lot 123 is next, the Magimix and the one-and-a-half-ton car jack …'

I knew I had struck gold when I paid my bill and took the first close look at the outside cover of my book. Beneath the title appeared the words 'A facsimile reprint of the trench magazine: the Wipers Times.' There was also a line-drawn cartoon of a languid junior officer dressed in military cap and tunic over plus fours and golfing shoes.

My interest in Trench Humour had already led me to the cartoons of Bruce Bairnsfather and I am a collector of the Grimwades china plates on which the famous drawings featuring Old Bill and his sprog sidekick Bert were faithfully reproduced;

We are at present staying at a farm;

Who made that 'ole?…Mice.

The book was made up of collected issues of The Wipers Times and its successors. The name of the paper changed as the production staff moved around the Western Front with the Pioneer Battalion who originally located the Press and produced the paper. It was printed in facsimile to make it appear like the original issues of the trench newspaper. Print and paper were poor quality and both were disintegrating fast. On leafing through the brown-edged pages for the first time I discovered that the work was almost completely anonymous apart from a regular series of poems credited to Gilbert Frankau and the signatures of Roberts and Pearson who appeared after the first editorial. I telephoned Timothy d'Arch-Smith, a school-friend with whom I shared the discomfiture of Cheltenham College in the early 1950s. He was a grandson of Frankau and I received by return of post a copy of 'Self Portrait', the poet's autobiography. My determination to unravel the riddles of Wipers can be explained by the following quotation from this book.

I – returning to the front – continued to write poetry for..... our divisional trench journal, *The Wipers Times*.

The origin of this peculiar sheet, which changed its title whenever we shifted to a new part of the line, had been the discovery by an enterprising Sherwood Forester, F.J. Roberts, who commanded the battalion and is still amongst my best friends, of an "old printing house just off the square at Wipers".

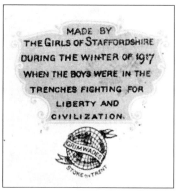

Reverse of Bairnsfather plate.

You can read the rest in his preface to the facsimile edition published by Herbert Jenkins in 1918 and beautifully printed on a copy of the original paper by William Brendon and Son, Ltd of Plymouth.

The 'advertisements' are still a joy to those of us who can solve their riddles …

It was not only the advertisements in *The Wipers Times* that contained riddles to be solved. There were articles and correspondence columns; racing tips, agony aunts, serials, prose and poetry, and through every page of uneven print ran a rich seam of humour, riddles, fantasy, wit and wisdom and everywhere the 'In Jokes' which only those initiated into the unrealistic existence of the front-line soldier actually serving in the Ypres Salient would appreciate.

When the first issue of *The Wipers Times* was distributed, the war had been in progress for about eighteen months and there were two years and nine months of fierce fighting to come before the Armistice. The huge battles of the Marne and Verdun had been fought, as had the Aisne and 'First Ypres'. Half of the Mons men, the BEF, the 'Contemptible Little Army' were already dead. The front lines were in stalemate. The General Staff were planning to break through at the Somme but this disastrous battle was still five months ahead. The first tanks were being built in England but had not yet been tried in action. Horses and mules played important roles right up to the front line and men struggled for survival in holes in the ground.

From some of the many books that have been written about the First World War, I gleaned as much factual information as I might one day require about the events that led up to the extraordinary military stalemate that was being fought out between two opposing armies around Ypres in 1916. I also learned that I was by no means the first writer to realize that facts alone could never portray the drama, the horror and the triumph of the human spirit that took place every day in the Salient. Ypres had been an obsession for others before me and the more I read the more I realized that I was embarking on research that would occupy my thoughts, probably for the rest of my life. Perhaps the fading pages of *The Wipers Times* would tell me more of daily life in the Salient than the factual print of the Ypres bibliography.

There was an interwoven thread of circumstance that ran through the fabric of my research into this extraordinary journal which was of interest in itself.

Let us start with Gilbert Frankau, grandfather of my school friend Timothy d'Arch-Smith, and regular contributor to *The Wipers Times*.

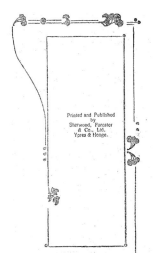

Gilbert Frankau was diagnosed as suffering from neurasthenia, or shellshock, as a result of war service at Ypres.

He was offered recuperation at the shellshock hospital at Craiglockhart by Lord Horder, who was the leading expert on these matters. Horder went on to become the Royal Physician and after the Second World War resided at Ashford Chase near Petersfield. He was a renowned horticulturist, as well as a distinguished doctor and located in his magnificent formal gardens at Steep was an open-air theatre. Here they put on Shakespeare plays every summer and for two years in the 1950s my sister and I were minor members of the company, the Steep Shakespeare Players. During the evenings we dined at Lord Horder's table. I remember him as a gruff, moustached gentleman who allowed us aspiring actors discreet access to his sherry decanter and attempted to educate our immature palates with fine wines. I recall being much amused by what seemed to be an eminent doctor's scorn for the modern way as demonstrated by an elegant oriental blue and white baluster jar that stood on his hall table. 'Leeches' was its simple label. Horder claimed to have often administered leeches in his medical career.

'I slapped a couple on George V,' he chortled, 'but they didn't do him much good.'

Lord Horder, Frankau and Scottish hospitals for neurasthenia led me to the First World War poets. Robert Graves and Siegfried Sassoon wrote verse while they were at Craiglockhart as did acerbic shell-shocked Wilfrid Owen. My sister, enthusiastic about my research into the Men of Wipers lent me two books: ' More songs by the Fighting men', an anthology of First World War verse, and 'Goodbye to All that' by Robert Graves. I had my own well-thumbed book of Wilfrid Owen.

The thread of coincidence ran on, for one of the fighting men whose poems were published in the anthology was Major Geoffrey Crump of the Essex Regiment. Geoffrey was stage director of the Steep Shakespeare Players who were gracious enough to include me as Third Soldier in Henry IV performed with much joy in the gardens of Lord Horder's mansion. At a post-production party Geoffrey Crump enthralled me and certainly contributed to my fascination with soldiers' poetry by reciting in the measured tones for which he was rightly renowned 'Today We Have Naming of Parts.' Robert Graves, although never in the Ypres Salient, was to my mind the best descriptive writer of the First World War and I devoured his book in a single sitting. To complete the circle of coincidence I would record that the present Lord Horder, who inherited the title when his father succumbed to a heart attack, sadly when the Players were in rehearsal for 'As You Like It', is a publisher and associate of Timothy d'Arch-Smith who, you will recall, is Gilbert Frankau's grandson.

Geoffrey Crump used to lecture on the Spoken Word and my next meeting with this, the most academic of 'The Soldier Poets,' came when I was attending a Royal Air Force course for junior staff officers. Geoffrey, an honoured visiting speaker, was stressing the inefficiency of strong language as a descriptive device and explaining how it soon lost its value as an emphatic.

'There were two uneducated working men sitting opposite each other in a train … (The sleepier members of the audience became alert as the master speaker launched into one of his justly renowned jokes.) One of them is reading, with difficulty, from a popular newspaper.

"Hey Bert," says the first, "What's this mean, 'One man one vote'?"

"Well," says the second after some deliberation, "It means, well, er, one fucking man, one fucking vote."

"Oh I see," says the first. (A pause, perfectly timed by Crump the Actor
   Poet) "Well why can't they fucking well say so?'"

The point was made and the joke, as always, well received, but at this
moment things went disastrously wrong. Among the sixty-strong male
audience in the lecture hall there was a lone woman; a WAAF Flying Officer
who in 1961 was boldly blazing the trail for the unisex Air Force. Geoffrey
Crump noticed her before the laughter died down. He blushed scarlet,
mumbled an apology to the lady and left the podium, never, I believe, to
return as lecturer to the Junior Command and Staff School, RAF Bircham
Newton. What a strange notion it now seems that it was in some way indecent
even accidentally to submit a lady to strong language; a sort of verbal 'Flash'.
But that notion was ingrained in Geoffrey Crump as it was in the other First
World War writers, including the correspondents of *The Wipers Times*.

For thirty years I have remembered Geoffrey Crump and his stories.
When I first met him, eye-witnesses of the First World War were
everywhere. Anyone interested could ask a man, fifty years of age or more,
'What was it like?' and, if the reticence of old soldiers could be successfully
overcome, some kind of an answer could be obtained. But now, when only a
dwindling number of grand nonagenarians survive to bring tears to our eyes
on Armistice Day, there is hardly anyone left to relive, for those who were
spared the horror, the magnificent, but infinitely tragic story of Ypres and
the First World War.

But *The Wipers Times* incorporated eyewitness reports on every page if
only an admiring student could solve the Riddles …

Members of the 16th Lancashire Fusiliers Old Comrades Association marching down
Chapel Street to attend Thiepval Day Service at Sacred Trinity Church 1932. An issue
of *The Wipers Times* was being prepared while these men fought at Thiepval.

Part One

What Was it Like?

Chapter 1

Trench Warfare

The *Wipers Times* was born of trench warfare. Without the relatively static, confrontational nature of the battlefield around the city of Ypres, editorial staff would not have had the time to compose and print the paper and distribution would have been impossible. There are a few articles and poems in *The Wipers Times* of a lyrical nature describing the unexpected beauty of some part of the battlefield or outlining the soldier's longing for home. On occasions we find correspondents denigrating the competence of the General Staff and those who were running the war; however, the lion's share of the paper, whether factual or in riddles, whether serious or cynical, seeking laughter or tears, is about the reality of trench warfare.

Warfare 1914-style was all about the occupation of territory. Germany had convinced herself that she should take over Europe and as a first step had

A communication trench in the Salient: possibly 'Grafton Street'. The dugout roof has been reinforced with railway lines.

To Grafton Street.

——: b:——

Now Hope lies buried, all that once
          could give
A satisfaction, or could soothe the eye,
With signs of work, which, being done,
          would help
Those others who with jar of rum did
          hasten
About their nightly duty in the line ;
And who with ease could lightly scuttle
          on
By duckboard or by traverse ; now un-
          :done
And by a cruel and unseemly fate
Are made to nightly journey on a road
Well set with pitfalls, crump holes, and
          their feet
Must hasten to their journey's end, or
          else
Some quick and hasty whizz-bang meet
          them full
Upon the jar and break it ; awful
          thought ;
For Grafton Street our fond and cherished
          child,
No mother ever saw with fonder eyes
Her offspring, than did we our traverses ,
Our fire-bays, height and end of our
          desires,
Our dug-outs roomy, gaze upon them
          now
And say with me our nightly hymn of
          hate ;
Oh ! Grafton Street in vision I have seen
A newer better namesake of thine own.
It's duckboard walk resounds with night-
          ly tread
Of hosts which shelter in their dug-outs
          sound
A dressing station which shall be replete
With every comfort human can devise.
Poor Hun in folly set, on folly bent,
To kick the pricks, of better knowing
          naught
Think ye that Grafton Street can signify
A ruin so complete as that to which
Your own must be ; the day now hastens
          on
And e'er the evening falls on men at
          peace
Your cries for mercy shall in truth arise,
And mercy thou shalt have when all is
          done
And Justice truth and peace shall reign
          alone.

simply sent her troops marching into Belgium and France. In 1914 invasions were supported by well-developed and accurate artillery, but of course there were no tanks and no air strikes. Initially the Germans marched on, flattening towns with their guns, driving out civilian refugees and occupying territory. They could only be stopped by an equally powerful army blocking their way. When the advance was finally halted in November, 1914, the occupation of land assumed a new meaning. At the beginning, the German Army was ordered to take over countries and continents, but gradually they were forced to reduce their ambitions; a town was taken here, a feature there, a canal crossed or a bridgehead occupied. No invading nation in the world could sustain the losses inflicted by the murderous efficiency of the machine gun and the disciplined small-arms fire of well-trained infantrymen. And when all momentum was lost, the soldiers of both sides simply dug themselves into the ground like animals. Holes became slits, then whole networks of trenches with dugouts and command posts, communication systems and gun emplacements and the opposing armies moved ten feet down into Mother Earth whose filthy absorbency gave them the only protection that there has ever been from the wholesale slaughter of machine guns.

Stalemate was reached and now the objective of each of the opposing armies was to maintain occupancy of their own trench systems and to force the enemy to abandon theirs.

'Grafton Street' was the nickname of a secure communication trench used for night resupply of such essentials of trench warfare as ammunition, fuel, food and the rum ration. The poet seems to have been involved in the construction of this trench which has now been destroyed. The whole area of the Ypres Salient was subject to murderously accurate sniper fire as well as observed artillery shelling from the surrounding hills. To travel eastwards from the city you came out at night; you moved wherever possible along

The only railway that ran towards Menin is visible on the left.

communication trenches and if you were ever above ground when a flare went up you dived for your life into the nearest hole, regardless of what you might find at the bottom.

An earlier poem, also about trench systems with London street names, is signed 'A Pioneer.' It contains the couplet, '*Here Foresters make nightly play, and in the mud hold revel high.*' The apocryphal publishers of *The Wipers Times* are given at the end of each issue as Sherwood and Forester which feebly disguises the name of the regiment in which the editor, Colonel

Hotel des Ramparts (Tradesman's Entrance).

Roberts, was serving. Thus, although we do not know his name, we can attribute 'To Grafton Street' to a Pioneer attached to the Sherwood Foresters who was in charge of men building trenches and dugouts in the Ypres Salient. He was probably a close friend of Roberts.

Could a soldier in the Ypres Salient in the Year 1916 compose a Shakespearean poem extolling the aesthetic appeal of a now-defunct communication trench and add a few words at the end offering sympathy and mercy to his enemy? Apparently our Pioneer friend could, and that is part of the magic of *The Wipers Times*.

'Wipers' of course was Ypres, and 'Menin' is a familiar name for anyone who has studied the First World War, but what of 'Fish-hook' and 'Gordon Farm Station'? And what was the joke hidden in this advertisement? There has never been a railway line connecting the two cities, but there was an infamous road and the front line between the British and German Armies straddled the Menin Road from 1915 to 1918. Upwards of 200,000 men were killed as the Germans struggled to take Ypres and the allies tried to push towards Menin.

So the notion of a day trip between these two points was just a light-hearted fantasy for men who needed a two-day artillery barrage and a huge build up of reinforcements if they were going to advance even fifty yards along the Menin

WIPERS FISH-HOOK & MENIN
RAILWAY.
— o —
DAILY EXCURSION TICKETS ARE
ISSUED TO

MENIN.

TRAINS WILL LEAVE DAILY AT 8 A.M. &
1 P.M., COMMENCING FEB 1ST, 1916.
FOR FURTHER PARTICULARS SEE SMALL
BILLS
————
Until further notice trains will not go beyond Gordon Farm Station, line beyond that closed for alterations.

UNDER ENTIRELY
NEW
MANAGEMENT.
——o——
HOTEL
DES RAMPARTS.
——o——
NO EXPENSE HAS BEEN
SPARED BY THE NEW
MANAGEMENT IN THE
RE-DECORATING AND
RE-FITTING OF THIS
FIRST-CLASS HOTEL
————
SPECIALLY RECOMMENDED
TO BUSINESS MEN.
————
New Electric   5 Private Lines.
Installation.   Tel Pioneers, Ypres.

Wipers Times. 12 February 1916.

Road. Fish-hook and Gordon Farm were well-known landmarks for the Pioneers and Suppliers who moved up after dark repairing dugouts and trenches and re-stringing the barbed wire entanglements.

'Line beyond Gordon Farm closed for alterations,' means 'Menin Road impassable at this location due to heavy shelling from both sides.' This piece of information should probably have been excised by the censor, but censoring of the written word was headquarters staff work and took place well behind the lines. Rear echelon men probably missed the subtleties of *The Wipers Times*, a fact that would have added to the pleasure of the slightly cynical readers of the paper in the dugouts and trenches around Ypres.

It has been suggested that the Railway advertisement was in fact an oblique reference to the light railway that was built by the British Army for supplying outposts of the Salient. This was of a narrow gauge and horses and mules were used to pull mine wagons along a line

The Communication Trench. Problem – whether to walk along the top and risk it, or do another mile of this.

located somewhat to the south of the Menin Road. This railway survived to the end of the war, but, as it never extended to Menin, we should think of the 'Excursions' offered in the advertisement as simply a product of the editor's unusual sense of humour.

The key to the Hotel des Ramparts advertisement lies in the telegraphic address, 'Pioneers Ypres.' The Royal Engineers were the scientific corps in the British Army. Armed with theodolites and slide rules, it was the Engineers who mined under the enemy walls and built bridges over rivers. The Pioneers were the bodging builders. They were the men, carpenters, farriers and simple handymen in civilian life who built camp sites and shored up trenches and above all, in the Salient, they made dugouts. And while they bodged up wonderful underground shelters for everyone else, human nature being what it is, we can be certain that the safest and most beautifully appointed dugout in Ypres would have been the residence of the Pioneers themselves.

In all editions of *The Wipers Times* and its successors there was a correspondence column based upon the London *Times* of the day. No one will be surprised to know that many of the letters in the Ypres variant

---:0:---
To the Editor.
Sir,—May I encroach on your valuable space to a small extent. We had a somewhat heated argument at Unity Villa the other night, and wish you to give us a ruling on the point. The question raised was, " Are the engineers better pioneers than the pioneers are engineers." The argument was continued at the neighbouring estaminet, but no definite conclusion was arrived at.—Thanking you in anticipation,

I am, yours faithfully,
ONE WHO HAS TRIPPED
AND FALLEN.

To the Editor,
" New Church " Times.
Sir,
May I encroach upon your valuable space to draw your attention to the fact that for some days now, the clock in the tower of the church at Wulverghem, has not received the amount of attention necessary to its good running.
This fact has caused many of the workers in our little village to miss their early morning trains to Messines.

I am, etc.,
" TEMPUS FUGIT "

concern when and by whom the first cuckoo was heard in the Salient. Most of the letters and indeed the replies were in fact written by the Editor, Colonel Roberts, and reflect his wry wit and his ability to make the paper read as though it was composed in the depths of peacetime England.

So, the Pioneers had the best dugout in town; of such permanence and security that envious infantrymen in trenches and converted shell holes in the Salient could well have imagined it a 'Hotel'. And where was it located? In the Ramparts of the old city of Ypres, naturally. A quotation from the editor's introduction to the '*Collected Wipers Times*' indicates the location of his own office and the print room.

The editorial den was in a casemate under the old ramparts built by Vauban – heaven alone knows when! Though why the dear old bird built a wall fifty feet thick to keep out grape shot – or whatever the Hun of the day threw around – is hard to say. However, God rest his soul! He gave us the only moments of security we had for three long months, and often we drank to his shadow.

Read and admire the work of an anonymous Second Lieutenant who has clearly lived through a terrible experience and gains some comfort from writing about it. Written into this parody of the Rubaiyat of Omar Khayyam is something of the animal fear that pervaded dugout life in the trenches. Readers will probably understand that 'Crumps' and 'Whizz-bangs' are nick-names for enemy shells. Fuller translations can be found in the chapter on Artillery.

Many educated young men fighting in the First World War took with them a prayer-book- sized copy of Edward Fitzgerald's translation of the Rubaiyat of Omar Khayyam. These little leather-bound books were usually inscribed by a loved one and carried a message of hope and encouragement. Was there, perhaps, something in the nature of a talisman about the Rubaiyat that made men want to carry a copy into the dugouts and trenches of Ypres? Did they gain comfort in their horrific living conditions from the romantic symmetry of the lines and the unashamed sensuality of the images?

> Here with a loaf of bread beneath the bough,
> A flask of wine a book of verse and thou
> Beside me singing in the wilderness
> And wilderness is Paradise enow.

Maybe the 'Line' subaltern carried the same little volume or, if not, he must have learned the Rubaiyat by heart. For that we must admire his study because, the 'Moving finger writes, and having writ', appears in the 51st verse.

How young he must have been. Note the double use of the word 'Tummy.' On both occasions scansion and sense would permit the more adult 'stomach' or the biblical 'belly'. 'Tummy' seems such a nursery word for a man shortly to go 'o'er the top' and the date of this issue of the paper and the clear evidence that the men were being 'psyched up' for a big push reminds us that the Battle of the Somme was imminent. We must hope our poet survived, but statistics make this unlikely.

This consideration of the realities of trench warfare concludes with two vignettes

RUBAIYAT OF A "LINE" SUBALTERN.

The passing whizz-bang shrieks and bullets hum
Yet, gentle stranger, to my dug-out come;
To you I'll unfold knowledge which may help,
But first methinks will ope a jar of rum.
—§ ‡ §—
This is a cheery place you will allow,
A tin of beef, a jar of rum, and Thou
Beside me, squatting in a pool of mud,
And dug-out is not Paradise enow.
—§ ‡ §—
Alas! Alas! When M.G.'s spat I swore,
I swore and swore—and then again I swore!—
While on my tummy lay in dank pool deep,
And bullets through my fav'rit breeches tore.
—§ ‡ §—
And then! And then with five-nine crump you bet,
The wily Hun bust up our parapet,
Blew off my roof, and made that blooming hole,
Through which you're now so quickly getting wet.
—§ ‡ §—
The surly blighter shoots, and having shot
Moves on, while you are cursing quite a lot,
And on your tummy crawl through feet of mud,
Nor pause till you've retaliation got.
—§ ‡ §—
But hist! 'Tis secret known to only few,
We're going "o'er the top," and going through,
And then! And then! Old Fritz will pay in kind
The debt he owes the likes of me and you.

If I were King! Ah! Bill, if I were King,
I wouldn' touch an "A" frame or a thing,
I'd watch the sergeant split his blooming thumb,
And, when he wasn't looking, drink his rum,
I'd make the corpr'l rations to me bring,
If I were King! Ah! Bill, if I were King.

of life in the salient; the use of the 'A' Frame to reinforce the sides of trenches and dugouts and the affection in which soldiers held their pet dogs.

'A' frames were so called because of their shape. They were smaller versions of the pre-fabricated timber sections that are used today to support the roofs of newly built houses. The triangular 'A' shape with cross piece possesses good physical load-bearing characteristics in all directions. In the trenches they were used in two ways. Either the 'A' was inverted and the frames inserted across a trench enabling a duckboard to be laid along the cross pieces; or two upright 'A' frames were used opposite each other against bulging or falling trench walls. The apexes of the triangles could then be forced apart to shore up the walls. 'A' frames were constructed by Pioneer carpenters in makeshift workshops in the cellars of the City and carried out to the front line trenches by overnight working parties, one to a man. They made an awkward and heavy load and Pioneers hated them deeply.

Terriers were the best pets because they were affectionate to man; they appeared to thrive in the tunnels, dugouts and trenches and they killed rats, the bloated, carrion-eating rats which were part of the filthiness of the trench existence.

"STICK IT."

What matter though the wily Hun
With bomb, and gas and many a gun
In futile fury, lashes out,
Don't wonder what it's all about—
                    " Stick it."

—o—o—o—

When soaked in mud, half dead with cold,
You curse that you're a soldier bold ;
Don't heave your " A " frame through the night,
And, though it's wanted, travel light—
                    " Stick it."

J I M.

—:o:—

A hard little, scarred little terrier,
With a touch of the sheep-dog thrown in—
        A mongrel—no matter,
        There's no better ratter
In trenches or billet, than Jim.

—:o:—

A tough little, rough little beggar ;
And merry, the eyes of him.
        But no Tartar or Turk
        Can do dirtier work
With an enemy rat, than Jim.

—:o:—

And when the light's done, and night's falling,
And the shadows are darkling and dim,
        In my coat you will nuzzle
        Your little pink muzzle
And growl in your dreams, little Jim,

                    R.M.O.

Chapter 2

Daily Life in the Salient

A number of writings from *The Wipers Times* can be used to make up a picture of daily life in the Salient. There are references to the scenery and the weather and the sights and sounds of Ypres. It is in this section that we can find out a little about circumstances unconnected with the actual process of fighting that affected the men. We see what they had to contend with in their everyday life that made sufficient impact to merit a line or two in the next issue of the paper.

There is a possibility that 'The Padre' was in fact 'Tubby' Clayton, the renowned army chaplain in the Ypres Salient. He was founder of 'Toc H' which was named after the original Talbot House in Poperinghe. He is known to have been a close personal friend of Roberts and Gilbert Frankau.

The 'Military Definitions' are written by the editorial staff and are mostly light-hearted. It is not, however, the only occasion in which some part of the Salient is likened to Hell; Hell in the biblical sense, pictured in Dante's Inferno. There is a much mouthed but little understood section from 'Messiah';

> For thou didst not leave his soul in Hell nor didst thou suffer thy Holy One to view corruption.

Corruption there was aplenty at Hooge and Roberts would have been horribly familiar with it, as this was the section of the Line where his battalion worked most often at its night-time task of constructing earthwork defences and repairing shell damage to redoubts and gun emplacements.

Military Definitions.

Hooge	....	See Hell.
Rum	....	See Warrant Officers.
Dump	....	A collection of odds and ends, sometimes known as the Divisional Toyshop.
Hell	, ...	See Hooge.
Fokker	....	The name given by all infantry officers and men to any aeroplane that flies at a great height.
Adjutant	...	See grenades or birds.
Infantryman	..	An animal of weird habits, whose peculiarities have only just been discovered. It displays a strange aversion to light, and lives in holes in the earth during the day, coming out at night seeking whom it may devour. In colour it assimilates itself to the ground in which it lives.

Reflections on Being Lost in Ypres at 3 a.m.

I wish I had been more studious as a youth. Then I should not have neglected the subjects I disliked. Then I should not have failed to cultivate the sense of geography. And thus I should not have contrived to lose myself so often in Ypres in the small hours of winter mornings.

Lost in Ypres. It is an eerie experience. Not a soul to be seen not a voice to be heard. Only far out on the road to Hooge, the quick impulsive rattle of the British machine guns answers the slower more calculating throbbing of the Hun variety. If a man would understand what hate means, let him wander along the Menin Road in the evening, and then let him find some poet, or pioneer, or artilleryman to express what he feels concerning the Hun operator in that concrete, machine-gun redoubt.

Lost in Ypres at night: in the daytime it is a difficult feat to accomplish. Transports and troops pass and re-pass along the ruined streets. From almost every aspect, through gigantic holes torn in the intervening walls, the rugged spikes of the ruined cathedral town mark the centre of the town. From time to time, too, the heavy thud of a " crump," (like some old and portly body falling through a too frail chair with a crash to the floor), is an unerring guide to the main square.

But at night all is different. The town is well-nigh deserted. All its inhabitants, like moles, have come out at dusk and have gone, pioneers and engineers, to their work in the line. Night after night they pass through dangerous ways to more dangerous work. Lightly singing some catchy chorus they move to and fro across the open road, in front of the firing line, or hovering like black ghosts, about the communication trenches, as if there were no such thing as war. The whole scene lights up in quick succession round the semi-circle of the sallient as the cold relentless star-shells sail up into the sky. Here and there, a

" grouser " airs his views, but receives little sympathy, for the men are bent on their work, and do it with a will.

All this while, however, I have been standing lost in Ypres. I cannot steer by the star-shells, for they seem to be on every side. And at night, too, the jagged spires of the cathedral are reduplicated by the remains of buildings all over the city. Like the fingers of ghosts they seem to point importunately to heaven, crying for vengeance. It is a city of ghosts, the city of the dead. For it and with it the sons of three nations have suffered and died. Yet within that city, not many days ago, a little maid of Flanders was found playing. That is an omen. Ypres has died, but shall live again. Her name in the past was linked with kings; but to-morrow she will have a nobler fame. Men will speak of her as the home of the British soldier who lives in her mighty rampart caverns or in the many cellars of her mansions. And even when the busy hum of everyday life shall have resumed its sway in future days, still there will be heard in ghostly echo the muffled fumbling of the transport, and the rhythmic tread of soldiers' feet.

By " The Padre."

◁ O ▷

EDITOR

SUB-EDITOR

From *The Realities of War* by Sir Philip Gibbs:

Bodies and bits of bodies, and clots of blood, and green, metallic looking slime, made by explosive gasses, were floating on the surface of the water below the crater banks when I first passed that way (Hooge), and so it was always. Our men lived there and died there within a few yards of the enemy, crouched below the sandbags and burrowed into the sides of the crater. Lice crawled over them in legions. Human flesh, rotting and stinking, mere pulp, was pasted into the mudbanks. If they dug to get

On the Menin Road between Ypres and Hooge.

> During the First World War HOOGE, situated along the Menin Road, used to be one of the most dangerous sectors in the Ypres Salient and had a very bad reputation amongst the British troops.
>
> On July 19th 1915 the chateâu was in German hands and the British 175th Tunneling Cor, H.E. exploded an underground mine making a crater 16 meter deep with a diameter of approximantely 40 meters. The galery was 65 meters long and the charge was 3.500 lbs. of Amonal. The crater was immediately occupied by 2 companies of the 4th Middlesex, 8th Brigade, 3rd Division, This crater still exists and is now a small pond within it the remains of a German bombproof concrete shelter built in 1916.

deeper cover, their shovels went into the softness of dead bodies who had been their comrades. Scraps of flesh, booted legs, blackened hands, eyeless heads, came falling over them when the enemy trench-mortared their position or blew up a mine shaft.

Interpretation of the 'Sporting Notes' and 'Stop Press' give a poignant reminder of some of the worst features of the soldier's daily lives.

The story of the 'Spring Handicap' is in fact a description of a gas attack. Both sides were using poisoned gas in 1916 in an attempt to break the stalemate in the front lines. The gas, usually chlorine or phosgene, was released behind the defenders' line and the antagonists relied on the

Sporting Notes

The Spring Handicap, was run for on the Hooge Course last Wednesday, and the sport was all that one could desire. The course being in rare condition—as stated in our last number—and the candidates trained to an ounce. The locally-trained animal "East Wind" just managed to catch the judge's eye first, but the much fancied "Chlorine" fell at the Culvert. The greatly advertised continental candidate "Fritz" took fright at the "gate," and so figures amongst the "also ran." "Whizz-bang" who was intended to make the running for "Fritz" started off at a great pace, but soon shot his bolt. "H.E." then took the lead, but was audibly broken before the distance was reached. "Tommy" and "East Wind" soon had "Frost" cold, and they went on to finish an exciting race, "East Wind" winning, as previously stated, by a nosecap.

Stop Press News.

3.30 HOOGE.

Whizz-bang	1
H.E.	2

Others fell. 8 runners.

The crack is' widening in' the cathedral spire. Steps must be taken.

Mr. Krump has arrived in town.

4 p.m. Question asked in the House, by Mr. Toothwaite, as to what measures had been taken to stop the war. Mr. Pennant answered "Tape Measures." (Loud Cheering.)

'Some Crack'.

THE old firm of NUNTHORPE, Cox and Co., are still going strong. Their Splendidly staffed offices in the Ramparts are always open to the public for business. Best odds always on offer. Latest business :.

5 to 1 Mist

11 to 2 East Wind or Frost.

8 to 1 Chlorine.

Others at proportionate market prices.

ADVT.

Correspondence.

To the Editor,
   "Wipers Times."

Sir,
   May 1 draw your attention to the fact that the gas mains of the town seriously need attention. I was returning from the Cloth Hall Cinema the other night, when a big leak broke out in the Rue de Lille; and it was only by promptly donning my helmet-gas, that I was able to proceed on my way.

I am, etc.,
   A LOVER OF FRESH AIR

prevailing wind to carry the evil cloud to the other side to blind and choke the enemy. Thus our army was always on alert when the wind was in the east. Wind strengths had to be low and therefore gas attacks were more likely in anticyclonic conditions, which in winter meant clear, frosty nights. 'The Culvert' was a large dugout and shelter on the Menin Road west of Hooge. It was here that 'Tommy' felt and overcame the gas attack by using his rudimetary gas protection; he was probably helped by a change of wind.

'The crack is widening' means that the spire has been knocked down by enemy bombard-ment. 'Mr Krump has arrived in town' explains that the city was being shelled by 5.9 inch (150mm) howitzers while the paper was being produced. The reference to Questions in the House indicates a fighting soldier's familiar contempt for politicians and the niceties of democratic government as viewed from the battlefield.

It seems that there was a small intelligence cell in the Divisional Headquarters in Ypres whose task it was to forecast the probability and location of German poisoned gas attack. The officers' names, possibly encoded, were Nunthorpe and Cox. They could well have been conscripted meteorologists who did their best to warn the front line troops when the wind was expected to blow from a 'dangerous' direction. They were not always successful. *The Wipers Times* and its successors advertise the Firm as bookmakers and carry numerous reports supposedly from disgruntled and unsuccessful punters.

In 1916 the military solutions to gas attack were simple; Warning and Protection.

Protection was the P.H.G. Helmet (Phenate Hexamine Goggle). It, like the Second World War gas mask, was to be carried at all times. Warning took the form of gas alarms, usually hooters or gongs, which were positioned all over the Salient. Commanders and Staff organized practice alerts at inconvenient moments.

There aren't many jokes about gas in the paper. This contrasts with the repeated light-hearted references to the enemy artillery. It is probable that such was the horror of gas attack in those early and only partially protected days that even the wit of Roberts and his writers found it difficult to dream up anything to smile about. The Dranoutre Electric Palace advertisement was placed in an edition that came shortly after a horrific gas attack on the 24th Division, the parent organization of *The Wipers Times* and most of its readers. Five hundred men were killed or incapacitated as a result of inhaling chlorine gas. The advertisement, heavily disguised, apparently to confuse the enemy and the censor, appears to promise retaliation.

The main fear that was induced by the use of gas as a weapon of war lay in its universality which, again, is in contrast to the artillery. A fighting man is sustained by the certainty that the sword thrust, the shell, the bullet or the

DRANOUTRE ELECTRIC PALACE

—o—o—o—o—

This Week—That Stupendous Film Play

GAS

Will be Released.

IN THREE PARTS—10,000 FEET LONG.

Featuring TWEN TEFORTH in an entirely new role.

—o—o—o—o—

OTHER ITEMS.

—o—o—o—o—

EVE AT THE FRONT.

IN TWO PARTS.

—o—o—o—o—

PEASANTS LEAVING HOOGE, etc., etc.

PRICES AS USUAL

Oh! To be in Flanders in a gas alert.

How I love a "stand to" in a little shirt

When the wind's erratic, and you're

dining in Berloo,

Don't forget your P.H.G. and take it in

with you.

A DAY FROM THE LIFE

OF A "SUB"

IN DIVISIONAL RESERVE.

BY HIMSELF.

—o—o—o—

12·40 a.m.—Sleeping peacefully.

12·45 a.m.—Not sleeping peacefully.

12·50 a.m.—Awakened by a noise like a fog-horn gone quite mad.

12.55 a.m.—Realise someone has smelt gas, cannot find gas-helmet or shirt.

1 a.m.—Grope about for matches and candle—find out to my discomfort several extra articles of furniture in the hut—curse volubly.

1·5 a.m.—People rush in to remind me that I am orderly "bloke." Have heated altercation with "next for duty" as to when term of office ends. Matter settled by the entrance of C.O.—AM orderly officer.

1·15 a.m.—Stumble round camp—rumour of "Stand-to"—curse abominably.

1·30 a.m.—Rumour squashed—gas alarm false — somebody's clockwork motor-bike horn came unstuck—curse again—retire to bed.

---

bayonet is always going to hit someone else. A rolling evil yellow cloud of chlorine gas had everyone's name on it and the unreasoning fear of gas attack became a feature of everyday life.

Should any reader be in doubt as to the horrors of chemical warfare, let him view the painting 'Gassed' by John Singer Sargent in the Imperial War Museum. Refer also to Wilfrid Owen's words on the suffering caused by chlorine gas; from the poem '*Dulce et Decorum Est*':

Gas! Gas! Quick, Boys! An ecstasy of fumbling,
Fitting the clumsy helmets just in time;
But someone still was yelling out and stumbling,
And flound'ring like a man in fire or lime....
Dim, through the misty panes and thick green light
As under a green sea I saw him drowning.
In all my dreams, before my helpless sight,
He plunges at me, guttering, choking, drowning.

'Green misty panels' refers to the face mask of the P.H.G. 'Dranoutre' is a village North West of Bailleul (Berloo) much subject to gas attack. When the

British mounted retaliatory attacks, the actual generation and release of gas was the work of Pioneers. Hall Caine and Marie Corelli were popular novelists of the day.

There is a poignant and descriptive poem in *The Wipers Times* of 6 March, 1916. It is a parody of Gray's 'Elegy Written in a Country Churchyard' written by an anonymous Subaltern with a good education and an up-to-date knowledge of daily life in the Salient. The poem captures a little of the jittery existence of the men in Ypres. It tells of the sounds of a city under bombardment and we should note the practised ease with which the writer identifies the noise of the various projectiles that flew lethally through the night air; 'six-inch, whizz-bang, and crump'. 'Five rounds rapid' is the sentry's nervous response to a moving shadow that might be an enemy.

Correspondence.

To the Editor,
"New Church" Times.

Sir,
A correspondent in your last issue made a quotation from the writings of Call Haine. The following quotation from the works of that famous author Carle Morelli seems to bear on the subject, viz:—

God made the horse,
The mule and eke the ass;
R.E.'s do all the work
And Pioneers the gas.

Yours, etc.,
JUSTISSIMUS.
—§ ‡ §—

Ypern — Rechts die Norderseite der Tuchhalle.

Ypres – Right, the north side of the Cloth Hall.

A DWELLER IN WIPERS' ELEGY TO THAT TOWN.

—o—o—o—

(With apologies to Grey.)

A six-inch tolls the knell of parting
day.
The transport cart winds slowly o'er the
lea.
A sapper homeward plods his weary
way,
And leaves the world to Wipers and to
me.

—§ † §—

Now fades the glimmering star shell from
the sight,
And all the air a solemn stillness holds ;
Save where a whizz-bang howls it's rapid
flight,
And " five rounds rapid " fill the distant
folds.

—§ † §—

Beneath the Ramparts old and grim and
grey,
In earthy sap, and casement cool and
deep ;
Each in his canvas cubicle and bay,
The men condemned to Wipers soundly
sleep.

—§ † §—

Full many a man will venture out by
day,
Deceived by what he thinks a quiet
spell ;
Till to a crump he nearly falls a prey,
And into neighbouring cellar bolts like
hell.

—§ † §—

A burning mountain belching forth it's
fire,
A sandstorm in the desert in full fling ;
Or Hades with it's lid prised off entire,
Is naught to dear old Wipers in the
Spring.

TO MELT A STONE.

Kindly manager of Cox,
I am sadly on the rocks,
For a time my warring ceases,
My patella is in pieces ;
Though in Hospital I lie,
I am not about to die ;
Therefore let me overdraw
Just a very little more,
If you stick to your red tape
I must go without my grape,
And my life must sadly fret
With a cheaper cigarette,
So pray be not hard upon
A poor dejected subaltern,
This is all I have to say,

"IMPECUNIOUS," R.F.A.

Reproduction Interdite. — Photo Antony, Ypres.

Campagne de 1911. — Ruines d'YPRES
Incendie de l'Eglise Saint-Martin.
Fire of St-Martin's Church

'The smoking ruins that the guns have left behind'.

"Yes, you are, one pound nineteen and elevenpence overdrawn, and that includes next month's pay"

Bruce Bairnsfather
(one who 'ad some)

Cox's

When one feels rather in favour of floating a War Loan of one's own

'Sap' is a mediaeval siege warfare term and refers to a trench or tunnel dug at right angles to a city's walls to enable defenders to move out and probe the enemy positions. The Royal Engineers are proud to be known as 'Sappers'.

Hell and Hades, as always, get a mention.

After recalling such horrors it is anticlimactic to talk of anything so mundane as officers' pay. However, in times of war the armed forces are meticulously paid either on regimental pay parades or through English clearing banks, with an attention to detail that somehow seems to accentuate the chaos of war. *The Wipers Times* reminds us that although Ypres daily life was more hazardous than those at home could conceive, this didn't stop Cox's, the London bank, pressurizing army officers about minute overdrafts.

We should remember that these young men were overdrawn on life as well as on Cox's.

Chapter 3

The Guns

In the history of warfare between developed countries, the gun had reached its peak of influence in 1915. The lockable breech, the rifled barrel and the invention of high explosive meant that the big guns were as near masters of the battlefield as any militant nation could wish. Back in the 1880s, Kipling wrote that '*Nothing stood up to the guns.*' and in the Ypres Salient we learn that the sky was often darkened by the sheer number of projectiles hurtling from one side of the line to the other. However, big guns don't win wars. As military commanders have discovered in campaigns from the Great Siege of Malta to the murderous Serb onslaught on Sarajevo, from Waterloo to Beirut via Vietnam, the big guns destroy, demoralize and depopulate but the war isn't won until the soldiers, the muddied and maligned poor bloody infantry, march in and *occupy* the smoking shambles that the guns have left behind.

Men against machine-guns; the grim results.

A CHRISTMAS CARD, 1914.

"They've evidently seen me."

Laying and loading a German mortar. Accuracy was poor but a chance direct hit was lethal.

In 1916 in the Salient the German guns had achieved nearly everything they could, strategically. They had flattened Ypres, Neuve Eglise, Wulverghem, Messines and Hooge. They had uprooted every tree in Zouave and Railway Woods and virtually blasted the top off Hill 60. (Artillerymen identify hills by the printed height above sea level that usually appears beside the summit on a map.) All but the most stubborn of the Belgian inhabitants had fled; the farms were destroyed, the canals drained and the roads and bridges pulverised, but the German infantry could not march into the devastated land until something or someone dislodged the opposing armies dug into the soft earth of the Flanders countryside. Hindenberg had already been taught that a frontal attack on entrenched troops who have machine-gun support was more costly in human life than even the German war machine could support.

So why did the enemy not turn their big guns on the trenches and simply blast the British, French, Canadians, Belgians, New Zealanders and Indians, along with their machine guns, their barbed wire, their hospitals their ammunition dumps and their poor terrified mules and horses, into the next world? They had the fire power and the ammunition, but they lacked the pin-point accuracy that such an offensive would require. There was no radar in 1916, no laser-guidance to help the gunners. They depended on the time-honoured 'Right 30, up 10' technique which enabled them to 'find' targets by amending the aim of the previous shot. This system required Observation Posts and OP-to-gun communications which, on the German side of the lines, were notoriously inefficient and subject to disruption by the Allies. Both armies needed to knock out the other's observation posts and to 'blind' the opposing artillery.

Statistics came to the aid of the men in the Salient. Let us say that, in the defensive role, the trenches were manned by a soldier every five yards of their length. At fifty-yard intervals there were machine gun redoubts with interlacing fields-of-fire in preparation for any frontal attack. Along the trench there were dugouts which sheltered commanders, off-duty sentries and a few immediate reserves of men and ammunition. Everything was below ground. Even the men actually standing in the trenches observed no man's land in front of them through periscopes. A heavy HE shell exploding at ground level made a crater of approximately fifteen yards in diameter and twenty feet deep. It hurled hot metal over a distance of about fifty yards at ground level but its killing area below ground was much reduced, say about a yard greater in any direction than the ''ole' it made in the mud. From these approximations a statistician might be able to calculate how many shells with an accuracy of plus or minus fifty yards over a range of 3,000 would have to be fired to be certain of killing one soldier in a ten-foot-deep, two-foot-wide trench in the Flanders mud, scoring a direct hit on a dugout, or bursting actually in a machine-gun nest. The answer is probably more shells than one gun could fire in a year. This demonstrates the need for the artillery barrage or 'strafe' as it was known in *The Wipers Times*, when long-range artillery compensated for its inaccuracy by sheer volume of projectiles fired.

Fifty guns firing at one section of trench with fire control and observation points could be fairly certain of blowing holes in the wire and killing most of the defenders. However, once an enemy barrage became apparent the defenders would first try to silence it with their own guns; a battery in action soon betrayed its position and artillery duels developed as each side tried to knock out the other's weapons. In the muddied trenches the survivors of the original barrage would withdraw and prepare for the infantry attack that was bound to follow and endeavour to assess the precise moment

War.

—:0:—

Take a wilderness of ruin,
Spread with mud quite six feet deep;
In this mud now cut some channels,
Then you have the line we keep.
Now you get some wire that's spiky,
Throw it round outside your line;
Get some pickets, drive in tightly,
And round these your wire entwine.
Get a lot of Huns and plant them,
In a ditch across the way;
Now you have war in the making,
As waged here from day to day.
Early morn the 'same old "stand to"
Daylight, sniping in full swing;
Forenoon, just the merry whizz-bang.
Mid-day oft a truce doth bring.
Afternoon repeats the morning,
Evening falls then work begins;
Each works in his muddy furrow,
Set with boards to catch your shins.
Choc-a-block with working parties,
Or with rations coming up;
Four hours scramble, then to dug-out,
Mud-encased, yet keen to sup.
Oft we're told "Remember Belgium,"
In the years that are to be;
Crosses set by all her ditches,
Are our pledge of memory.

when the enemy guns were forced to cease firing to protect their own troops. The ultimate battle would once again be resolved by the relative killing efficiency of either side, with small-arms and machine gun fire.

Of course it would be far easier for the German forces to make conditions so unpleasant for the defending troops in the Salient that they vacated the trenches of their own accord. The French army suffered a mutiny when for a short time the infantry simply refused to carry on fighting. So the artillery shells rained down indiscriminately on the Salient. The German gunners fired at any crossroads or assembly point behind the lines where the death-per-round-fired average could be improved. They disrupted supply lines so that men in the trenches would run out of rum or ammunition or four-by-two or food or replacements. Shells were lobbed at the front line to make the British troops aware of the permanent possibility of violent and unexpected death as a stray burst of shrapnel rained down into a trench or a Russian Roulette mortar broke through the timber roof of a dugout.

In 1916 in the trenches of the Ypres Salient it was the task and the duty of the British Forces simply to endure and survive. By the end of that year every man in the battle must have been suffering from some degree of psychological disorder due to the action of the enemy guns. If they weren't wounded or

'Dawn strafe on the Somme. As the British found to their cost even such a huge concetration of gunfire can not be certain to take out entrenched troops and machine guns.'

In this aerial photo of troops advancing over shell-cratered territory, an assessment may be made of the impossibility of halting the ant-like progress of infantry even with saturation shelling. The picture also demonstrates that in this type of warfare infantry depended on good fortune alone to survive.

physically damaged from nearby explosions, their minds had probably been unhinged by daily butcher's shop scenes of slaughter and the realization that only chance and good fortune would decide whether the next shell over- or under-shot their position by enough to permit them to live another day.

On every page of *The Wipers Times* there is a reference to the German shells; sometimes jocular, sometimes with hatred, sometimes with fear, but the paper's psychological success was to de-traumatize the horror of the German guns simply by talking about them, cracking little jokes and making oblique references to the drama of being on the receiving end of unopposed artillery fire. It also appears to help if soldiers give silly names to the machines of war. Remember the general pur-pose helicopter that carried Americans into battle in Vietnam and brought home the pathetic shapeless body bags? They called it the 'Jolly Green Giant'.

The printing errors and unexpected use of the triangular symbol are indications of the inexperience of the off-duty soldiers who were producing the paper. The apostrophe in the middle of the word Cinema in the right-hand advertisement indicates, simply, that the printers had run out of capital Es. A happier solution might have been to make the first item on the programme at the Cloth Hall the FIVE Duds or better still the FOUR.

To understand the joke about the 'Johnsons' we move first to Poperinghe, a town eight miles due West of Ypres. Poperinghe, abbreviated to Pop by the soldiers, was the final railhead en route to the front line. It was here that organized supply and re-enforcement reverted to chaos. The town was just within artillery range of the German big guns and by 1916 there was always the possibility of air attack.

An In-fringe-ment

" Look 'ere. Bert, if you wants to remain in this 'ere trench be'ave yerself "

Bert is rehearsing a now-forgotten schoolboy gesture of derision that would have been accompanied on the playground by a cry of 'Tee hee you missed me.' The poignancy of the cartoon lies in the application of gestures which are usually associated with paper pellets flicked on rubber bands, to shellfire which is far too close for comfort.

Stretcher bearers on the road from Boesinghe to 'Pop.' Photo IWM

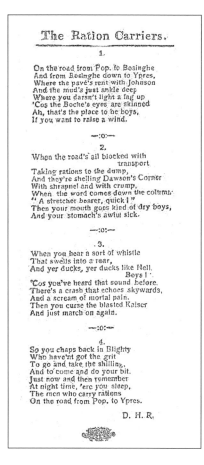

The Ration Carriers.

1.

On the road from Pop. to Bosinghe
And from Bosinghe down to Ypres,
Where the pavé's rent with Johnson
And the mud's just ankle deep
Where you darsn't light a fag up
'Cos the Boche's eyes are skinned
Ah, that's the place to be boys,
If you want to raise a wind.

—:o:—

2.

When the road's all blocked with
transport
Taking rations to the dump,
And they're shelling Dawson's Corner
With shrapnel and with crump,
When the word comes down the column
" A stretcher bearer, quick ! "
Then your mouth goes kind of dry boys,
And your stomach's awful sick.

—:o:—

3.

When you hear a sort of whistle
That swells into a roar,
And yer ducks, yer ducks like Hell,
Boys ! .
'Cos you've heard that sound before.
There's a crash that echoes skywards,
And a scream of mortal pain.
Then you curse the blasted Kaiser
And just march on again.

—:o:—

4.

So you chaps back in Blighty
Who have'nt got the grit
To go and take the shilling,
And to come and do your bit.
Just now and then remember
At night time, 'ere you sleep,
The men who carry rations
On the road from Pop. to Ypres.

D. H. R.

Reproduction Interdite. — Photo Antony, Ypres
Campagne de 1914 — Ruines d'YPRES
Incendie du Belfroi (22 novembre 1914)
Fire of the belfroy.

'The best ventilated hall in the town'.

Everything went through Poperinghe: rations and ammunition, horses, wounded, tanks, wagons, guns, and hundreds of thousands of men. It was here that both newcomers to active service experienced the first inklings of doubt that anyone was actually in charge or knew what was going on. Poperinghe was an example of the military bedlam that only war can produce.

The short poem tells of conditions on the resupply route from Poperinghe to Ypres. It is an example of a familiar military concern with the amount of courage required to carry out a particular duty. Resupply men were always at pains to explain that their work was every bit as dangerous as that of men in the firing line.

'... to raise a wind.' is a phrase now in disuse. It means 'to be really frightened.' Rhymes in the poem give confirmation of the difficulties British soldiers had with pronouncing 'Ypres'.

'The pavé's rent with Johnson,' is the significant line. 'Pavé' is the French name for a paved road, but what was 'Johnson'? In *Fragments, The Life of*

Bruce Bairnsfather a reference is made to the famous cartoon, 'Well if you knows of a better 'ole.'

'No cartoon of the war,' the writer states, 'in actual fact, hit the public so much as that of the two desperate men in the Johnson 'ole ...'

'Johnson' was Salient slang for the noisy, black-smoking, contact-bursting, death-dealing, hot metal scattering, German heavy artillery shells that slammed into the salient in 1916 at the rate of some 2000 per day.

In Gilbert Frankau's biography there is a passage, on a completely different subject, that likens something black to the skin of Jack Johnson, the heavyweight boxer who's name the soldiers of the BEF gave to the black-smoking bursts of high explosive from German artillery. Apparently this feature was most recognizable in explosions of enemy shells of '5.9' calibre.

Jack Johnson was the first negro heavyweight champion of the world. His skin colour gave rise to a ribald music hall song before the war in which the singer claims to have fought the champion. The man was at an unfair disadvantage because the lighting was poor and he couldn't see his dark skinned opponent coming. The imagery survived to the Second World War where night-fighter pilots endeavouring to intercept German bombers without the assistance of radar claimed that the whole excercise was like looking for 'Jack Johnson in a cellar'.

Leafing through *The Wipers Times* we come across many nicknames for enemy artillery. 'Bertha' or 'Big Bertha' was the largest German artillery piece. It fired a 16/17 inch projectile. Smaller projectiles were referred to by their exact dimensions. '*After issue No 2 was published*,' writes the editor in a foreword to the facsimile edition, '*the Hun "found" our works with a 5.9*'. 'Shrapnel' was the name of the inventor of this murderous anti-personnel weapon. The first head protectors issued to the British Army in 1914 were designated Shrapnel Helmets before they became known as the more familiar Tin Hats. 'Crump' is an onomatopoeic word used to describe any exploding projectile larger than rifle and machine gun bullets. A 'Whizz-bang' was obviously identified by the noise it made. The name was probably used to differentiate between artillery shells which travelled supersonically and mortar rounds which have a slower, steeper trajectory and make a very different sound in flight. The Whizz-bang gave rise to much front-line lore including the questionable theory that if you

Answers to Some of Our Many Correspondents.

Jock. (Zouave Wood).—No, when on patrol work and you hear the words—"Ach Gott! ich bin ganz fed-up gerworden "=issue from an unknown trench, this does not necessarily signify that you have worked too far over to your left and stumbled into the French lines.

Motorist. (Popperinghe).—Yes, we have had other complaints of the suspected police trap on the Menin Road, and advise caution on the stretch between "Hell Fire Corner" and the Culvert.

Wind Up. (Hooge).—Certainly not, A "Whizz Bang" does not leave the gun *after* it hits your trench, but just before.

T.T.O. (H 23 B 56).—We sympathise, but when unknown females write to you with requests for photographs, it would be safer to send for references first.

heard the Whizz and the Bang the shell had already missed you. It was 'curtains' if you only heard the Whizz.

The 'Answers' appeared in the first edition of *The Wipers Times* and there have, of course, been no correspondents. The letters are the work of the editorial staff and reflect exactly the puckish, inventive humour of the paper. 'Zouave Wood' and 'Hooge' were famous locations where fearful battles were fought by the BEF in 1914. Now they were fortified outposts of the Salient.

A 'Minnie' was a *Minenwerfer* or mine thrower; it was in simple terms a high-trajectory heavy mortar that delivered a bomb fused to explode below ground. This used the earthquake effect of delayed action explosions to collapse trenches and dugouts. If the shock waves from an adjacent Minnie didn't kill you outright the chances are that you would be buried alive in your subterranean shelter. The infantry of Ypres hated Minnies, and they weren't too enamoured of Trench Mortars (Toc Emmas) either.

'O Pip,' (OP) was an observation post for artillery spotting and any elevated position was important to both sides for this purpose. This is why Hill 60 was fought over so many times.

The Article 'Adieu to the Salient' was written by a soldier whose unit was being pulled out of the line for 'Rest'. For a few weeks he will be just out of range of the enemy guns and we hope he will have some respite from the lethal detonations which have entered his soul. And a word about Archie; anti-aircraft fire, although at a later date known by the Signallers' abbreviation of Ack Ack, was more commonly referred to by the troops as 'Archie'. What was the lethality of anti-aircraft

Jack and Jill on top of a Hill
Had built an O Pip Station,
But Frightful Fritz blew it to bits
To their great consternation.

ADIEU TO THE SALIENT.

—o—o—o—

The news is confidential! At least, as yet, it is not known to everybody. Nevertheless it is true. Had I the vocabulary I could tell you what I think of this charming spot. Words having failed me, I bid it "Good-bye" with a silence more eloquent than words. For we are leaving the Salient and going into "rest"!!—

Whatever trials "rest"? may hold, whatever the future may have for us, I think that always I shall be glad to have seen the Salient. A month there holds more than a year elsewhere, "Wipers"! He's a strange man who can gaze on that unmoved. Who, that has known it, will forget the high-strung tension of the Menin Road, who, unmoved, can pass those fields of crosses? The Menin Road and all it means. To know all the by-paths and alternative ways so as to dodge when shelling starts! To know all its holes and ditches when machine guns loose! Can there be any emotion to equal that of lying prone in a crump-hole with a machine gun ripping across your back. Hell Fire Corner! aptly named. The span from there to Hooge, who that has slithered along it in gum boots thigh will ever forget. And now I no more to ponder as to which route to use. No longer the old question "where are they putting 'em to-night? For we're going back to "rest"!!

But not all—some of us remain. Poor lads: There they stay in the Salient and crosses mark the price they paid. Always, when the strain of the Salient may have left us, the memory of those crosses will remain, and those true hearts who sleep there may rest assured that we, who worked with them, fought with them and hoped with them, will exact the price. Ypres, and all you mean farewell! To those who come after us good luck! We are going back to "rest"!!!

```
╔══════════════════════╗
║      TO MINNIE.      ║
║   ┄┅╾╼┅┄   ║
║ (Dedicated to the P.B.I.) ║
╚══════════════════════╝
```

In days gone by some aeons ago
That name my youthful pulses stirred,
I thrilled whene'er she whispered low
Ran to her when her voice I heard.

—:o:—

Ah Minnie! how our feelings change,
For now I hear your voice with dread,
And hasten to get out of range
Ere you me on the landscape spread.

—:o:—

Your lightest whisper makes me thrill,
Your presence makes me hide my head,
Your voice can make me hasten still—
But 'tis away from you instead.

—:o:—

You fickle jade! you traitrous minx!
We once exchanged love's old sweet tales
Now where effulgent star-shell winks
Your raucous screech my ear assails.

—:o:—

No place is sacred, I declare,
Your manners most immodest are,
You force your blatant presence where
Maidens should be particular.

—:o:—

You uninvited do intrude,
You force an entrance to my couch,
Though if I've warning you're about
I'll not be there, for that I'll vouch.

—:o:—

Name once most loved of all your sex,
Now hated with a loathing great,
When next my harassed soul you vex
You'll get some back at any rate.

NO CHILDRENS PARTY COMPLETE WITHOUT IT.

———

ARCHIE

THE NEW MECHANICAL INVENTION.
NOT A TOY.
NOT A COMPLICATED MACHINE.
A CHILD CAN USE IT.

—o—o—o—

With Belt and Five Cartridges. In Highly Polished
Box, 4s. 6d. Extra.

SOLE AGENTS FOR YPRES AND DISTRICT: MESSRS. ANTI, AIRCRAFT AND CO.

fire which has failed in its primary object of knocking down aeroplanes?

Did the constant overhead barrage present any real danger to men on the ground? The answer appears to be that an exploded AA shell was so fragmented that falling metallic particles had little penetration and injuries on the ground were unlikely. This, however, was not the case with unexploded or dud 'Archie' which caused many casualties among *Wipers Times* readers. Such accidents caused comment in the paper because it was a singularly unfortunate way for a man to 'Stop one.'

A chapter on artillery must include a word about mines. The First World War mining operations, masterminded by General Plumer, were an attempt to break the stalemate. If the guns could not dislodge the enemy from trenches and dugouts, a possible alternative was to burrow under

Things We Want to Know.

—:o:—

The name of the Camp Commandant who bought up all the whiskey in Bethune owing to early advice of the coming drought.

? ? ?

The name of the M.O. who is not a doctor.

? ? ?

If it is true that he takes an umbrella on his walks, as "Archie" duds are so plentiful.

? ? ?

Whether two notorious red-hats were disappointed over a little question of "Who's HE taking with him."

? ? ?

Ref. G.R.O. Q.M.G.'s Branch No. 2073 :—(A)—What is a BONA FIDE rum drinker. (B)—Whether whiskey cannot be supplied on the same terms to BONA FIDE whiskey drinkers.

```
┌┄┄┄┄┄┄┄┄┄┄┄┄┄┄┄┄┄┄┐
│        GONE        │
└┄┄┄┄┄┄┄┄┄┄┄┄┄┄┄┄┄┄┘
```

Gone are the days of the Seventythird,
When never a quail or a grouse was heard,
Gone are our smiles—each eye has a tear
For gone is our priceless Brigadier;
We ne'er shall forget his cheery face,
Tho' we've got another to take his place.

—§†§—

Gone is the Transport Officer too
"Dear old Charles" whom all ranks knew,
Knocked out by a shell for a Bosch who flew,
They say that the air for miles went blue;
We ne'er shall forget his cheery face,
Tho' we've got another to take his place.

—R.I.B.—

Charge; 91,000 lbs of Ammotal explosive manhandled along a 500 yard tunnel.

Blown; 7th June 1917.

Crater diameter; 250 feet.

Depth; 40 feet

Diameter of complete obliteration; 430 feet.

The Spanbroekmolen mine crater, now a Peace Lake sponsored by Toc H.

A STIRRING DRAMA,

ENTITLED:

MINED

A MOST UPLIFTING PERFORMANCE.

—0—0—0—0—

ALL THE LATEST PICTURES.

ENTIRE CHANGE OF PROGRAMME WEEKLY.

—0—0—0—0—

Best Ventilated Hall in the Town.

PRICES AS USUAL.

---

hostile positions and explode vast tonnages of high explosive. The courage of the tunnellers was legendary, facing as they did the every-day possibility of being buried alive. Mines were opposed by counter-mines and, when the two tunnels broke into each other, claustrophobic hand-to-hand battles took place between miners

Don't sit up for the mine, Daddy! don't sit up for the mine!
Let's go to our Chateau at Walton Heath, and to bed at half-past nine,
Mary can call us for zero hour, if she wakes us about 3·9,
We'll hear the big bang at 3·10, you see, so don't sit up for the mine.

THE PATRIOT.

—o—o—o—

HE other evening, as I was taking my usual walk before dinner by way of an appetizer, I saw someone off towards the Bosche lines digging in the ground. After a long and careful scrutiny it became evident that the man was alone, and from his bent shoulder and general air of weariness, I judged that he was old. Taking my six-shooter in one hand and courage in the other, I carefully stalked my prey and effected a capture. My joy was short-lived, for my man was a Tommy, old, and armed only with a spade. He had been digging holes in the ground, until that part of the field looked like a colander.

Now actions like these need explaining. The man was either exposing himself to a sniper's bullet in hope of ending all, or else there may be treason in this. Signals to aeroplanes or something.

On asking him what was his idea of digging shell holes in the fields so near the Bosche lines he said :—" Sir, it takes hundreds of men to get iron mined and treated. This iron is made into shells. These shells are then placed into costly guns or howitzers, and with the aid of a bag or two of cordite sent on the rest of their journey. All this costs money, two three or maybe five pounds a-piece, and the work of many people " The old man stopped and counted the holes he had dug eight in all. " You see, sir," he said, " I have saved my Government twenty to forty pounds, and if you had not interrupted me I would have saved it more, for that is all these shells are doing, digging holes, and I can do it cheaper."

I took the man's name and number, and reported the incident to the C.O. at mess that night. The poor old man was sent to Blighty by the Artillery M.O., who had heard the tale and diagnosed the case as " N.Y.D.—'Mental."

But this winter, while you and I are out here in this country, in a little cottage in Yorkshire you might see our old friend with his people all about him, the fire burning brightly. In a corner there is a spade all cleaned and polished, and as the old man sees it there is a twinkle in his eye. While out here the Artillery M.O. is slowly writing on scraps of paper:" Mental—Query ? "

H. DAVIS.

SONG OF ANY INFANTRY BRIGADIER TO HIS MEN.

In my dug-out (where the plans are laid)
I sing this song to my Brigade.
You chaps who in a scrap have been
Will " compris " fully what I mean.
Just lately in the stunts you've struck,
You haven't had the best of luck.
You've had the kicks without the pence,
And always struck a stiffish fence.
You've had the mud: you've had the wet:
You've had the shells as well. And yet
You never grumble—just hold on
When all except your pluck has gone.
We know the cheery way you curse
When things are getting worse and
                                            worse,
Yet if I ask for further work,
There's not a dammed one here would
                                            shirk ;
The Higher Staff quite understand,
But know the old Division, and
They know that they have but to ask,
And you will carry out the task,
So I have pledged my knightly word
To stick it out until the Third.
And though I pledge it with remorse
I pledge it hopefully, because
I know the stuff of which you're made,
I know the old " Umpteenth " Brigade.
I know you'll always play the game
(Although it is a b * * * * y shame),
And so in tempest and in rain,
In shells and shells, and shells again,
Just understand (it's nothing new ?)
How proud I am of all of you.

wielding shovels and pick handles. Mines were completed and detonated all over the Salient, the most successful ones being at Hooge, and the vast explosions that just about blew the top off the Messines Ridge at 3.10 a.m. on the 7 June, 1917. The explosions were tactically of only minor effect because such was the shock and confusion felt by both sides that, by the time the dazed infantry could be summoned to occupy the still-smoking devastation, the enemy had recovered themselves as well.

The short poem is based on a Victorian sentimental music-hall song '*Don't go down in the Mine, Daddy*'. The song was sung by a child who had a premonition of a coal mining disaster. Trench maps have failed to show exactly where the '*Château at Walton Heath*' was located but there can have been no problem in hearing the sounds of the mine explosions; the noise and shock waves were felt in London and all over the south of England and the Prime Minister was awakened by it in his office in Downing Street, having fallen asleep at his desk.

The realization that the infantry were harried to the point of desperation by regular yet random casualties from enemy artillery is shown in the 'Song of Any Infantry Brigadier'. So is the fact that the PBI were never broken by it; a triumph of courage and endurance that is chronicled on every page of *The Wipers Times*.

The last word is left to the 'Patriot' who with the clear-sightedness of the supposedly insane (Not Yet Diagnosed – Mental) has not only produced a telling comment on the wasteful inefficiency of shelling open spaces, but engineered a 'Blighty' into the bargain.

Chapter 4

Shellshock

In 1995 news reports were heavy with the phrase 'Terrorised to the point of madness by the enemy guns,' used to describe the helpless citizens of former Yugoslavia; a lady psychiatrist from Sarajevo had chronicled her personal descent towards insanity. Yet nowhere in modern wars can the enemy shells have been endured for so long and in such numbers as they were by the defending armies in the Ypres Salient. *The Wipers Times* makes no mention of 'shellshock', the name used during and after the First World War for the unbearable mental trauma of warfare, but if one reads between the lines it figures on every page.

Gilbert Frankau's poem in *The Wipers Times* of 20 March, 1916, gives some idea of his mental state at the time. Frankau, a gunner officer, has seen front-line service in the Battle of Loos and has been moved, probably by a sympathetic and understanding CO, to work in 'Requisitioning and Re-Supply', one step behind the front line. Here he was in the doubtful position of taking no active part in the fighting, but still living within range of the enemy guns.

The four cart-horses of the apocalypse routing Kaiser Wilhelm with 'plum and apple': can we respectfully suggest that Gilbert Frankau himself was shellshocked when he wrote these lines?

In later years he freely admits it himself.

From *Self Portrait* by Gilbert Frankau:

Some half a mile to the left was Geoffrey Weldon's 'regular' battery. On a quiet afternoon I walked over to have tea with him. Returning to the coffin-shaped hole where I spent my nights, I found a shell crater just outside it, in the exact place where I should have been sitting had I stayed at home. Within a few hours another shell, falling on his battery position, wounded Geoffrey to the death. The worse soldier was to write the better's epitaph:

> 'Brother take heart! God's world is clean and wide for you
> Regret not one whose pride is that he died for you'

'That 16-inch Sensation'.

It is possible that a certain shell which had decapitated the infantryman at my side, knocking me flat and embedding three tiny pieces of grit behind my left ear, was already affecting my behaviour ...

(Lord) Horder said, 'Have it your own way and report for duty if you insist. You'll never be sent back to the front; but you will eventually be sent to the shellshock hospital at Craigellachie. It's a nice place – if you like fellows jumping head first from the top storey on to the terrace just while you're having your after breakfast stroll there'.

He gave me full details of that actual happening – and eventually a chit which stated that, in his opinion, I should be granted three months home leave. Horder's word on 'Shellshock and neurasthenia' must already have been law. I forwarded the chit to the competent authority and was granted leave almost by return of post.

SOME DREAM.

In Wipers, where the whizz-bangs
      dance,
I mused upon the Great Advance.
I read (though most by heart I knew)
Ream upon ream from G and Q.
Which fearsome reading nearly done,
I slept—and dreamed we smashed the
      Hun:
Dreamed we had left our sodden
      trenches—
The well-known holes, the well-known
      stenches—
And forward stormed for wealth and
      wenches.
(Even in dreams, my eagle mind
Perpended Prussia's womenkind—
Deciding, if it came to shooting,
I'd rather I were shot for looting)
Rifle nor mortar, gun nor lance
Had wrought—at last—our Great
      Advance:
Our freshest troops, our A.S.C.
It was that gave us victory!
Yea! 'Twas the Army Safety Corps
Drowned Belgium's swamps in German
      gore.
Wagon on wagon, team on team,
I watched their quarter-locks agleam,
Mad squadrons of my whiskied dream.
' Whips over' on each ' heavy draught '
They leaped the wire; and, leaping
      laughed;

Then furious with uplifted crops
Hacked their red path through Clonmel
      Copse;
The while their deadly Fifty-fives'
Took countless toll of limbs and lives.
Black columns down the Menin Road.
In endless streams their motors
      flowed . . . .
Vainly, the flower of William's flock
Strove to withstand this awful shock,

No human force could hope to dam
Those waves of Plum and Apple jam;
Bavaria's stoutest infantry
Paled at the sugar, black with tea;
Proud Prussia, trained to meatless
      days,
Reeled and fled back in sheer amaze
As, joint to joint and knee to knee,
Charged home Fred Karno's Cavalry . . .
And now, alone, in Glencorse Wood,
Undaunted, little Willie stood,
And eyed the foe, and eyed the food :
Too long he tarried ! F—sch—r
      smote
Full on that gorged and greedy throat
With a faked requisition note . . . .
'Twas Mine ! Chill terror at my
      breast,
My traitor soul, in dreams, confessed;
And woke to find—not Army Scandals
But shortage in our ration candles.

GILBERT FRANKAU.

13/3/16.

It gives the writings of Gilbert Frankau much extra poignancy when one understands that these poems were the product of a mind already becoming unhinged by shellshock. In his introduction to the facsimile edition Roberts apologizes for the fact that his correspondents' hilarity was more often hysterical than natural. It appears that one of the early symptoms of shellshock was to prompt men, unusually, to compose verse. Could it perhaps be that the regular rhythms of jingles and stanzas gave some kind of comfort to a mind becoming punchdrunk from the irregular and unexpected detonations of guns, shells and bombs?

It is certainly not far-fetched to suggest that most of the correspondents and readers of *The Wipers Times* were suffering from shellshock to some degree, and Roberts was on occasions swamped by the numbers of aspiring copy-writers who pressed him to publish their verse.

NOTICE.

We regret to announce that an insidious disease is affecting the Division, and the result is a hurricane of poetry. Subalterns have been seen with a notebook in one hand, and bombs in the other absently walking near the wire in deep communion with the muse. Even Quartermasters with books, note, one, and pencil, copying, break into song while arguing the point re boots. gum, thigh. The Editor would be obliged if a few of the poets would break into prose as a paper cannot live by "poems" alone.

Stop-gap.

—:o:—

Little stacks of sandbags,
Little lumps of clay ;
Make our blooming trenches,
In which we work and play.

Merry little whizz-bang,
Jolly little crump ;
Made our trench a picture,
Wiggle, woggle, wump.

An awful thought has come to me
Of sad disaster that might be ;
Just suppose a 12 inch shell
Fell right on this dug-out—well ;
This train of thought I'll not pursue,
(That fills the gap, and so will do !)

Robert Graves, *Goodbye To All That*:

For the first three weeks, an officer was of little use in the front line; he did not know his way about, had not learned the rules of health and safety, or grown accustomed to recognizing degrees of danger. Between three weeks and four weeks he was at his best, unless he happened to have any particular bad shock or sequence of shocks. Then his usefulness gradually declined as neurasthenia developed. At six months he was still more or less all right; but by nine or ten months, unless he had been given a few weeks' rest on a technical course, or in hospital, he usually became a drag on the other company officers. After a year or fifteen months he was often worse than useless. Dr. W.H.R. Rivers told me later that the action of one of the ductless glands – I think the thyroid – caused this slow general decline in military usefulness, by failing at a certain point to pump a sedative chemical into the blood. Without its continued assistance the man went about his tasks in an apathetic and doped condition, cheated into further endurance.

AFTERWORD.

—o—

And now, Old Girl, we've fairly had our
whack,
Be off, before they start to strafe us back!
Come, let us plod across the weary Plain,
Until we sight TENTH AVENUE again :
On, up the interminable C.T.,
Watched by the greater part of Germany:
And, as we go, mark each familiar
spot
Where fresh work has been done—or
p'r'aps has not :
On, past the footboards no one seems to
mend,
Till even VENDIN ALLEY finds an end,
And wading through a Minnie-hole
(brand-new),
We gingerly descend to C.H.Q.,
Our journey ended in a Rabbit-hutch—
" How goes the Battle? Have they
Minnied much?"

P.B.I.

Another symptom of shellshock seems to have been a stubborn, indeed suicidal, determination not to give up. This behaviour is allied to the guilt that we now know that sufferers feel simply to have survived some horrifying disaster. Frankau threw a spectacular tantrum when shellshock was diagnosed, and he did not rest until he had lied and fiddled his way back to his unit at Ypres.

Graves tells us of traumatised men going about their business in an apathetic and doped condition; in the next poem, 'Afterword' one can recognize other symptoms. The writer has completed a hard and dangerous night's work. On his way home he is depressed to note that things appear to be broken down faster than they can be repaired. He feels exposed as though the whole world is sniping at him and when he finally makes it back to comparative safety, he is exasperated when some one asks him a damn-fool question about the conditions outside. ('Tenth Avenue' and 'Vendin Alley' were communication trenches; 'CHQ' the company headquarters dug-out; 'PBI' Poor Bloody Infantry man.)

'Your Loving Sister Edie,' was an officer from Ypres sent home and hospitalized with general debilitation arising from shellshock.

Shellshock was widely assumed to be caused by the constant but unpredictable concussive detonations of shells from the big guns. This was compounded by the realization that violent death or terrible injury was always probable and never unlikely. A recently published list of stressful occurrences in 20th century life places 'Death or serious illness of a close relative' high up among traumas that contribute to mental breakdown. Two poems from *The Wipers Times* remind us that troops would have suffered the same emotional disturbance from the death of a close comrade as, in more peaceful times, a man might experience from the loss of wife or child. Even at the height of the war in the Ypres trenches a soldier could get compassionate leave on the death of a relative, but, if he lost a comrade, all the poor man could do was to prop up the body by the roadside with a G.R.C. (Grave Registration Cross) and march on. Maybe a follow-up burial party would give the closest friend he ever had a decent burial.

THE B.E.F. TIMES.

LETTERS FROM EDIE.

—o—o—o—

Tuesday.

My very dearest Clarence,

Your long-awaited, anxiously opened, and merrily perused epistle just to hand, and here I am answering it per return. You MUST be ill, you will doubtless exclaim in your inimitably witty manner. Ah, but your hazard is a correct one, I HAVE been ill—aye and sorely so—yea verily. Two ulcers and many spots did make their abode in my throat, and did cause me to suffer much. "Yes, dear boy, the little woman nearly slipped through our fingers this time, but we've managed to pull her through."

(PHOTOGRAPHS UNREPRODUCEABLE.—ED.)

Dear Sir,

Above is a photograph, life size, of the throat of my grandmother, Femina Muggins, aged 96 years. For 60 years she could eat nothing but gin and bitters, and her throat was in a fearful state—one mass of itching sores indeed a grim sight. After one application of your hair-lotion her throat and breath were like a little child's, and notwithstanding food regulations, she consumed an entire ox for her breakfast. You are at liberty to make what use you like of this letter and photographs.—Yours truly, Jerusha Juggins (Mrs.), 595 Semolina Avenue, Tooting.

Excuse the digression. I'm up for the first time, sitting in an armchair in my bedroom, and looking charming as usual in :—(A) a mauve silk nightie, with spiders' webs embroidered on it—most seduc; (B) a black silk kimono, with almond blossoms all over it; hair done on top à la Chinois, and with large mauve bow. "The dainty dear!" I hear you and your contrades ejaculate - "How true" I can only echo.

Elsie—prepare for a shock—has just taken a post as assistant cook in a hospital at Barnet! She starts this week, and is most delightfully vague about everything. She calls it her "part" of cook, and is at present very occupied in getting a nice uniform.

England is, as you doubtless know, in a ferment at present because :—Our leading halfpenny journal is raising its price from a halfpenny to a penny—the "Daily Mail" says so, so it MUST be so.

I've been writing many decadent and Futuristic poems while in bed, they needn't rhyme, and are very simple and so effective. I'll send you some for your little paper if you like. One was called "Worm" and went something like this (you probably won't appreciate it, not having read much Futuristic poetry, but you may take it from me that its an excellent specimen of the kind of stuff that is sold in orange paper covered books with black scrolls on the covers) :—

WORM.

Thou thing—
Slimy and crawling.
Oozing along.
Not brown,
As men's eyes see.
But reddish green,
And moist.
Death meaning nought
To thee.
Who livest
And breedest
During many æons
Billions more yellow horrors
Like thyself.
Oh, Hell!

Believe me or believe me not, but I dashed that marvellous thing off in a few moments! Swonderful.

Got to have dinner now (i.e.—beef tea and junket, ugh!) so no more. Heaps of best love to you, and "kind thoughts and remembrances" to the Major and your other little friends.

Your Loving Sister,

EDIE.

From '*Wipers*' by Tim Carew:

It was at Ypres that the word 'Chum' first acquired its real meaning. In the Old Contemptibles Association, every member, whether Field Marshal or Private, carries the appellation 'Chum' before his name. On all sides in the stinking holes which went by the name 'trenches' could be heard the comfortable words of the Contemptibles and the word 'Chum' was the most comfortable of all;

'Want a light off my fag, chum?' Drawing by E. Kennington, Talbot House Poperinghe.

GOD-SPEED.

For a year we've taken what came along,
We've fought or worked and we've held
our line,
Till August finds us " going strong,"
The game's afoot and the goal's the
Rhine.

—:0:—

Through summer's heat and the winter's
gloom
We've tasted the joys that the Salient
holds,
A filthy dug-out our only room,
Where our only comfort a jar enfolds.

—:0:—

We've learnt the game in a grim hard
school,
Where mistakes had a price that 'twas
hard to pay,
With Death sitting by and holding the
rule,
And conducting our studies by night and
day.

—:0:—

But we've also learnt, and 'tis good to
know,
That the pal of a dug-out's a friend worth
while,
For friendship made 'neath the star-shell's
glow
Means " Help every lame dog over a
stile."

'Lean on me, Chum...'
'Have a swig from my bottle, Chum.'
'Want a light off my fag, Chum'
'Won't be long now, Chum ...'

On burial details there were very few chaplains to read the burial service; graves were dug – the regulation six feet of earth – and as often as not the body was tipped in without ceremony, with the accompanying farewell, 'In you go Chum – God bless.' Many a soldier has a worse epitaph.

To My Chum is one of the strongest poems from *The Wipers Times* and even after countless re-readings it is hard to be unmoved by its sentiments. It seems to express so completely the unrelenting sadness of the whole terrible war. Where is the Victory? Where is the Glory? What triumph can there be if all a man carries on fighting for is to ensure that his best friend has not died in vain?

Shellshock occasionally so traumatized a soldier that he turned and ran from the battlefield – if the poor man had any sense of direction left and could work out which way to run. We can not leave this subject without consideration of the consequences in 1916 of 'Cowardice in the face of the enemy,' which were summary court-martial and death by firing squad. It is perhaps surprising that such an advanced and anarchic newspaper as *The Wipers Times* should not give some indication of the horror that civilized people feel nowadays for the heartless cruelty of such punishment. In explanation we should remember that when the paper was being printed no one knew what the outcome of the war would be. What was certain was that all would be lost if soldiers ran from the battlefield in any numbers and mutiny caught hold in the British Army. Such a result would undoubtedly ensue if shellshocked soldiers were feather-bedded away from the battlefield by sympathetic psychiatrists and told to take leave away from it all. The whole shocking business must be understood as part of the horror of war and a reminder that when nations fight each other it is the common soldier who finds out at first-hand the de-civilizing process that ensues.

The following abridged quotation is from '*Shot at Dawn*', a history of executions in World War One by Putkowski and Sykes, published in 1989:

> As they approached their destination the Pioneers moved on to the high ground of Pozières Ridge. Whether the party moved across the open or passed along the trenches is unclear. Evidence given at the trial however tends to suggest that the men were in the open … When the party were within 500 yards of the intended place of work a shell crashed down just 25 yards from Private

TO MY CHUM.

No more we'll share the same old barn,
The same old dug-out, same old yarn,
No more a tin of bully share,
Nor split our rum by a star-shell's flare,
    So long old lad.

——:0:——

What times we've had, both good and
    bad,
We've shared what shelter could be had,
The same crump-hole when the whizz-
    bangs shrieked,
The same old billet that always leaked,
And now—you've " stopped one."

——:0:——

We'd weathered the storm two winters
    long,
We'd managed to grin when all went
    wrong,
Because together we fought and fed,
Our hearts were light ; but now—you're
    dead
    And I am Matchless.

——:0:——

Well, old lad, here's peace to you,
And for me, well, there's my job to do,
For you and the others who lie at
    rest,
Assured may be that we'll do our best
    In vengeance.

——:0:——

Just one more cross by a strafed road-
    side,
With it's G.R.C., and a name for guide,
But it's only myself who has lost a
    friend,
And though I may fight through to the
    end,
No dug-out or billet will be the same,
All pals can only be pals in name,
But we'll all carry on till the end of the
    game
    Because you lie there.

Botfield. Evidence given at the court martial stated that the accused was seen to run away and that in a subsequent search he was not found.

The working party continued to their destination and worked till 3.30 am. completing 250 yards of digging. Three hours after the detail's return, Private Botfield was seen back in his Bivouac near Bécourt Wood, and soon after the disciplinary process began.

Botfield told the court that after the shell exploded he jumped into a trench, adding weight to the theory that the party were in the open. The Private continued that he had later attempted to rejoin his party but had met another soldier who must have given him incorrect directions.

Botfield then admitted that he had sat down in the trench, fallen asleep, waking the next day at 4am, and then returned to camp.

Private Botfield made no statement in mitigation and perhaps unwisely called no one to give him a character reference. The court did however note his previous crime. Sir Douglas Haig confirmed the sentence of death on 14 October and three days later the prisoner learned of his fate. At dawn on 18 October Private Botfield was shot at Poperinghe …

Note that, as nearly always, it was a bursting shell that caused this poor man to run away.

The paper does not keep its well-disciplined silence in respect of Field Punishment No. 1. This was another British Army barbarity which was applied for any indiscipline short of 'Cowardice in the Face of the Enemy'. The loss of a weapon or ammunition, not obeying orders, persistent drunkenness, sleeping while on sentry duty and Absence without Leave; these were the misdemeanours that attracted Field Punishment No. 1. In addition to suffering long periods of pack drill and hard labour, the malefactor was tied by hands and feet to a post or gunwheel in an attitude of crucifixion for a period of up to 24 hours.

LANCELOT'S LETTERS TO LONELY LADIES.

FLANDERS

May, 1916

YOU poor little Dears :—

I heard such a funny one about one of our majors the other day. He lost his way in a bit of the country he was ill acquainted with. The day was hot and dusty, the major was hot and thirsty when—lo and behold—he saw, leaning in a somewhat negligent attitude against a gate a private soldier.

" Which way to the Officers' Mess of the Umpshires ?" shouted our tired and weary major

" Along the road about half a-mile, on the left, sir, answered the Tommy, nodding his head in that direction, but otherwise motionless

" Why the — — don't you spring to attention when an officer addresses you ? " roared our friend now thoroughly roused

" Because sir," said the man very meekly. " I'm doing F.P. No. 1, and am tied up to this 'ere gate "

And he's a nice little major man too.

Good-bye and God bless you all.

LANCELOT.

Chapter 5

Communications

The next section of observations on *The Wipers Times* is loosely concerned with Communications. Word of mouth and electronically assisted communications play such a vital part in military operations that it is not surprising to find them referred to directly and indirectly on most pages of a '*Trench Journal*'.

Imagine the simplest form of inter-unit communication – the runner. This man has to receive and remember a message correctly; he then has to make a

12340

Telephone and pigeon-men in a shell hole; telephone lines are broken so messages are being sent by carrier pigeon. Note: this photo would have been censored by reason of the dead or seriously wounded British soldiers clearly visible. Photo Imperial War Museum.

Correspondence.

To the Editor,
"Somme-Times."

Sir,

I should like to draw your atten
tion to a recent discovery of ours which
we have made by judicious inter-breed-
ing. It is the "Parrotidgin " and it is
the result of crossing the parrot and the
pigeon. It should be of immense use
to the War Office as the bird can deliver
its message by word of mouth. It
requires careful feeding and judicious
handling. Our efforts in this direction
are still proceeding and we will advise
you of any further results.

We are, sir
Yours faithfully,
GRANDPA and NICKETT,
Ornithologists.

Answers

to Correspondents.

—:0:—

COLONEL.—We are surprised that you
should have sent such a story to an
earnest periodical like this.

LOVER OF NATURE.—We've had just
about enough of you and your birds.
The mere fact that you've found a
cuckoo's nest with three eggs leaves
us cold. If it costs us 500 francs just
because you heard a gas-horn and
mistook it for the cuckoo, we shudder
to think what might happen if we
don't nip your natural history nosings
in the bud.

SUBALTERN.—Yes, every junior officer
may carry a F.M.'s baton in his
knapsack, but we think you'll discard
that to make room for an extra pair of
socks before very long.

KNOWLEDGE.—No, Ypres is not pronounced " Wipers " because it was
once the centre of the handkerchief
industry.

STAFF-OFFICER.—We sympathise with you
in your little trouble, and advise you
to write to " Cynthia," our love-
expert, about it.

ANXIOUS ONE.—No, its no good worrying
us. The judge will go through all
answers in good time, and the prizes
will go to their proper destination. We
also regret to say you put ten answers
on one coupon, and it's either another
nine francs or nothing doing.

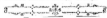

Oh where and oh where is Nick-it-and-run,
And whom does he call 'my dear,
At dead of night on the telephone,
When he tells you secrets the Boche has
known
For the better part of a year ?

perilous journey to a specified destination and
pass the message on, hopefully undistorted, to a
listener who does not expect to receive a
message and usually is not in a position to apply
logic and common sense when interpreting it.
Thus, as we all remember, the recipient of the
message, 'Advancing tonight, send re-
enforcements,' understands perfectly well that
somewhere some one is 'dancing tonight,' but
can not understand why it is deemed necessary
'to send three-and- fourpence.'

To counteract difficulties arising from
variations in the pronunciation of locations
abroad, so often the subject of military
messages, the British soldier shows remarkable
ingenuity in anglicising foreign place names.
In *'Oh What a Lovely War'* much play is made
of the confusion caused in the early years over
the Belgian town-name 'Huy' and the
disastrous results that stemmed from
minimally French-speaking staff officers
confusing Huy with the French for Yes. Not
so Tommy. He would have christened the
town 'Hughie' and the name would have
passed into the language forthwith.

The most obvious example is 'Wipers'
itself. 'Plug Street' is a typical British
corruption of the name of the Belgian village
of Ploegsteert. The letter concerning carrier
pigeons is used as a reminder of the primitive
state of inter-unit communications at this
stage of the First World War.

A small interjection here to illustrate how
the anonymity of the correspondents who
composed *The Wipers Times* is gradually being
broken. Nickett and Grandpa, although their

There's a line that runs from Nieuport
down into Alsace Lorraine,
Its twists and turns are many, and each
means a loss or gain ;
Every yard can tell a story, every foot
can claim its fee,
There the line will stay for ever from
Lorraine up to the sea.

Places memorised by symbol, little things
that caught the mind,
As at Loos 'twas but a lone tree which in
mem'ry is enshrined ;
Perhaps at Wipers 'twas a corner, shell
bespattered, held our sight,
Or a nightingale at Plug Street, sending
music through the night.

Little things, yet each implanted when
the nerves are tension high,
And in years to come remembered how,
while gazing, death passed by :
So the line for all has sign posts, and a
dug-out oft can hold
Little memories to haunt one as the
future years unfold.

Though this line will be behind us as we
push on to the Spree,
Yet to all it will be sacred, mud-encased
though it may be;
In the future dim and distant they will
tell the tale again—
The ghosts of those who held the line
from Nieuport to Lorraine.

"OURS OR THEIRS."

SCENE 2 : AN O.P.
TIME : 2.30 P.M.
TEMPERATURE : ZERO.

Adjutant is discovered sitting in readiness. He has a pair of binoculars slung round his neck. He has forgotten his British Warm.
Thirty minutes elapse.
Enter M.T.M.O. and H.T.M.O. with brace of telephonists.
Both (cheerily) : So sorry. Afraid we're a bit late. Hope we havn't kept you waiting ?
Adj. (shortly) : Not at all.
H.T.M.O. : Never mind. We'll start right away. They've got their line and range. Tell 'em to report when ready.
No. 1 Tel. : Hallo, there. Hallo, hallo, hallo, No. 1 gun, hallo, hallo, HALLO ! !
No. 2 Tel. : Is that No. 3 gun ? Report when ready please
No. 1 Tel. : Hallo, HALLO, HALLO ! ?
H.T.M.O. : Damn that wire.
M.T.M.O. : Thank Heaven, my wires all right. Fire.
M.T.M.O. : Curse. Its a dud. Tell 'em to repeat.
No. 1 Tel. : Hallo, HALLO, HALLO.
H.T.M.O. : It's no darn good. The blasted wire's gone. You'd better slip along and put it right.
M.T.M.O. : What the blazes is wrong with No. 3 gun ? Tell 'em to wake up a bit.
No. 2 Tel. : Misfire, sir. Rifle mechanism blown out, sir. Just trying another, sir. Hallo No. 3, No 3 fired, sir.
M.T.M.O. : There she goes. Good. A beauty. See all that timber and corrugated iron go up? There's a duckboard and two old buckets. Excellent. Repeat.
No. 1 Tel. (returning) : All right now, sir. Hallo there No. 1, can you hear? Right. No 1 ready to fire, sir.
H.T.M.O. : Fire.
No. 2 Tel. : Hallo, hallo, hallo, hallo, No. 3 gun, HALLO, HALLO.
H.T.M.O. : Good Lord. It's a short. Thank Heavens, it's a dud. Wait a bit though, I used a 19 fuse.
(A gigantic explosion is observed).
M.T.M.O. : Bad luck, old man.
No. 2 Tel. : Hallo, No. 3, Hallo, hallo, HALLO, HALLO. No good, sir.
M.T.M.O. : Darn these infernal wires.
(Enter battalion runner completely out of breath.)
Runner (to Adjutant): Captain Jones, sir, 'as sent me to tell you as 'ow the cook 'ouse and men's latrines 'ave been blown up, sir. A toffee apple landed right between 'em, sir.
M.T.M.O. : Oh, damn. I'm awfully sorry.
No. 1. Tel. (to H.T.M.O.) : Gun out of action, sir. Bed jumped out sir.
Adj. (shivering) : Thank God. A most interesting afternoon, you fellows. Let me know what time the hymn of hate comes off to-morrow. Cheero !
Both : ! !   !   J. H. W.

letter is spurious, were real people, probably brigade intelligence officers. Nickett, so named for some light-fingered exploit, figures in *The Nuts of the Old Brigade* by Gilbert Frankau, and Grandpa, an officer clearly of relatively advanced years, is signatory to a comic 'intelligence' report in a later edition of the paper.

And now back to 'Plug Street'.

Patrick Beaver, who introduced and annotated *The Wipers Times* in 1973, explains that British soldiers, particularly telephonists and signallers, soon came up with an acceptable version of the Belgian place name 'Godevaers-velde'. They called it 'Gertie wears velvet.' which would prove to students of phonetics that the first O was probably accented in Flemish to indicate a French OE sound.

The battalion runner gradually gave way to the field telephone and rudimentary wireless telephony by morse code. Portable leather-cased telephones of First World War vintage are still to be found. They have twist-on terminals for the connecting wire and a crank-handle to ring the bell at the other end. Trench to trench, company to company, battalion to battalion and back and across, the Salient was a maze of wire, black signallers' wire that joined field telephones to rudimentary exchanges and generals to company commanders. The wires proliferated like pondweed because when they were broken they were re-laid, never repaired. Wire got lost in the mud; it became entangled, it was cut by shellfire and broken by angry stretcher-bearers hopelessly enmeshed in the slithery darkness. When a message was shouted into a telephone at one end, it was a miracle if it was recognizable when it crackled out of the earpiece at the other.

Read how Robert Graves describes his first progression along a communication trench to the front line.

> The guide gave us hoarse directions all the time. 'Hole right', 'Wire high', 'Wire low', 'Deep place here Sir', 'Wire low'. The field telephone wires had been fastened by staples to the side of the trench, and when it rained the staples fell out and the wire fell down and tripped people up. If it sagged too much, one stretched it across the trench to the other side to correct the sag, but then it would catch one's head. The holes were sump pits used for draining the trenches.

It is with communications cock-ups that 'friendly fire' accidents begin; In '*Ours or Theirs*' we read of a Trench Mortar (Toffee-apple) landing amongst friendly troops. In '*Desert Storm*' it was a missile fired on allied soldiers from the air, but in both cases the accident was caused by a breakdown in communications between front line, fire control agency and the point of weapon release.

'Toffee-apple' mortar bombs; 1917. Photo IWM

M.T.M.O.: Medium Trench Mortar Officer
H.T.M.O.: Heavy Trench Mortar Officer

The '*Hymn of Hate*' was a rabble-rousing anti-British propaganda song. It was popular in Germany at the start of the First World War. The last lines,

> 'We love as one, we hate as one,
> We have one foe, and one alone –
> ENGLAND!'

are typical of the general sentiment. Artillery barrages became known as 'Hymns of Hate' probably in reference to this song.

> 'Advancing tonight; send reinforcements.'
> 'I understand you are dancing tonight …'
> 'No, No, NO; Advancing Ad-Vancing …'
> 'I can't hear you; line is very bad; spell first word.'
> 'Aie Dee Vee Aie Enn See …'
> 'Understand Kay Ee Ee Jay Emm Dee …'
> 'Wrong. I spell A Ack, D Don, V Vic, A Ack, N Nan,'
> 'Got you now. Understand Advancing. Query three and fourpence.'

The first phonetic alphabet evolved during the time that *The Wipers Times* was being produced. Originally B could stand for 'Baby' or 'Blood' or 'Bullet' or whatever came into a half-deafened signaller's head. Gradually it became apparent that the spelling was more easily understood if B always stood for the same thing; 'Beer'. The most common letters to be clarified in this way were the ones which sounded similar or which were only phonetically differentiated by first or last consonant. 'Bee, Cee, Dee, Gee, Pee, Tee, Vee; Ay, Jay, Kay and Emm and Enn'. Phonetic words like 'Beer' and 'Pip' moved from the signallers' language into everyday conversation and thence to *The Wipers Times*. 'O Pip' and 'I Beer' are interesting because neither the O nor the I were considered to sound sufficiently like any other letter to merit a phonetic stand-in.

There is a reference in the paper to the Distinguished Conduct Medal. It becomes the Don C Emma which indicates that there was nothing in normal use for C to stand for. Perhaps it was the only one of the 'EE' sounds not to be given a permanent phonetic equivalent.

'T27 B' is the designation of an allied trench. It is not difficult to imagine the progression towards a 'friendly fire' accident if a message calling down artillery fire on a German trench, say at G27P, became garbled in the telephone system. A friendly 'toffee apple' polishing off the Nuts of the Old Brigade? What a disaster!

'Baloo' is a soldier's corruption of the French town name of Bailleul.

'I. Beer' means IB which means Infantry Brigade.

It is typical of the behaviour of a close-knit community living under unusual circumstances that the soldiers of Wipers modified the language in their own particular way. By referring to 'Toc twenty-seven beer' Gilbert Frankau was proclaiming that he belonged. He was one of the unfortunates who had been there. A visiting war correspondent would have to ask what it meant, so would a staff Major from safer areas in the rear. In conversation many years later, survivors of the First World War would revert to Pip Emma and Ack Emma when telling the time. It was their way of reminding themselves that they had been there and they were proud of it. The custom survived the introduction into the military of both the twenty-four-hour clock and the 'Alpha Bravo Charlie' phonetic alphabet.

Oh give me the Nuts of the old Brigade
The Nuts of the right good cheer!
I wish I were with them, wherever they
went,
Though I'd rather it wasn't The
Salient . . . .
And so would the old I. Beer.

GILBERT FRANKAU.

19/6/16.

Oh where are my lost interpreters,
And what the deuce do they do ?
Are they buying port by the wagon-load,
Or galloping hard on the hard high road
To draw their pay in Baloo ?

Oh where are the Nuts of the old Brigade,
The Nuts that used to be here ?
They have left their Gunners and motored
away,
Shall I find them at Kemmel or at
Fleurbaix
Or in Tock Twenty-seven Beer ?

The prisoner with mournful look just
sadly murmured " Who'd
Have thought that Prussia's best should
thus so quickly have been looed ?"
" Ho yus," said Tommy with a grin,"and
bloomin' well napooed."

The privit to the sergeant said
" I wants my blooming rum."
" Na poo," the sergeant curtly said,
And sucked his jammy thumb.
" There's soup in foo' for you to-night."
The privit said, " By gum !"

Brief consideration should be given to the word 'Narpoo'. It is a corruption of a French or Belgian negative; either 'Ne pas' or 'Il n'y a plus'. The following shades of meaning seem to be covered by ' Narpoo' when it occurs in literature of the First World War:

'I have none.
You have none.
There are none.
Finish.
No Good.
There are no more.
There never were any.
I am no more.'

Thus the long-running *Wipers Times* serial, 'Narpoo Rum' would translate as 'There is no rum.' 'Rum Narpoo' would mean that the Rum was no good, or perhaps that it was finished. Note that the universality of 'Narpoo' in the First World War was matched by that of 'Okay' in the Second. In almost every case 'Okay' meant the exact opposite of Na- or Nar-poo.

'Looed' refers to the battle of Loos which, although militarily at best a draw, was put across to the British troops as a famous victory.

'Kultur', the German for culture, was a propaganda word used by both sides. In Berlin it was the enlightening and uplifting greater German way of life that it was the Hohenzollern duty to impose upon the world. Amongst the Allies 'Kultur' was used to describe the arrogant, overbearing, un-Christian and uncivilized philosophy from which Europe had to be protected.

The strange tendency for equipment officers and the Quartermaster branch of the British Army to speak backwards has given amusement to front line troops over many years. There seems to be a humourless pomposity about 'Pots chamber one' that is missing if this

K'S for the KULTUR beneficent Huns
Endeavour to force down our
throats with big guns :
They send shells in packets, they send
them in ones :
But Kultur's NAR-Poo in the trenches.

particular item is referred to as a 'Chamber pot'. This is compounded if the fuller service nomenclature of 'Pots; chamber, crested, senior officers for the use of,' is recited.

In the Quartermaster's inventory, which is supposed to list every item of clothing and equipment that a generous government could need to issue to servicemen, entries are tabulated under plural generic headings. These headings are then modified by as many descriptive adjectives that a history of cock-ups as old as the British Army, deems necessary. 'Send More Boots,' a harrassed Quartermaster wrote home from the Crimea; and we all know what he got. What he should have asked for was 'boots cold-weather marching left' *and* 'boots cold-weather marching right.' Then perhaps we might not have lost so many soldiers to frost-bite because they had to wear a balaklava helmet on one foot.

Contributors to *The Wipers Times* often mocked the Quartermasters by reverting to 'equipment-speak' when mentioning service-issue items. It was not done solely for laughs. Front-line fighting troops undoubtedly felt that it was irrelevant to the messy, bloody and dangerous process of fighting a war in the trenches, to be pestered by the comparatively secure Q branch for handwritten returns to regularize the issue of almost anything. Ammunition, food, weapons and clothing had to be indented for before delivery and accounted for at regular intervals. The equippers were trying, quite properly, to control the ruinous expenditure of resources that fighting a war involves. Proper and well-meaning the process may have been, but it drove the men in the trenches mad.

'Gum Boots Thigh' were waders in equipment-speak, though 'Boots Gum Thigh' would be more quartermasterly. When he wrote '*Urgent or*

'Indent now for gum boots thigh'

From 'Urgent or Ordinary' by Gilbert Frankau. *Wipers Times* 2/3/16

" For information "—" Urgent "—
" Confidential "—
" Secret "—" For necessary action,
please "—
" The G.O.C. considers it essential "—
My soldier-soul must steel itself to these ;
Must face, by dawn's dim light. by
night's dull taper,
Disciplined, dour, gas-helmeted, and
stern,
Brigades, battalions, batteries, of paper.—
The loud ' report,' the treacherous
' return,'

Division orders, billeting epistles,
Barbed ' Zeppelin' wires that baffle
G.H.Q.
And the dread ' Summary whose blurred
page bristles
With ' facts ' no German general ever
knew,
Let the Hun hate ! We need no beer-
roused passions
To keep our sword-blade bright, our
powder dry,

The while we chase October's o'erdrawn
rations
And hunt that missing pair of ' Gum-
boots, thigh.'

GILBERT FRANKAU.

2/3/16.

RATS.

I want to write a poem, yet I find I have
no theme,
" Rats " are no subject for an elegy,
Yet they fill my waking moments, and
when star-shells softly gleam,
'Tis the rats who spend the midnight
hours with me.
—o—o—o—
On my table in the evening they will
form " Battalion mass,"
They will open tins of bully with their
teeth,
And should a cake be sent me by some
friend at home, alas !
They will extricate it from its cardboard
sheath.
—o—o—o—
They are bloated, fat and cunning, and
they're marvels as to size,
And their teeth can penetrate a sniping
plate,
I could tell you tales unnumbered, but
you'd think I'm telling lies,

Of one old, grey whiskered buck-rat and
his mate.
—o—o—o—
Just to show you, on my table lay a tin
of sardines—sealed—
With the implement to open hanging
near,
The old buck-rat espied them, to his
missis loudly squealed,
" Bring quickly that tin-opener, Stinky
dear ! "
—o—o—o—
She fondly trotted up the pole, and
brought him his desire,
He proceeded then with all his might
and main,
He opened up that tin, and then—'tis
here you'll dub me " Liar ! "—
He closed it down, and sealed it up again.

Have you seen one, should a rival chance
to spoil his love affair,
Bring a bomb, Mills, hand, and place it
underneath
The portion of the trench where that said
rival had his lair,
And then he'll pull the pin out with his
teeth.

Ordinary' Gilbert Frankau was one step back from the front line, having been moved from his battery to serve as a middleman in the endless paper battle between rear echelon equipment depots and the guns that were actually firing. This meant that he was bombarded with forms from both sides as he worked by candlelight on a makeshift table in an unsafe dugout within the city walls of Ypres. The rather laboured puns on the words 'Report' and 'Return' which mark Frankau down as an artilleryman are typical of his style of writing. Nowadays puns elicit groans but in the days of Wilde, Frankau and Coward no 'witty' verse was without them.

The poem about rats is included to demonstrate the 'Q' description of the Mills Bomb, an early form of anti-personnel grenade. Readers will also note the vivid description of Trench Life that the writer conveys almost unconsciously. This particular issue of the paper celebrated Christmas 1916.

'God rest you merry gentlemen ...'

An Ode to Q.

—o—o—o—

Listen reader, while I tell you
Stirrings deeds both old and new
Tales of battles during which we
—Chits received from Batt. H. Q

—:o:—

Fought we had a losing battle
All the day and all the night.
All communications broken,
Never was there such a plight.
Now the Hun comes o'er the sandbags
In one long unbroken mass—
Just in time—the welcome message
" Indent now for helmets gas

—:o:—

Shelled they'd been for three days solid
In a trench just two feet high.
Couldn't get retaliation
Matter not how they might try.
Binks's men had held the trenches
(Binks is NOT his proper name),
Savagely he sent the message
" Carn't you stop their purple game ?"
Anxiously they wait the answer,
What a brave but serried band.
Here it comes—Binks grabs the paper
" Deficiences not yet to hand ! "

—:o:—

Have you ever heard the tale, lad,
How we took the trench at A ?
Said the good old 92nd.
Here we are, and here we'll stay
What a tale of awful trial,
Cut off was our food supply.
If we do not get some bully
—Bread or biscuits—we shall die.
The foe comes on in countless thousands
Bearing down with savage cry.
Jones receives a frantic message
" Indent now for gum boots thigh."

—:o:—

Thus you see, O gentle reader;
Why the O. C. Coys are grey.
These and other kindred worries
Are their portion day by day.

Part Two

The Readers

Chapter 6

Below the Waist

The examination of personal characteristics and physical attributes of the average *Wipers Times* reader starts at ground or mud-level and, in this chapter, we move slowly upwards to the waist.

Napoleon suggested that the most important physical attribute of a soldier was his stomach, but in the First World War we must allow that the feet took pride of place. With what envious eyes the survivors of Ypres must have looked on the Armoured Personnel Carriers that are now considered essential to the conduct of any war where infantrymen are involved. The unarmed personnel carriers of 1914-1918 were the soldiers' feet. When moving up to the front for a spell in the trenches or moving out for 'Rest', they marched. To pull out when the 'strafe' got too intense, to hurry back to oppose the consequent frontal attack, to patrol no man's land and to carry back the wounded, the men of Ypres were completely dependent on their feet. The infallible 'Blighty' which was guaranteed to

Going up to the trenches 1916.

TO HARASSED SUBALTERNS.
—o—o—o—o—
IS YOUR LIFE MISERABLE? ARE YOU UNHAPPY?
DO YOU HATE YOUR COMPANY COMMANDER?
—o—o—o—o—
YES! THEN BUY HIM ONE OF
OUR NEW PATENT TIP DUCK BOARDS
YOU GET HIM ON THE END—THE DUCK BOARD DOES THE REST
—o—o—o—o—
Made in three sizes, and every time a "Blighty."
—o—o—o—o—
" If once he steps on to the end,
'Twill take a month his face to mend "
—o—o—o—o—
WRITE AT ONCE & ENSURE HAPPINESS
THE NOVELTY SYNDICATE, R.E. HOUSE   Tel.: " DUMP '

QUESTIONS A
PLATOON COMMANDER
SHOULD ASK HIMSELF.

ENGRAVED BY SAPPER COUZENS R.E.

1: Am I as offensive
as I might be.

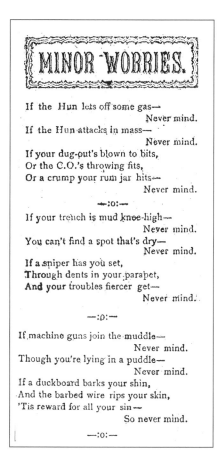

MINOR WORRIES.

If the Hun lets off some gas—
Never mind.
If the Hun attacks in mass—
Never mind.
If your dug-out's blown to bits,
Or the C.O.'s throwing fits,
Or a crump your rum jar hits—
Never mind.

—:o:—

If your trench is mud knee-high—
Never mind.
You can't find a spot that's dry—
Never mind.
If a sniper has you set,
Through dents in your parapet,
And your troubles fiercer get—
Never mind.

—:o:—

If machine guns join the muddle—
Never mind.
Though you're lying in a puddle—
Never mind.
If a duckboard barks your shin,
And the barbed wire rips your skin,
'Tis reward for all your sin—
So never mind.

—:o:—

engineer repatriation was a wound to the foot, and that is where a man shot himself if a self-inflicted wound was his only hope of survival.

There are many references to the feet in *The Wipers Times*. We read of irregular variations on army issue footwear the most common of which was the 'Gum boot thigh' or wader-boot which was an attempt to keep the feet dry in trenches which invariably penetrated below the water table of the Flanders plain. Fungal and parasitic disorders were common (trench foot and pediculi). Another problem stemmed from the duckboards that were laid along the bottom of trenches in an attempt to elevate the walkway above water level. These boards never made a firm footing and would twist or fly upwards when trodden on by the muddy feet of passing men. Imagine the travails of the stretcher-bearers as they manoeuvred their dead-weight load along a narrow trench with right-angle corners. The duckboards tilted and gave way as they passed, their wounded passengers groaned at every shock, and a sniper's bullet or shrapnel awaited if their helmeted heads momentarily projected above the parapet.

CLOTH HALL, YPRES.

—o—o—o—

SAPPER AND PARTY.

IN THEIR SCREAMING FARCE, ENTITLED:
"STUCK IN A GUM-BOOT."

—o—o—o—o—

JOCK McGREE

IN HIS FAMOUS SONG
"Trenches Ain't the Proper Place for Kilts,"

—o—o—o—o—

POPULAR PRICES.

—o—o—o—o—

Ventilated throughout by Bosch and Co.

Take the case of poor Bill 'Arris
Deep in love with Rosy Greet,
So forgot to grease his tootsies,
Stayed outside and got " trench feet."

P'S for PEDICULI, horrible pests,
    They make themselves happy in
        trousers and vests ;
Though dear little fellows, they're un-
        welcome guests
To the P.B.I. in the trenches.

ARE YOU GOING OVER THE TOP?

IF SO BE SURE TO FIRST INSPECT OUR NEW LINE OF VELVETEEN
CORDUROY PLUSH BREECHES.

BE IN THE FASHION AND LOOK LIKE A SOLDIER.

ALL ONE PRICE, 9s. 11d.

THOUSANDS OF TESTIMONIALS FROM ALL FRONTS.

SEND FOR THESE AND ILLUSTRATED BROCHURE ENTITLED:
" Breeches And Their Wearers " Or
" Legs Make The Officer."

Address : POND & CO., WULVERGHEM.   Agents all along the line

An off-duty Subaltern of
the 19th Lancashire
Fusiliers wearing the
discredited pale-coloured
breeches.

MY own pet extravagences are shoes
and stockings. I wish you could
see my new bottines, black toes
and white uppers, of course, à la " Eve,"
and so high; for not a scrap of a gap
must there be between boot tops and
skirt-edge, and the latter is still at a
deliciously high level. A windy day
witnesses many revelations, some more
fearful than beautiful, and only those of
us who are conscious of our—ahem !—
" stockings " being faultless dare face a
real gale.

Answers

to Correspondents.

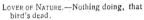

LOVER OF NATURE.—Nothing doing, that bird's dead.

PRO BONO.—Noise you complain of is our new metre gun. Certainly, will have it removed if it disturbs your sleep.

SUBALTERN.—No, the death penalty is not enforced in the case of murdering an adjutant, as you can always be able to prove extenuating circumstances.

YOUNG OFFICER.—It is not "the thing" to wear turned up slacks and shoes when "going over the top," in fact, you run the risk of being sent back to your unit if discovered.

TROUBLED.—Certainly think you have just complaint against people in next dug-out, and if you care to take the matter further there is no doubt that you will get damager. It certainly was scandal if, as you affirm, the picture was one of Kirschner's.

Routine Orders about this time stated, rather pompously, that Platoon Commanders at no time should think only defensively. In fact they should make a conscious effort to be as offensive as possible. *The Wipers Times* milked this for every laugh possible, using 'Offensive' in its peacetime meaning of 'Giving Offence.' Note the footwear.

After the feet it is logical to move upwards a little and consider the legs. There is one reference in the paper to the notorious impracticality of the kilt as trench uniform. Some people will recall from history lessons that the soldiers in the Scottish regiments suffered from chaffing and sores on the legs brought on by the abrasive hems of mud-encrusted kilts. The story may be as much of a chestnut as the left-hand boots in the Crimea, but the matter is raised in *The Wipers Times*, in one of the Cloth Hall 'Entertainment' advertisements.

'Legs make the Officer' indeed, but the light-coloured breeches worn by junior officers

Over the Top – Battle of the Somme. Not the moment for the leader to advertise his position.

in the early years of the First World War made the wearers an immediate and special target for the enemy gunners when leading their men over the parapets for another hopeless charge against fortified positions. This advertisement is an example of the Editor's skill at getting in a dig at the general staff for a lethal military inefficiency, with-out crossing the border of insubordination.

This part of a poem by Gilbert Frankau points the way for the next investigation into the lives of *The Wipers Times* readers. We have considered the feet, the knees and the legs and next for study are matters sexual and lavatorial.

The popular but groundless rumour that Medical Officers and Quartermasters strove to lull the libidos of fighting men by the administration of bromide, usually in the tea, was still in circulation forty years later when young men were conscripted for National Service. This solves the riddle of 'bromo'. Chromolithography was a method of colourprinting that was perfected in Victorian times, and seldom bettered for mass reproduction of famous paintings. So, a 'Naughty Chromo,' was a colour print of a subject which, like 'bugger' and 'bloody', might offend the sensibilities of an Edwardian lady.

But who was Kirchner, and what were these naughty pictures that could divert Gilbert Frankau in his dugout bed from the more normal dreams of sleeping men in forward areas subject to enemy shell fire?

There was a Kirchner Girl in the Imperial War Museum exhibition of Forces Sweethearts. Singers, film actresses, music-hall stars, news-readers, nurses, tealadies, 'Sally Army' girls; all were on display there and the thread that held this strange disparity of females together was that at some time amidst the dirt, danger and discomfort of war, men had derived a moment's good cheer from their images. On display were Memphis Belle and Fertile Myrtle, lovingly painted on the fuselages of Flying Fortresses; and the impossibly-breasted Varga girls accompanied by verses of astonishing coyness. '*I know just what you're thinking, When you stare at me that way. Thank*

VIRTUE.

Now you subs of tender years
For your morals, it appears,
(You must admit they're open much to
question)
There is shortly going to be
A morality O.C.,
Who will see that vice does not spoil
your digestion.

His H.Q. is going to be
Close by Leicester Square, and he
Will parade his Batt. for duty every night,
In his ranks we'll shortly see
P'raps a Bishop or M.P.,
Who will see that virtue's path you tread
aright.

If on leave and pleasure bent
At Victoria, a gent
Will grab you as you're dodging off alone,
Will escort you to H.Q.,
When you'll quickly find that you
Are provided with an aged chaperone.

Your amusement will depend
On how much she'll let you spend,
And you'll dine at Lyons or an A.B.C.,
Should you dare to want a drink,
With a look she'll make you think
What an awful well of sin a sub can be.

You may smoke one cigarette,
Ere retiring you will get
All your orders for the morrow's pleasure
feast,
Hand your cash in charge, and then
Off to bed as clock strikes ten,
Feeling that in former days you were a
beast.

You will come to learn and love
Programmes as described above
For you must admit that you were most
immoral,
You will find when leave's expired
That your fancies will have tired
For the glass that sparkles, and for lips of
coral.

Urgent or Ordinary.

I dreamed of bloody spurs and bloodier
    sabre,
Of mentions—not too modest—in
    despatches ;
I threw my foes, as Scotchmen toss the
    caber,
And sent my prisoners home in wholesale
    batches ;
Led my platoons to storm the Prussian
    trenches,
Galloped my guns to enfilade his flank ;
Was it H.M.'s own royal hand, or
    French's,
That pinned the V.C. on my tunic ?
    SWANK !
Those dreams are dead : now in my
    Wiper's dug-out,
I only dream of Kirchner's naughtiest
    chromo ;
The brasier smokes ; no window lets the
    fug out ;
And the Bosche shells ; and ' Q ' still
    issues bromo

Entanglements

" COME ON, BERT, IT'S SAFER IN THE TRENCHES "

goodness I'm a painting, Oh what would mother say?' There was music; '*We'll Meet Again,*' promised Vera and people tapped their feet to '*Don't sit under the Apple Tree with Anybody Else but Me.*' And in a brightly lit display cabinet, in a section devoted to the First World War, there was a grey folder entitled 'War Time Lovelies – Drawn for the *Daily Sketch* by Raphael Kirchner.'

The star of the album was a girl dressed in what can only be described as a translucent – not transparent – combination garment which suggested rather than accentuated the conventional points of interest in the female form. She wore a casually draped red scarf, turban like, over her golden curls giving the clue to the picture's title: '*Miss Redcap.*'

The immediate impact of the Kirchner girls was in their innocence. Here was nothing lustful, nothing brazen or tarty. Miss Redcap was not portrayed to arouse but simply to be decorative; a glimpse into the boudoir of a girl who had, perhaps on purpose, forgotten to close the door as she changed for dinner. From this one could deduce that the readers of *The Wipers Times* themselves were equally innocent in their fantasies and so much more civilised in their attitude to women than the Germans and, sadly, generations of British men that were to follow them. Read what Gilbert Frankau has to say about the behaviour of men at war.

The idiot girl who sat dribbling by her mother's stove in Bailleul while our interpreter and I drank coffee had been raped at the age of sixteen in the open street by more than a dozen drunken Hun infantrymen while their officers looked on.

People with less prejudiced minds than my own may suggest that such behaviour is possible in all warring armies. I maintain that it would have been utterly impossible in ours.

For one lesson my fourteen months at the front did teach me; that the world's finest gentleman is 'poor bloody Tommy'.

Women who complain today about the increasing incidence of rape and the general dishonouring of females might do well to compare a Kirchner girl with a modern pornographic pin-up. Here is one clue to the de-civilization that has invaded the fantasies of the young men of this land.

The poems 'Tommy in France' and 'Virtue' serve as confirmation of the restrictions that British civilization placed on the sexual behaviour of the men fighting the First World War. Tommy and his mate are bewailing their constant failure to 'make it' with the few local girls that are still around. A drink in a cafe is a poor substitute. The 'Sub of Tender Years' is advised of the 'Morality Patrols' who apparently oversaw the behaviour of young men on leave in London.

Comparison should be made between the British Army and the armies of Germany, France and Italy who encouraged prostitution and brothels wherever there were accumulations of unattached fighting men. Look at the occupying armies of Pakistan in what is now Bangladesh, and the men of Serbia amongst the Muslims of Bosnia where rape actually became a soldier's duty.

The Nuts of the Old Brigade by Gilbert Frankau is a short poem bewailing the departure of some of the comrades he fought with in the early days of the war.

LOVE AND WAR.

—o—o—o—

In the line a soldiers's fancy
Oft may turn to thoughts of love.
But too hard to dream of Nancy
When the whizz-bangs sing above.

—§ † §—

In the midst of some sweet picture
Vision of a love swept mind,
Bang ! "A whizz-bang almost nicke\
  yer !"
"Duck, yer blighter, are yer blind ?"

—§ † §—

Then remember old Tom Stoner,
Ponder on his awful fate.
Always writing to his Donah,
Lost his rum 'cos 'e was late.

—§ † §—

Then again there's 'Arry 'Awkins,
Stopped to dream at Gordon Farm.
Got a "blightie" found his Polly
Walking out on Johnson's arm.

—§ † §—

Plenty more of such examples
I could give, had I but time.
War on tender feelings tramples,
H.E. breaks up thoughts sublime.

—§ † §—

"Don't dream when you're near machine
  guns !"
Is a thing to bear in mind.
Think of love when not between Huns,
A sniper's quick, and love is blind.

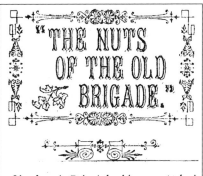

TOMMY IN FRANCE.

—o—o—o—

"Oh! madamerselle, chery madamerselle,
You come for a nice promenay ?
Yes, its always the same with your ' apres
la guerre,'
And your ' me no compris ' what I say,
Come along Bill to the old ' staminet,'
Though the beer may be rotten it still is
a ' wet,'
A hunk off a loaf and a glass, me and you,
What's that old lady ? Oh! damn it,
' Napoo.' "

"THE NUTS OF THE OLD BRIGADE."

Oh where is Bob o' the big moustache ?
An alien Adjutant shoots
For the Major-man that I used to know,
With his Kirchner ladies all in a row,
And his seventeen pairs of boots.

Frankau has just returned from leave in the UK to find the regiment and *The Wipers Times* printing office have been re-positioned. A lot of his friends are posted or have become casualties. Can we not just picture the eccentric mustachioed Major Bob with his dugout full of pin-ups and his highly polished boots? He probably called all women 'M'Dear' and doubtless an overworked orderly accom-panied him whenever he visited the trenches, carrying spare footwear to replace any that became muddied.

To indulge in any sort of sexual activity was something of a triumph for the soldiers in the trenches around Ypres. It was a triumph over military authority which forbade all erotic physical contact between the sexes while actively engaged in hostilities. It was also a signal victory over discomfort, danger and loneliness, and a man who managed to steal as much as a kiss from a waitress in a bomb damaged Belgian estaminet attained the status of a hero among his less fortunate comrades. But while the Army, from Lord Kitchener downwards, did its damnedest to ban fraternization and associated evils, no one could disallow fantasies. They tried to of course. Fantasies led to daydreaming and poor concentration which in those anti-'self-abuse' days were thought to be ultimately responsible for loss of energy, shaky hands and a poor aim with a rifle. Pictures of pretty girls in dugouts and places of rest were frowned upon by higher authority and consequently much admired by the lonely soldiers. Pin-ups also appeared to confirm that those who displayed them were slightly rebellious people who retained some individuality in a world where conformity equated with discipline.

The Wipers Times is ambivalent in these matters. Like *Tee Emm*, the Second World War aircrew training magazine, the paper gives the party line on the dangers of day-dreaming about the 'Girl Back Home' but at the same time it gives discreet adulation to those who achieve even the faintest

Things We Want To Know.

—◼—

The name of the brunette infantry officer whose man got hold of the carrier pigeons, (sent to this celebrated Company Commander when his communications in the front line had broken down) and cooked them.   Also who were his guests ?

—o—

The name of the M.O. who attended one of the leading lights of the Fancies, and was overcome by her many charms.

—o—

The celebrated infantry officer who appears daily in the trenches disguised as a Xmas tree.

—o—

Why the dug-out of a certain Big Man is so much affected by subalterns of tender years, and if this has anything to do with the decorations on his walls.

—o—

The weekly wage bill at the Fancies.

R. B.

Things We Want to Know.

—o—o—o—

The name of the Brig. Major, who, in relief orders, mentioned that one battalion of a famous regiment would find billets in three houses in Street Verbod te Wateren.

•   •   •

The name of the red trimmed officer who has a penchant for 5A.

•   •   •

The name of the Major who capitulated to the dark-eyed Belgique at the " Chateau."

The name of the M G.O. who has come to the conclusion that the only reason the Hun planes visit Pop. is to bomb his camp. (The personelle of which, we believe, is three N.C.O.'s and one private.)

•   •   •

Are we as OFFENSIVE as we might be.

sexual success. There is also much regard paid to those who display the most daring array of pin-ups.

'*Love and War*' is the practical anti-fantasy poem and is the nearest *The Wipers Times* ever gets to being a version of Battalion Routine Orders.

These columns of 'Things We Want To Know' (TWWTK) appeared in early editions of *The Wipers Times*. There is one reference to dugout decoration and two to 'The Fancies,' a concert troupe who occasionally appeared in a makeshift theatre in Poperinghe. There were two girls in the company one of whom was the daughter of an estaminet keeper in Armentières – possibly the original 'Mademoiselle'.

The second sequence of TWWTK contains news of a sexual encounter of sufficient importance to arouse the interest of the readers. Incidently, a translation of '*Verbod te wateren*' would be the Edwardian street sign, 'Commit No Nuisance', nowadays de-eulogised into 'Don't Piss in the Street.'

The solution to some of the 'Riddles' posed by the 'Things We Want to Know' column (page 55) can never be more than speculation. I would like to suggest that two junior officers might have been awarded the Military Cross in skirmishes at 'Strongpoint C2.' In a typically understated and obtuse manner, the Editor is offering congratulations by suggesting that that particular location should be known as 'MC 2.'

I was much amused by the story of the Officer who ate the carrier pigeons. I will take a small personal diversion here to solve the riddle of the infantryman disguised as a Christmas Tree, (see page 55).

I went to war in a Beverley transport aircraft; a giant slab-sided four-engined monster that flew, so its pilots said, 'like a Mexican brick-built shit-house', but landed with the elegance of a ballet dancer. We inched on to the 400 yard airstrip at Thumeir, north of Aden and came to rest in a dramatic cloud of reverse-thrusted desert dust.(See painting by David Shepherd hanging, I believe, in the great hall of the Royal Air Force College at Cranwell.) I disembarked in the searing dry heat of the Radfan mountains with some difficulty due to the diversity of equipment with which I was encumbered. I had been posted to the minor skirmish in the Radfan at the end of a tour in Aden and before embarking in the Beverley I drew from the equipment section at Khormaksar the appropriate scale of equipment issued to Officers proceeding on active-service (Desert) (Non-nuclear) (1955). I was presented with and not permitted to refuse;

Canvas collapsible wash stand;	2 Mess tins;
Water bottle;	Knife fork spoon plate;
Collapsible canvas chair;	4 tins of compo rations;
Safari-bed ;	Binoculars;
Field dressing;	Sunburn cream;
First Aid kit;	Anti-Malaria tablets;
Morphine;	Salt tablets;
Webbing belt pouch and holster;	Insect repellent;
.38 Smith and Wesson;	Toilet paper;
10 rounds for same;	Athletes foot powder.
Sun hat and mosquito net;	

Robert Graves records a not dissimilar issue on his departure for the Front in 1914. Since the débâcle of the Crimea, the British Army has ensured that while its strategies and its weapons might at times be inadequate it could never be accused of under-equipping its fighting men.

It was always possible therefore to spot the new arrivals, both at Ypres and in the Radfan, by their appearance; so hung about with accoutrements as to resemble a Christmas tree.

Graves uses this phrase as does The Wipers Times, although in the latter case we must presume that it was the officer's persistence in appearing 'disguised as an Xmas tree' that was of note. I certainly followed military convention and discarded as soon as possible this mound of redundant equipment that marked me out as a 'Sprog in the War Zone' adding an unopened kitbag full of service issue this-and-that to a huge pile in a tent that had been set aside for this particular purpose.

WANTED.

STRONG YOUTH as LAMPLIGHTER for Wytschaete—good wage paid if work satisfactory.—Apply Wytschaete Urban District Council.

AGENTS for ART. HILLERY'S HOT CRUMPETS—Good opening for a forceful young man.—Write Box 110, " New Church " Times.

ARE YOU TIRED, HOT & THIRSTY AFTER A LONG WALK? YES! THEN DROP IN AT BUS FARM THE NEW TEA SHOP.

—o—o—o—

Tastefully Fitted.
General Attractions.
Walloon Waitresses.

—o—o—o—

FAMOUS CRUMPET HOUSE.
AIRY TEA ROOMS.
SPECIAL ACCOMODATION FOR MOTORISTS.
SWITCHBACK NEAR BY.
TAKE THE TUBE OR GREEN 'BUS.
PARTIES CATERED FOR AND WEDDING BREAKFAST'S ARRANGED.

—o—o—o—

TELEPHONE : 102, HOP.
TELEGRAMS : " MOVING."

Things   We   Want   to   Know.

---:o:---

Who it is that makes an infernal din on a horn at 2 a.m.

? ? ?

Whether it is a fact that the amorous incarnadined major has again succumbed.

? ? ?

Whether the popular Artillery C O. helped the Belgian priest in his little trouble

? ? ?

Whether it is a fact that a noticeboard at the foot of Kemmel Hill reads .— ' Anyone proceeding up the Hill will please go by main road, as a patrol is established there to enforce the stringent regulations re passes, etc.   Persons going by other routes might miss patrol."

? ? ?

The name of the firm of estate agents which is trying to let Red Lodge.

? ? ?

How the poplars are coming up.

T.W.W.T.K. Explained.

It was probably a Gas warning horn that made the 'infernal din.'

'Incarnadined' means 'newly coloured red'. This Major has been recently elevated to 'The Staff' and has taken the opportunity to set up a liaison with a female somewhere a few miles to the rear of the Salient.

Clearly the Belgian Priest was having more success in illicit affairs than Tommy. The editor is expressing envy rather than disapproval.

The mathematically spaced Poplar trees planted along the Belgian roads were used by the German artillery to range on. British Engineers, Pioneers and Gunners did their best to knock them down. A Lover of Nature or Salient Environmentalist (probably named Phillpott) seems to have planted replacement seedlings somewhere close to *The Wipers Times* office.

That night as I retired to my Safari bed, the twenty-five-pound field-guns, in use for the last time on active service with the British Army, fired ranging rounds into the surrounding hills. Bangbang ..... Boomboom re-echoed around the camp and in the next tent a radio crackled as the O.Pip, sorry the Oscar Papa, called and corrected the fall of shot.

These extracts confirm that the sex life of the soldiers was virtually confined to harmless voyeurism. The 'Bus Farm' advertisement suggests that 'Tea and Sympathy' from willing Belgian girls might have been available at this particular location but the 'Walloon Waitresses' were probably pure fantasy. 'Crumpet' had no sexual innuendo in 1916 but merely referred, as ever, to the enemy guns.

… and a little more on the subject of the Poplar Nursery.

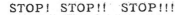

STOP! STOP!! STOP!!!

NOW THAT SPRING IS COMING
YOU REQUIRE SHADE.
WE ARE IN A POSITION TO OFFER THE PUBLIC
250,000,000 SAPLINGS
OF THAT FULSOME, PROLIFIC AND UMBRAGEOUS PLANT,
THE POPLAR
—o—o—o—o—
WHAT ARE YOU GOING TO HANG THAT HAMMMMOCK ON?
—SURELY NOT THE FISH HOOK—
Therefore Buy While Opportunity Offers.
—o—o—o—o—
OLD WORLD AVENUES A SPECIALITY.
—o—o—o—o—
ADDRESS: FILL, POTS & Co. RENINGHELST.

Stunted Poplar 'range-markers' can be seen in this picture of wagons near 'Hellfire Corner'.

THE SUB.

He loves the Merry " Tatler," he adores
the Saucy " Sketch,"
The " Bystander " also fills him with
delight ;
But the pages that he revels in, the evil-
minded wretch,
Are the adverts of those things in pink
and white.

—:o:—

They are advertised in crêpe-de-chine,
and trimmed with silk and lace ;
The pictures fairly make him long for
leave ;
And while he gloats upon their frills, he
cannot find the grace
To read the pars of PHRYNETTE, BLANCHE
and EVE.

—:o:—

Before the war, he'd hardly heard of lace
and lingerie ;
He didn't know the meaning of chemise.
But thanks to weekly papers, this
astounding mystery
Has been solved by dainty VENN and
dear LABISE.

—:o:—

Before the war, he only knew of corsets
and of hats,
All other vogues invoked a ribald "what-
ho."
But the last decree of Fashion is a dinky
nightie, that's
Embroidered with his regimental motto.

—:o:—

It's this war, that is responsible for
teaching simple youth
All sorts of naughty Continental tricks.
And already he's decided, when it's over,
that, in truth,
He'll buy mamma a pair of cami-knicks.

R.M.O.

CRICKET.

— o —

WITH APOLOGIES TO CAPT. F. B
WILSON (Late of the Daily Mirror.)

— o —

X. I. B. v. LOCREHOF.

— o —

It was a great game, we won of course,
and Roger Rum got a blob, bless him.
Anyway I won ten bob, and how Johnny
did love it. Small wonder too, as he
had actually registered more'n forty on
the tins before he had his middle ash
rather badly bent, watching 'em like the
meanest private watches dear Minnie at
Spanbroekmolen and connecting every
time too he was. What an innings, in
other words the real bons. As for the
Editor he revelled in it—he is rather
roguish with the crimson rambler. Was
I there? Search me as they say in Horace,
AND I may tell you that the day before
when the Editor was batting I removed
all three pegs with the second ball (the
only reason it was'nt the first was because
I'd previously arranged to let him get a
couple by serving up a full toss well
outside the crux peg providing he did the
same to me when I staggered into the
centre) well, as I've said, the Editor got
a couple and then went out—quick—and
during the remainder of the innings proceeded to prop up the bar at the regimental canteen during closed hours too—
the horrid florid Forester I By the time,
therefore, I took my stand he'd forgotten
all about our little do, and hanged if the
very first time he swung the spheroid at
me it was'nt accompanied by a fearful
crash of ash. He's no sportsman as you
may or may not know, but I'm getting
a trifle off the rails so I'll continue. The
Professor turned up for a moment, and
we assured him we weren't playing too
much cricket but merely combining same
with a little bombing practice. And
what about our sometime Rugger international ? I don't care to tell you how
many he got as he's my C.O. so ask the
Editor if you want the news. The
wicket was as beautiful as Tina, and we
had a priceless day although Bobbie
was'nt playing.

P.B.I.

There are two references to 'Tina' who ran a canteen or small bar in the
vicinity of Locrehof which was very much in the front line area around
Dranoutre. There is a half-hearted attempt to make her out as something of
a Mata Hari but surely her appeal was that of a friendly female face in a
situation where such sights were so rare as to seem miraculous? She
obviously charmed Roberts, the Editor, and we see, in the cricket report, a
rare glimpse of his persona. The game obviously did happen, as opposed to

the horse races and golf matches which were disguised references to sniping exchanges and gas attacks. The game at Locrehof provided some much-needed and riotous relaxation for those taking part. The style is a wickedly accurate caricature of Wilson of *The Mirror*.

Some snippets from 'Violet's Chronicles of Fashion' are used to conclude this section on the vestigial sex lives of the Ypres men.

Once a week *The Tatler* magazine from London was available in the trenches. The soldiers devoured every page of this unlikely reading material, not for the social tittle-tattle for which the magazine was famous, but for the sexy bits. These were heavily disguised as fashion reports and underwear advertisements and it is hard to imagine that anyone could find them titillating. However the numerous '... know what I mean' references in *The Wipers Times* indicate that the arrival of *The Tatler* in the trenches was the turn-on of the week. 'Eve' was the fashion writer for *Tatler* while 'Violet' wrote on fashion for the Wipers variant. It has not been possible to establish the identity of 'Violet' but perhaps we could imagine her/him as a hairy-arsed sergeant of Pioneers with a gruff voice and a wicked sense of the ridiculous.

'In olden days a glimpse of stocking ...'

So, regrettably, to the toilet.

The German gunners, you will recall, never missed an opportunity to improve their casualty-per-round-fired ratio. To do this they targeted any location where the enemy soldiers were forced to congregate. Attack assembly-points, bridges and

The name of the subaltern who told the Major that to take his wife to Nottingham Goose Fair was like taking a sandwich to the Lord Mayor's Banquet.

? ? ?

Whether the London papers are aware there are a few BRITISH troops on the western front.

? ? ?

What Fritz said when he hurriedly left his sausages the other day.

? ? ?

Whether Tina's knowledge of troop movements is more profitable than her canteen.

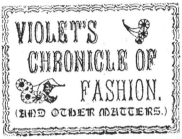

VIOLET'S CHRONICLE OF FASHION.
(AND OTHER MATTERS.)

(SUBS. NOT TO READ THIS—ED.)
—o—o—o—

YOU have doubtless heard of the sub. who defined a lady as one who wears stockings that are silk all the way up. (Which is perhaps hardly fair to those whose misplaced ideas of economy lead them to purchase what the shops call "silk-ankles.") Well, he will have to revise his definition, anyway. For not only our stockings must be silk nowadays, but all "les dessons." Never has lingerie been more fascinating,—or more extra-vagant; but girls whose war-work prevents the wearing of pretty frocks may be forgiven if they indulge in frillies instead. Garments are fairy-like in their filmy beauty,—camisoles are airy fragments of chiffon, lace, and ribbon just blown together, petticoats are real poems, while as for night-wear, even the simplest designs are artistic triumphs, and the materials are so dainty and sometimes so diaphanous that the result seems a mere ghost of a nightie!

crossroads were all pre-planned targets for a strafe or artillery barrage, and so were latrines and ablutions. The army had a routine even in the trenches. There was a stand-to at dawn when the night sentries came off guard and the day watch took over; rum and tea; breakfast and more tea and then a visit to the latrines and ablutions. More often than not the daily annoyance barrage from the enemy coincided with this moment of unpreparedness and the infantry were blown up in the bogs

WANTED.

GOOD GARDENER, must be able to drive motor car, clean boots, look after baby (male), tune piano and extract teeth. Trade Union men need not apply. —Ref. Box 111, N.C. TIMES.

YOUNG MEN for giving out Hand Bills in the Messines district Must know the country well. Chance of a rise.—Write Box 80, Advt. Dept.

AGENTS for '' Morning Hate '' Toilet Soap. Good commision. Excellent opening for an industrious young man.— Write Box 505, c/o this paper.

with their shirts off or their trousers down. This early morning barrage was christened 'The Morning Hate' and there is one reference to it in *The Wipers Times*.

The geography of Flanders and the fact that the City of Ypres and its environs are at sea level meant that, for a latrine or earth-toilet to have any depth of soakaway, the seat must be above ground level and the user thus deprived of the protection of a trench wall. The alternatives were the simple bucket,(but who empties it and where?) or the corner of the trench or dugout where the men were also living and eating and trying to survive. Army regulations are strict on latrines. Their depth and construction is laid down in a manual, as are the depths to which human waste is to be buried, the chemicals with which it is to be treated and the minimum distance away from places of work that 'ablutions' may be sited. Fatigue parties made up of soldiers who have incurred the sergeant's displeasure or committed some minor indiscipline would be detailed to empty buckets in the hours of darkness; one of the many after-sunset activities that went on in the Salient as the star-shells shot up and the indiscriminate snipers took aim at the glow of a cigarette smoked perhaps as a palliative to foul odours, by a regimental shit-shifter.

In 1916 the chemical issued for disinfecting latrines was chloride of lime. It was only partially effective because its action was to kill bacteria. This process sometimes delayed decomposition which often was the most satisfactory method of disposal. For this reason Medical Officers complained bitterly about a regulation bidding them to sprinkle chloride of lime on unburied corpses, a pointless procedure which served only to endanger the lives of the men detailed to do the sprinkling. There was also something called a *Vermoral* sprayer which was akin to an ordinary garden syringe. It was filled with a solution of creoline to combat bad smells and doubled as a primitive anti-gas spray.

Robert Graves, *'Goodbye To All That'*:

… awful swine, those Territorials; usen't to trouble about latrines at all; left food about to encourage rats; never filled a sand-bag.

Soldiers' Marching Song. (Sung lustily to the opening bars of *'Colonel Bogey.'*)

'We are the night shit-shifters. We shift shite by night..'

Although it is now three-quarters of a century since the First World War, we should not imagine that living in filth was any less revolting for the soldiers of Ypres than it would be for us. In a lot of ways the young men of the Edwardian generation were more fastidious than we are today, especially with regard to bodily functions. Symptomatic of this is the familiar circumlocution which survives, largely in the medical profession, to this day. ('How are the bowels this morning, Mrs Wilkinson?') Horses sweated, men perspired and women merely glowed. From the days of nanny and first potty-training, young men were taught to go to the lavatory regularly, cleanly, and in private. They were also instructed to leave the window open even in a blizzard to allow bad smells to disperse before anyone else could be inconvenienced.

If, in the nineteen-nineties, you are one of those people who are meticulous in the use of an aerosol air-freshener in the bathroom, or perhaps you recoil in horror if you venture unexpectedly into a continental 'ankle-splasher' toilet; if you regularly find yourself with legs crossed and bladder bursting in order to spare yourself the 'unpleasantness' of a public lavatory, remember the young men of Ypres and understand that one of the

OUR SPLENDID NEW SERIAL.

—o—o—o—

"NARPOO RUM."

—o—o—o—

BY THE AUTHOR OF "SHOT IN THE CULVERT."

—o—o—o—

DRAMATIS PERSONAE:

—o—

Cloridy Lyme — A Sanitary Inspector.
Madeline Carot — A French Girl.
Intfia Pink — A Pioneer.
General Bertram
Rudolph de Rogerum — The Earl of Loose.
Lord Reginald
de Kheathorpe -- His Son.
Q. Wemm — A Storekeeper.
L. Plumernapple — A Soldier.
Herlock Shomes — The Great Detective.
Dr Hotsam — His Admirer.

—o—o—o—

CHAPTER 1.

—o—o—o—

"MY DEAR Hotsam, nothing of the kind I assure you," said Shomes, in his comfortable dug out in Quality Street. "My methods are based on deduction   For instance, you hear someone coming up the stairs. Well, that is all the untrained ear can hear, but I know it's a soldier with many ribbons, an Irish accent and a friend named Reggie   How do I know? My dear fellow—   At that moment the door opened, and General Bertram Rudolph de Rogerum entered. Casting himself in a chair he demanded a cocktail. " Well, my dear general," said Shomes, placing his finger tips together, " how can I help you? "   " What! you know me? " gasped the general   " Oh yes! " said Shomes, as he tilted his vermoral sprayer and squirted a quart into his left arm

" Well," said the general, " I have come about a very mysterious affair   Three nights running the Brigade rum ration has disappeared "

" Good heavens! " ejaculated Hotsam " Aha! " said Shomes, " this promises to be a most interesting case."   With that he picked up his violin, and proceeded to play dreamily.   " Now I am ready, general, tell me all about it."

At the Brewery Baths

"You chuck another sardine at me, my lad, and you'll hear from my solicitors"

Breweries, with their huge vats which could be filled with steaming hot water to make communal baths, were ideal bath houses. The hot soak was one of Tommy's occasional luxuries, when he could rid himself from lice for a while and be issued with clean clothing.

GRAND   CHRISTMAS   BAZAAR.

HAVE YOU A FRIEND AT THE FRONT.

IF SO WHAT NICER PRESENT COULD YOU SEND HIM THAN OUR NEW

"VERMORLET."

This can be used either as a Soda-water Syphon or Anti-Gas Sprayer. Complete with 12 Bulbs for each purpose, 50 Francs.

—o—o—o—o—

ALSO OUR NEW

"Combination Respirator and Mouth Organ."

The dulcet tones of the Mouth Organ will brighten even the worst Gas Attack.

—o—o—o—o—

WE SPECIALISE IN NOVELTIES.

—o—o—o—o—

Come and View. You will not be urged to buy. Or drop a Field Post Card, and we will send you our Illustrated Catalogue Printed in Seven Languages.

—o—o—o—o—

See our new Waterproof Suits. They are made to resist the damp of the Trenches. and only the best Metal is used in their construction.

—o—o—o—o—

HEROD'S, UNIVERSAL PROVIDER.

hardest of their travails was the reality that, not only could they not keep clean, they were permanently and dehumanizingly filthy.

Robert Graves; *'Goodbye to all That'*:

In the interval between stand-to and breakfast, the men who were not getting in a bit of extra sleep sat about talking and smoking, writing letters home, cleaning their rifles, running their thumb-nails up the seams of their shirts killing lice …

And in *The Wipers Times* we find that one soldier, out of the trenches for a few days rest, is so enamoured of his shaving soap that he writes an ode in its praise.

'Vermorlet' is a mongrel of the popular *Sparklet* soda water maker and our friend the *Vermoral* sprayer. There is probably a connection between the respirator-cum-mouth-organ and the well documented order to unprotected troops subject to gas attack; 'Piss on your handkerchief; tie it round your mouth and then breathe through it.'

'Herod's' is, of course, Harrods; and did soldiers wear Full Metal Jackets before Vietnam?

THE SYBARITE'S SOLILOQUY.

Dearest, at break of Dawn, I need you most,
And, as you, in your silver shrouded dress,
Gambol before my eyes, I daily bless
The coins that made you mine, the trifling cost,
That sold you into bondage, such as this;
To be my Slave, Enchantress of my Soul,
To pay, afresh, each morn, the levied toll,
That I extort from you—a honied kiss.
And, as, upon my cheeks, my rugged chin,
Your scented lips, you passionately press,
In muscadine abandon, I caress
Your adipose delight, and with a grin,
Each morning, half awake, for you, I grope
Oh Stick of Superfatted Shaving Soap.
                                    C. L. P.

Chapter 7

Below the Waist: Some Conclusions

I believe I have made a fundamental error in the previous chapter when considering matters lavatorial and sexual. It would seem that my generalisations are insecure. The first shadow of doubt was cast by a letter I received from Tim d'Arch-Smith. Tim is himself a novelist and shares his Grandfather's love of words (and predilection for brackets).

Dear I-C,

I don't think you should lay down the law about the purity of the English Tommy until you've read a book by Dr Magnus Hirschfield (known to his mates in psycho-analytical circles as 'Auntie Magnesia') entitled *'Sexualgeschichte des Weltkriegs'*. There's a handy English (probably American) translation, Panurge Press, New York 1934. This will probably convince you that Grandfather Gilbert was a bit of an old innocent in these matters.

Well, narpoo to you and hoping you too are in the pink (Hunting Pink? or Shakespeare's Pink of courtesy?) Let me know how you get on.

Yrs Tim.

P.S. It would be interesting to do a bibliography of all the books printed in pocket form for use in the trenches. A.E.Housman was asked permission for a 12mo edition of *'A Shropshire Lad'* to be done for soldiers. He refused, saying that it would only be torn up for use 'After breakfast'.

So if Gilbert Frankau was not completely in touch with reality with regard to the gentlemanliness of the British Tommy in the Ypres Salient, I began to doubt my own assessment that the readers of *The Wipers Times* were surprisingly innocent and puritanical in their personal habits and sexual relations. This doubt became a certainty when I read more of Robert Graves. His platoon of Royal Welch Fusiliers, admittedly stationed in Northern France rather than in Belgium, had a hundred percent attendance

An Officer's Love-Life...... .....and a Private's.

Romance, 1917

"Darling, every potato that I have is yours" (engaged).

Nil Admirari

"Now, then, never mind about those demi-mondaines; look straight to your front!"

record at a local brothel in one evening. One of the men, whose letters home it was Graves' duty to censor, told his wife intimate details of each woman he made love to, but added that these various experiences only made him keener to survive the war and get back home to the marriage-bed because his dear wife was better than all of them. How could I equate this bunch of typically licentious soldiery with the innocents of Wipers and their antiseptic Kirchner pin-ups and furtive titillations in the *'Tatler'*?

Like so many other things in the British Army, it was all a matter of rank and the impenetrable divide between officers and soldiers.

Lord Kitchener addressed all troops, the officers, the privates, the non-commissioned men and even the teenage drummer boys and bandsmen in his famous message to the BEF in 1914.

'You are ordered abroad as a soldier of the King to help our French comrades against the invasion of a common enemy. You have to perform a task which will need your courage, your energy, your patience. Remember that the honour of the British Army depends on your individual conduct. It will be your duty not only to set an example of discipline and perfect steadiness under fire, but also to maintain the most friendly relations with those whom you are helping in this struggle. The operations in which you are engaged will, for the most part, take place in a friendly country, and you can do your own country no better service than in showing yourself in France and Belgium in the true character of a British soldier.

'Be invariably courteous, considerate, and kind. Never do anything likely to injure or destroy property, and always look upon looting as a disgraceful act. You are sure to meet with a welcome and to be trusted; your conduct must justify that welcome and that trust.

'Your duty can not be done unless your health is sound. So keep constantly on your guard against any excesses. In this new experience you may find temptations, both in wine and women. You must entirely resist both temptations, and, while treating all women with perfect courtesy, you should avoid any intimacy. Do your duty bravely. Fear God. Honour the King.'

In 1914 the soldiers would have taken all this with a healthy pinch of salt. By 1916 in the Salient the pinch had become a fistful. 'Safeguard your health; don't catch the clap; say thanks but no thanks to French girls …' Lord Kitchener could witter on all he wished but what's the point in safeguarding your health when the chances are that Fritz is going to shoot, bayonet or blast you to pieces within the next twenty-four hours? So Robert Graves' Royal Welch Fusiliers queued up for the brothel and, no doubt, as they unbuttoned their trousers they raised two fingers to Lord Kitchener in an irreverent rejoinder to his lordship's famous gesture in the 'Your Country Needs You' posters. The only ones who took any notice of Kitchener's directive were the officers – because they were supposed to lead by example. Robert Graves, who writes that he was a virgin on his wedding night some years later, felt duty bound to wait outside the brothel and to take no part in the proceedings except to 'Count them all in and count them all out again.' And Gilbert Frankau made the point in his

2nd Lt Rylands. 16th Lancashire Fusiliers (Salford Pals) Killed in Action November 1916. Aged 20.

Our casemate will always be vividly remembered by those who knew it. We had a piano—loot from a neighbouring cellar where it had been propping up the remnants of a house—a gramophone, a printing-press and a lot of subalterns. Can anyone wonder that we are but shadows of our former

selves? When Fritz's love-tokens arrived with greater frequency and precision than we altogether relished we would turn our whole outfit on together. The effect of "Pantomime Hits" on the piano, "Dance with Me" on the gramophone, a number of subalterns, and 5·9 and 4·2's on the roof, has to be heard to be realized.

At dusk, donning boots, gum, thigh, we would set off to Hooge to work till dawn in feet of liquid mud composed of—various things better left unsaid—trying to make a little cover for the lads who were holding on to the remnants of Belgium in the teeth of every disadvantage, discomfort and peril.

Yet always at the most inconvenient moment came a persistent demand from an ink-covered sergeant, "Copy wanted, sir!"

From Roberts' Introduction to a Collected Edition of *The Wipers Times.*

description of the rape of the Belgian girl that the German Officers made no move to restrain their troops. The British Tommy was certainly a great gentleman, not perhaps by nature, but by good discipline and the constant supervision of gentlemanly officers. I therefore tend towards the conclusion that the planned readership of The Wipers Times consisted largely of junior officers of whom the Line Subaltern who parodied the Rubaiyat of

While the soldiers fix bayonets, the officer who is to lead them exchanges a few words with a member of his platoon.

Omar Khayyam was typical; so much of the material in the paper seems to reflect the nature, the humour, the gallantry and the surprising unworldiness of this remarkable group of men.

Yet in spite of this I would conclude that *The Wipers Times* was read by all ranks and actually contributed to the maintenance of discipline in the front-line trenches. The paper achieved this by stressing the fact that the Officers, who were duty bound to issue some of the most dreaded orders that a soldier could possibly receive ...

'At Zero hour the artillery barrage will cease; I will blow three blasts on my whistle and the Company will follow me over the parapet and across the open ground in front of us. The objective is to occupy the German trench 150 yards ahead. Company, fix bayonets ...'

... were human themselves and fallible and frightened and well aware that their own orders were sometimes difficult or impossible to carry out.

The Wipers Times could not have existed in peacetime because in barracks the divide between officers and men was absolute. In front-line situations in war time, this gulf became eroded. First names were used instead of ranks; officers and men ate in the same surroundings, and washed and visited the latrines and got drunk in each other's company. The General Staff disapproved because they retained a barracks outlook on discipline, but they couldn't stop it. A whole new front-line discipline that was based on survival rather than tradition from the past suffused the Army at war and it probably fought the better for it.

Chapter 8

Food and Drink

From consideration of references to sex and the toilet that occur in the paper we have come to the conclusion that the target readership of *The Wipers Times* was young officers in the 19 to 22 age group, of good background and education, who were well indoctrinated with the Christian ethics of the day and who were constantly aware of their responsibilities as gentlemen. What is there to learn from consideration of their stomachs or more particularly what they ate and drank?

The poem 'Hoof Beats' is a good example of the sort of jingle that seems to have given relief to the shellshocked mind. The content is inconsequential, but the rhythm is strong and we can imagine the man who wrote it saying the words over and over in his mind as he makes his dangerous way to and from the front line trenches, carrying his load of rations.

Didn't *Maconochie* once produce *Pan Yan Pickle*? It sounds familiar, a half-remembered advertisement like 'Guinness is Good for You' or 'You're never alone with a ... what was it?'

Nestlés now make *Pan Yan*; before the take-over it was *Rowntrees*, and before that it was a firm dating back to Victorian times called *Maconochie* who indeed supplied tinned meat, preserves and pickles for soldiers fighting in the First World War.

The following recipe for 'Ragout Maconochie' is from a book about the Ypres Salient.

Open one tin of Maconochie rations. Warm gently until the greasy oil floats to the top. Remove this by blotting up with a piece of 'four-bi-two' flannelette. Place this on one side for later use. Remove the black lumps from the RationMac. These are potatoes. Squeeze out the greasy oil from the 'four-bi-two' into a frying pan and gently fry the potatoes. Take

Hoof Beats.

Maconochie ! Maconochie !
Bully beef and biscuits !
Hullo, damn it ! that's a crump,
How those bangs give me the hump ;
Here's another ! Where's she dropping ?
Duck ! or pieces you'll be stopping !
Plum and apple ! beef and biscuit,
Well, here goes, I'd better risk it ;
Just round here, there is no telling
When the Hun begins his shelling
How good my dug-out seems to me.
Maconochie ! Maconochie !

two handfuls of dried veg. (They look very much like any other dead leaves). Mix with a little water flavoured with Chloride of Lime and pat into croutons. These should be gently fried after the potatoes are cooked. Reheat the Mac. ration and serve the whole on a cold enamel plate.

There were many ways of dying in the First World War, but few soldiers were lost to actual starvation. Lines of communication were short and British sea power ensured secure passage of stores across the Channel. In *The Wipers Times* we read predictable soldier's gripes about diet; too much cold bully beef, too much *Maconochie* and too many indigestible home-made cakes sent by well-wishers at home.

> ## TO MY MARRAINE.
>
> I love you for your kindliness and grace,
> And wonder how it happens, that you deign
> To send me sweets and gifts, my dear MARRAINE,
> Across the intervening miles of space
> Your portrait, in the evening mists, I trace,
> While doing sentry, in the mud and rain,
> The sky is dark above ; but free from stain
> Or blemish, is your lovely visioned face.
>
> —o—o—o—
>
> However long this war goes on, MARRAINE,
> I'll love you, I'll adore you, to the end ;
> But all the Doctor's Magic cannot shake
> From my inside, this unaccustomed pain,
> I pray you, I implore you, not to send
> Another sanguinary HOME-MADE cake.
>
> THE M.O. (C.L.P.)

It was enemy action that disrupted the movement of rations from the railheads to the trenches. Convoys and wagon trains were shelled and, once the tins got to the front line, as often as not the food had to be eaten raw because cook-house smoke and camp fires attracted enemy shell-fire and bombs. As always there was tea, 'dixie' tea, a hot sweet drink boiled up with milk, sugar and a handful of tea-leaves, in any receptacle that would hold enough chlorinated water to make a brew. Sometimes the water-jacket of a machine gun was used, the heat being provided by firing endless belts of ammunition at grass-top level in the general direction of the Hun.

Fixed-arc machine guns which fired by day and night were not aimed at anything in particular but were used by both sides to deny segments of no man's land to the enemy. This principle gave rise to the surprising notion that it was safer to stand up when patrolling at night in no man's land than to crawl. Fixed-arc fire would only hit you in the ankle and such wounds were not life-threatening and held the promise of a trip back to Blighty. We are not told how this theory coped with the reality that a man falls down when shot through the ankles, presumably right into the spray of bullets that he was hoping to avoid by standing up. Anyhow, by reason of their protracted bursts of fire, fixed-arc machine guns made the best tea.

Though we now know about 'dixie' tea, these lines from Gilbert Frankau's verse '*Urgent or Ordinary*' need a little more

> —o—o—o—
>
> There was a time when first I donned the Khaki—
> Oh, martial days in Brighton-by-the-Sea !—
> When not the deepest draught of Omar's Saki
> Could fire my ardent soul like dixie tea.

Two Quatrains from the 'Rubaiyat';

Ah, fill the Cup;-what boots it to repeat
How time is slipping underneath our feet;
Unborn TOMORROW and dead YESTERDAY,
Why fret about them if TODAY be sweet.

And fear not lest existence closing your
Account, should lose, or know the type no more;
The Eternal Saki from that bowl has poured
Millions of bubbles like us, and will pour.

explanation. Twenty-Four Division, stout defenders of the Ypres Salient and parent unit of most readers of *The Wipers Times* as well as the paper's contributors, was formed and 'worked up' in Sussex. Most of the volunteer officers were billeted in Brighton and manoeuvres and exercises were carried out from tented camps on the Downs. These were days of high morale and confidence in the future and a good time seems to have been had by all.

'Omar's Saki' is a typical laboured Gilbert Frankau rhyme. Omar Khayyam was a philosopher of the 'Eat Drink and be Merry' school which probably explains his popularity with the young officers of the First World War. He was a Persian poet and astronomer who wrote in the 12th Century and who drank plenty of red wine.

It was one of the ironies of Royal Air Force survival courses in the 1950s that pilots were advised in the classroom that alcohol was useless as a protection against hypothermia and, shortly afterwards, received a service issue of Navy Rum. On dinghy drills, after they had been helicoptered from the February-grey waters of the Bristol Channel, Hunter pilots were set down, frightened and shivering, on Westward Ho! golf course. It was in

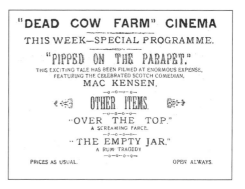

"The Spirit of our Troops is Excellent."

"DEAD COW FARM" CINEMA

THIS WEEK—SPECIAL PROGRAMME.

"PIPPED ON THE PARAPET."

THIS EXCITING TALE HAS BEEN FILMED AT ENORMOUS EXPENSE, FEATURING THE CELEBRATED SCOTCH COMEDIAN,
MAC KENSEN.

OTHER ITEMS

"OVER THE TOP."
A SCREAMING FARCE.

"THE EMPTY JAR."
A RUM TRAGEDY

PRICES AS USUAL.   OPEN ALWAYS.

this unlikely location that a regulation tot of Navy Rum was administered by a grinning orderly who measured out the dose as though it was Syrup of Figs. During the First World War no such fine decisions were made between what did you good and what made you feel good. Rum was issued to the soldiers in the same way as it had been doled out to sailors at sea for hundreds of years. In *The Wipers Times* we read on almost every page about some problem with the rum issue. It also turns up in '*Oh What a Lovely War*'

> 'If the Sergeant steals your rum, never mind,'

This should be amplified slightly. It was the Quartermaster-Sergeant's duty to dispense rum to sentries and troops in the front line positions. Usually this was done on the 'One for you, one for me' principle, with the result that by the time the rum jar reached the most exposed, far flung and dangerous trenches the jar was empty and the Sergeant drunk.

Historically the early years of the century were a time of uncertainty and hypocrisy with regard to alcohol, that led up to Prohibition in the United States. Lloyd George, who was Chancellor of the Exchequer and Prime Minister during the First World War, espoused Temperance in his political pronouncements even though he was known to indulge quite liberally in alcohol in his private life. Do-gooders and Temperance Societies tried to get the rum issue and all boozing banned from the British Army.

One would like to think that it was such pleas from the front line soldiers that held the forces of Prohibition at bay in the British Army. However, it was just as likely that the Generals had not missed the point that soldiers sometimes perform acts of superhuman courage and endurance when under the influence of alcohol. Inexperienced troops cowering in the trenches came to dread the 'Double Rum Issue' as an indication of an impending 'Push'. Pride in the most heroic deeds of arms carried out by individual British soldiers should perhaps be tempered by the knowledge that these were often the result of adrenalin and deliberately induced drunkenness.

Officers usually drank whisky which they bought to augment the free but unreliable service issue rum. There can be no doubt that the young men in the Salient were made to feel guilty for their near universal alcohol dependence. *The Wipers Times* opinion on the subject is that the actual amount of booze

---

WITH APOLOGIES TO RUDYARD KIPLING.

—o—o—o—

When you're waiting for zero, to go o'er the top,
And yer mind gets a-wondering what you will stop,
Just go to yer bottle, and neck a wee drop,
Cos thinkin' ain't good for a soldier.

TO THE P.B.I.

AN APPRECIATION.

Gone is the Summer, and gone are the
flies,
Gone the green hedges that gladdened
our eyes ;
Around us the landscape is reeking
with rain,
Gone is all comfort—'tis Winter again.
—§ † §—
So here's to the lads of the P.B.I.,
Who live in a ditch that never is dry ;
Who grin through discomfort and danger
alike,
Go " over the top " when a chance comes
to strike ;
Though they're living in, Hell they are
cheery and gay,
And draw as their stipend just one bob
per day.
—§ † §—
Back once more to the boots, gum, thigh,
In a pulverised trench where the mud's
knee-high ;
To the duck-board slide on a cold wet
night,
When you pray for a star-shell to give
you light ;
When your clothes are wet, and the rum
jar's dry,
Then you want all your cheeriness, P.B.I.
—§ † §—
They take what may come with a grouse
just skin-deep,
In a rat-worried dug-out on mud try to
sleep ;
Do you wonder they make all the
atmosphere hum,
When some arm-chair old lunatic grudges
them rum ;
And they read in the papers that "James
So-and-Such
Thinks that our soldiers are drinking too
much."

Leave the Tommy alone Mr. James
So-and-Such.
There are vices much nearer home waiting
your touch ;
Take yourself now for instance, examine
and see
If your own priggish virtue is all it
should be ;
Give those of a larger life chance to enjoy
A charity wider than that you employ.
—§ † §—
Don't let Tommy's vices shatter your
sleep,
When you write to the " Times " stick
to " Little Bo-Peep,"
As a subject she's really much more in
your line
Than licentious soldiery, women, and
wine,
So here's to the lads who can live and
can die,
Backbone of the Empire, the old P.B.I.

PIONEER.

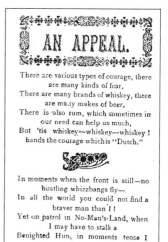

AN APPEAL.

There are various types of courage, there
are many kinds of fear,
There are many brands of whiskey, there
are many makes of beer,
There is also rum, which sometimes in
our need can help us much,
But 'tis whiskey—whiskey—whiskey !
hands the courage which is "Dutch."

In moments when the front is still—no
hustling whizzbangs fly—
In all the world you could not find a
braver man than I !
Yet on patrol in No-Man's-Land, when
I may have to stalk a
Benighted Hun, in moments tense I
have recourse to " Walker."

consumed should remain a naughty secret shared by the readership but hidden from those at home.

A social comment on whisky dependence is contained in the sub-plot of *'Journey's End'* by R.C. Sherriff. After years at the front, Stanhope, the hero, survives on a minimum of two bottles of Scotch a day, a not unusual rate of consumption, confirmed by Robert Graves.

He is aware of his lapse into drunkenness but is ashamed of it and resorts to censoring mail in order to prevent news of such dishonourable behaviour getting home to his family and fiancée. It is clear that among the officer class drink was taken in excess in an attempt to make the intolerable tolerable. Such behaviour was seen by the stern unsympathetic women at home as weakness and the men were ashamed and guilty about their addiction. How things have changed in the intervening seventy-five years.

NOW THE WINTER NIGHTS ARE
WITH US NO BETTER TONIC
CAN BE HAD THAN

RHUMATOGEN

Cures   FLATUANCE.
COLD FEET.
ETC., ETC.

CAN BE TAKEN WITH TEA OR
SIMILAR BEVERAGE. OBTAINABLE
FROM ALL Q, M. STORES.

'Rhumatogen' is a mongrel of Rum and the already popular 'Sanatogen' nerve tonic.

ALBERT - POZIERES - BAPAUME CIRCUIT.
–o–o–o–o–
Grand Touring Concert Party.
BY SPECIAL ARRANGEMENT WITH
P R O F E S S O R   S C R A P P E R.
–o–o–o–o–
THE FOLLOWING WILL BE THE PROGRAMME (W.P.)
–o–o–o–o–
TROUPE   OPENING   CHORUS.
1. Song—"When the midnight choo-choo leaves
   for Pozieres."
2. Solo—" Up I came with my little lot."
   Enrico WALTHALLO.
3. Concerted item—" Come along over the garden wall."
   BY THE TROUPE.
4. Grand chorus and glee—" I'm   much   more
   happy than when I was free."
   Sung by Messrs. BOSCH.
5. Song and Chorus—"Pray tell me gentle
   Hunlet are there any more at home
   like you."
6. Grand concerted number---" Another little
   drink would'nt do us any harm."
   BY THE TROUPE.
–o–o–o–o–
BOOK EARLY.   PRICES DOUBLE.

The Axis of the proposed advance in the Battle of the Somme.

Refers to a defeated U-boat commander 'Franz Walther'

It is in the use of euphemistic words for hard liquor such as 'a spot' and 'a jar' that the *Wipers Times* staff indicate that heavy alcohol consumption is something that is understood in the Line but must be kept secret from shrinking violets at home.

Who that has known it can forget the joy of a spot in the Culvert dug-out?

Good luck be with you all, and when we pull out – well – call in at the editorial sanctum for a spot and a chin.

Through summer's heat and the winter's gloom
We've tasted the joys that the Salient holds,
A filthy dug-out our only room,
Where our only comfort a jar enfolds.

There is a jolting conclusion to the officially sanctioned consumption of alcohol amongst servicemen on active service that students of life in the Salient should not ignore. Copious quantities of rum, whisky, gin and any other nerve-deadening potions were administered, with military approval, to those unfortunates condemned to die at dawn by firing squad for cowardice, mutiny or desertion. The famous silhouette of a soldier tied to a chair awaiting execution arouses sympathy for many reasons, not least that the poor man was by this stage probably too drunk to stand. The use of alcohol to deaden the nerves before a moment of inconceivable horror was as old as the story of the crucifixion of Christ.

'And they gave him to drink wine mingled with myrrh'

Chapter 9

Hearts and Minds

As we work our way through *The Wipers Times* and unravel the riddles and allusions, we come across a familiar story of endurance and courage in the face of a uniformly awful daily existence. Many students of the First World War feel that the high morale of the men in the trenches is perhaps the greatest riddle of all the Wipers story.

Most of modern military thinking on the subject of morale stems from the First World War. Montgomery and Slim, two generals who wrote extensively about this subject, based their advice on personal experiences from the Western Front. These treatises were condensed and incorporated into training manuals for all three Services. Instruction on this subject is unchanged today and Morale remains high on the list of compulsory studies for aspiring officers in the Armed Forces.

'Morale is a mental state,' the manuals explain, 'that is influenced by the following material conditions; universal knowledge of and adherence to the Aim, good training and good discipline; esprit de corps is important along with good leadership and sound administration. Morale is low if an army is poorly equipped and nothing enhances morale more than being on the winning side.'

'Sound administration' means that every aspect of a soldier's life must be organized to contribute to, and not detract from, fighting efficiency. For example, men must be well fed, with regard to variety as well as nutrition. They need satisfactory accomodation and even in the most trying circumstances they must be regularly paid; they must have leave and medical attention, mail from home and minimum family worries; casualty evacuation should be seen to be efficient and the spiritual needs of soldiers, which are historically greater than those of men at home in peacetime, should be well catered for.

In the Ypres Salient the British Army was not well fed, accommodation was appalling and pay was a constant niggle.

THE 'OUT SINCE MONS' MAN, WHO HAS INSPIRED SOME OF BAIRNSFATHER'S MORE SERIOUS SKETCHES.

[To face p. 80

"O
Jean

A terror hangs above our heads.
I scarcely dare to think
Of that awful doom, that each one dreads
from which the bravest shrink
———— " ————

It's not the crashing shrapnel shell
Or yet the snipers shot.
It's not the maxims bursts of Hell
These matter not a jot
———— • ————

It's a far worse thing than that my son
With which we have to grapple
It's if we see another one————
More tin of PLUM and APPLE.
————• • ————

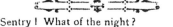

Sentry ! What of the night ?
The sentry's answer I will not repeat,
Though short in words, 'twas with feeling
                              replete,
It covered all he thought and more,
It covered all he'd thought before,
It covered all he might think yet
In years to come.   For he was wet
                And had no rum.

In a poem published in *The Wipers Times* of 29 May 1916, Gilbert Frankau writes an open letter in verse to the owner of *The Daily Mail* who, before the war, had published some of his work. The subject is a pay differential. The men of the BEF who had absorbed the initial thrust of the German invasion of Belgium and France and even now were holding the line in the Ypres Salient were not happy about the pay and conditions offered to the recruits of Kitchener's New Army, who were to reinforce them on the Western Front. Pay was one shilling per day for those who had been ' out since Mons' …

… One hundred pounds per annum plus separation allowance for the New Army.

Lord Derby instituted a scheme wherby men were recruited into the army and then loaned back to their civilian employers until such time as the military training machine could accomodate them.

THE "NEW CHURCH" TIMES

WAILS TO THE MAIL.

NO. 1.

(Married men of the latest armies will receive 104 pounds per annum in addition to the usual separation allowance.)

Northcliffe, my Northcliffe,
  In days that are dead
The bard was a scoffer
  At much that you said,
A fervid opponent
  Of " Daily Mail " Bread.

The bard never dreamed
  That it mattered a jot
If you trusted in soap
  Or put peas in your pot,
Or how many aeroplanes
  England had not.

And when you backed Blatchford
  To bark at the Bosche,
Or when you puffed Willett
  As wiser than Josh—
Northcliffe, my Northcliffe,
  I own I said " Tosh."

Northcliffe, my Northcliffe,
  Now here at thy feet
The poet craves pardon
  Tho' vengeance be sweet
As the peas that thou prizest
  In Carmelite Street.

Forgive me past trespasses,
  Hark to my trope,
To my words that are softer
  Than Lever's Soft Soap,
For only through thee,
  Has a suppliant hope !

Northcliffe, my Northcliffe,
  Ah ! greater than Mars
Or double-faced Janus
  Whose portal unbars
The flood-tide of battle
  Napoleon of " Pars."

Whose words are uncensored,
  Whose leader compels
Greys, Asquiths, McKennas,
  And eke double L's,
With contraband cotton
  And scandal of shells,

Who rulest the Seas,
  And the Earth and the Air
And the manifold medals
  " Base " Officers wear,
Northcliffe, my Northcliffe,
  Now hark to my prayer !

When the " Hide-the-Truth Press "
  And the " Slack 23 "
Have yielded sword, money,
  And trident to thee
And K.J. and Boosey
  And Pemberton B.

Remember, while paying
  The Derby man's rent,
His rates, his insurance,
  And more than he spent,
That others SAID NOTHING,
  GOT NOTHING, but WENT.

They were somewhere in France,
  While the Derby man bucked
To his wife, and in sheets
  Was connubially tucked . . .
But no one pays them
  For the homes that they chucked.

They were crouching to crumps
  While he cried at a Zepp,
He was dancing what time
  They were taught to "Keep step,"
And he gets a hundred
  Per an. PLUS the Sep-

-aration allowance !
  By Carmelite House,
If a Man be worth anything
  More than a Mouse,
Northcliffe, my Northcliffe,
  THESE CHAPS HAVE A GROUSE.

GILBERT FRANKAU.

22/5/16.

Students of morale should note that it was not the amount that the soldiers were paid which set them grousing, though goodness knows it seems a niggardly reward for offering life and limb in defence of one's country, but an unfair differential in rates of pay. *The Daily Mail* was already a great champion of the fighting men and Frankau and *The Wipers Times* often successfully prompted press campaigns for their benefit.

Examples such as those quoted indicate that the High Command during the First World War could not look to 'sound administration' to account for the high morale of the British soldiers in the trenches. Analysis of the requirement for good equipment would also indicate that the morale of the men remained high in spite of and not because of the efforts of the British Army, although this is not quite as straightforward as would first appear.

Moans about unserviceable or inefficient equipment are as familiar in stories about the First World War as are the 'left boot' tales from the Crimea. Although the fighting men of Ypres had plenty to moan about, 'equipment' in the 'morale' context refers more to the tools that the men were issued with, than to do the actual fighting. The 'scandal of the shells' referred to in Frankau's '*Wails to the Mail*' was a problem of inadequate equipment in the early years of the war, but by 1916 the British Army was as well armed in artillery, machine guns and small arms as their opponents. Therefore, as a factor affecting morale, 'equipment' was probably neutral or slightly beneficial. Some consideration should be given to the notion that a soldier's morale is, perversely, slightly improved by having something to moan about.

It is difficult to review the morale of the men without being influenced by the fact that we know the outcome of each individual battle and of the War itself. It is facile for military thinkers to stress the importance of 'success' in maintaining morale because soldiers are always much more concerned about the future than the past. Before a fight, a

When One Would Like to Start an Offensive on One's Own
RECIPE FOR FEELING LIKE THIS—Bully, biscuits, no coke, and leave just cancelled

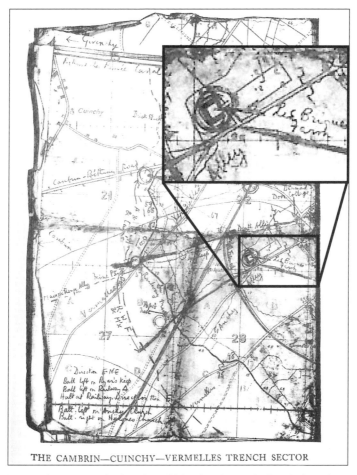

THE CAMBRIN—CUINCHY—VERMELLES TRENCH SECTOR

'Les Briques Farm', the First Objective, is marked and ringed on
this Trench Map reproduced from 'Goodbye to All That.'

track record of success and a clear superiority in all military aspects is
required if there is to be any heightening of morale attributable to being on
the winning side.

Lieutenant Robert Graves of 'A' Company, 2nd Battalion, Royal Welch
Fusiliers recieved a briefing along with fellow officers, one of whom was
known as 'The Actor' for an attack on La Bassée. The briefing officer was
Captain Thomas.

FIRST OBJECTIVE – Les Briques Farm. The big house plainly visible
to our front, surrounded by trees. To get this it is necessary to cross three
lines of enemy trenches. The first is three hundred yards distant, the
second four hundred, and the third about six hundred. We then cross 2

railways. Behind the second railway is a German trench called the Brick Trench. Then comes the Farm, a strong place with moat and cellars and a kitchen garden strongly staked and wired.

SECOND OBJECTIVE - The Town of Auchy - this is also plainly visible from our trenches. It is four hundred yards beyond the Farm and defended by a first line of trench half way across, and a second line immediately in front of the town. When we have occupied the first line our direction is half-right, with the left of the battalion directed on 'Tall Chimney'.

THIRD OBJECTIVE - Village of Haisnes - Conspicuous by high-spired church. Our eventual line will be taken up on the railway behind this village, where we will dig in and await reinforcements.

When Thomas reached this point the 'Actor's' shoulders were shaking with laughter.

'What's up?' asked Thomas irritably.

The Actor giggled; 'Who in God's name is responsible for this little effort?'

'Don't know,' Thomas said. 'Probably Paul the Pimp or some one like that.' (Paul the Pimp was a Captain on the divisional Staff, young, inexperienced, and much disliked. He wore red tabs upon his chest and even on his undervest.) 'Between the six of us – and you youngsters must be careful not to let the men know – this is what they call a Subsidiary Attack. There will be no troops in support. We've just got to go over and keep the enemy busy while the folk on our right do the real work. You

---

Monday. 31st July. 1916.

THE CONTALMAISON OPERA HOUSE.

—o—o—o—o—

THIS WEEK.

The Great Spectacular Drama, Entitled :

"THERE'S ONE MORE RIVER TO CROSS."

INTRODUCING THE CELEBRATED MALE IMPERSONATOR,

LITTLE WILLIE.

—o—o—o—o—

THE THREE LORELEI

IN THEIR SONG SCENA, ENTITLED :

"OH WILLIE COME HOME BEFORE YOU GET HURT."

—o—o—o—o—

The Original Bottle-nosed Comedian,

FRITZ

IN HIS NEW SKETCH

"I'VE HAD SOMME."

—(—o—o—o—

PRICES AS USUAL.   BOOK EARLY.

notice that the bombardment is much heavier over there. They've knocked the Hohenzollern Redoubt to bits. Personally I don't give a damn either way. We'll get killed whatever happens.'

We all laughed.

Robert Graves continues:

That afternoon I repeated the whole rigmarole to the platoon, and told them of the inevitable success attending our assault. They seemed to believe it. All except Sergeant Townsend.

We do find in *The Wipers Times* many examples of 'Talking up' military successes. Commanders never used the paper to improve morale by propaganda; more likely those who wrote the columns and stories were themselves convinced that significant victories were occurring every day and that the end of the war was only weeks away. Only a few men doubted that the 'Big Push' – the Battle of the Somme – was going to be a walkover and also the beginning of the end of the war.

> Should this issue be very much delayed we hope our readers will understand and excuse it on account of the many calls on our time. Since the above was written certain things have happened which have decided the name of the present issue. Whether we shall have time or not to fill all the pages is another thing, and our readers will understand if the number is produced with a blank page or two. We think it better to take this course than wait till after the show to produce a full number. And now there is one thing we would wish to do, that is, to wish God-speed to all our pals in the Division. We've all had many weary and many good times together. Who that has known it can forget the joy of a spot in the Culvert dug-out, and the many other haunts known to most of us? Whatever comes we can rely on the old Division to give a good account of itself. So here's to you all, lads, the game is started, keep the ball rolling and remember that the only good Hun is a dead Hun. Good luck be with you all, and when we pull out—well—call in at the editorial sanctum for a spot and a chin.
>
> **THE EDITOR.**

The objective in the Somme Campaign was for Allied troops to advance to and cross the Rhine. 'Willie' was Crown Prince Wilhelm, Commander of the German Army.

The need to make the most of any military good news can be seen at its most simplistic in this column of 'People We Take Our Hats off To,' a regular feature of the Paper.

It is from the issue dated 3 July, 1916 and during the previous month some of the most important events of the war so far, took place.

The Royal Navy fought the Battle of Jutland. This, the only head-on confrontation between the British and German fleets, is now considered to have been inconclusive, with most historians suggesting a 'points' win for Germany. In terms of ships and men lost the outcome

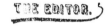

People We Take Our Hats off To.

——:o:——

The British Navy.

——:o:——

The Russians.

——:o:——

The French.

——:o:——

The Canadians.

was undoubtedly in favour of the enemy. There were, however, moments of glory for the Royal Navy and, with little to shout about on their own front, we can understand the boys in khaki raising a few cheers for their colleagues in navy blue.

The Russians too had a moment of glory in May and June, 1916. The Brusilov offensive was spectacularly successful in its early stages and well worth a ragged cheer and the raising of a few tin hats. The readers of the '*Kemmel*' variant of *The Wipers Times* could not have been expected to foresee that before the next issue of the paper, at the end of July, the campaign was to turn sour with the loss of a million men and this would lead ultimately to the collapse of Russia as a military power.

The French? The heroism of their stand at Verdun against the all-out assault of the German Fifth Army certainly merited a respectful

"Ils ne passeront pas"
"Old soldiers never say die, they'll simply block the way"

Bairnsfather's view of the French at Verdun.

and admiring recognition, even though, by May 1916 it became very clear that an Allied counter-offensive elsewhere to ease the pressure on Verdun was essential. Hence the Battles of the Somme. After 1 July 1916, not a single German division was sent to reinforce the Fifth Army.

The cry 'Ils ne passeront pas' was General Pétain's when he assumed command at Verdun.

To continue for a moment on the subject of Verdun;

In '*Spring-Time Thoughts*' the correspondent 'Amateur' humbly suggests that an Allied counter-attack at Verdun might be less hazardous than a head-on advance against prepared German positions. He has obviously heard rumours of the planned campaign in the Somme area. His prescience is quite tragic.

To complete the examination of people to whom *The Wipers Times* editorial staff felt that hats should be raised in early July, 1916, we should consider the Canadians. There were many Canadian troops in the Salient and they distinguished themselves in the Second Battle of Ypres. They were to do so again at Passchendaele. However, there is no report of a

SPRING-TIME THOUGHTS.

Thank Heaven we are running out of winter and into spring. " Oh, to be in Flanders now that April's there !". Now that summer has begun to arrive naturally everyone is asking " What is going to happen ?" and the air is full of rumours. Is it as impossible for us to go through as it was for the Germans at Verdun ? The differences, are distinct contrasts. On the one hand—perfect organisation, but indifferent fighting material. On the other—indifferent organisation, with perfect fighting material. The German is temperamentally a poor uphill fighter, and once his organisation, is upset he will crumble. Obviously then the thing is to upset his organisation. The easiest way to do this is to suddenly make him reverse his plan of campaign, and attack him where his organisation is prepared only for attack. The point lying ready to hand for this is obviously Verdun, and, by sudden concentration there, one might achieve an overwhelming success at much less cost than will an organised and obvious push at a place prepared and ready for defence. Neuve Chapelle and Loos show us the cost of breaking through prepared ground, and the result is infinitesmal gain. Possibly the loss would be as large at Verdun, though a well calculated attack there could not easily be more unsuccessful than the two already mentioned. Also it would have the advantages of surprise and of forcing a sudden complete reversal of positions, a state of affairs which might easily prove too difficult for even the German organisation. True, the German artillery is there ready, but so it will be at any front elsewhere. Already the seeds of failure are sown in the German, troops there, and it would be easier to turn this into an absolute demoralisation than to butt up against a new army on a new ground.

AMATEUR.

recent skirmish that would prompt the raising of hats in July, 1916, and Roberts was probably acknowledging their indomitable and gallant spirit that stiffened the resolve of all the Allies in the Salient. We can also be sure that the now-forgotten achievement of the Canadians had as great an impact on the lives of *Wipers Times* readers as did any of the other events mentioned.

There is also a monumental unanswered riddle in this 3 July, 1916 issue of the *The Kemmel Times*. From start to finish of the paper there is not the smallest, most shrouded, most insignificant or most oblique reference to the Battle of the Somme which started three days before publication, on 1 July. In the next edition – *The Somme Times* of 30 July – we can find only three references to the battle, namely Roberts' Editorial which has already been quoted when he invites friends to call into the Editorial Den for a drink before they march off southwards to join the slaughter, the laboured puns of the Opera House programme and the 'Optimism' advertisement which scarcely disguises the composer's bitterness.

How was it possible, we must ask, for the biggest battle, the greatest tragedy, the most almighty cock-up that the British Armed Forces were ever involved in to go unreported in the pages of this newspaper; a soldiers' journal that was printed within a few days and a few miles of the scene where the British alone suffered nearly 60,000 casualties in one ghastly period of twenty-four hours?

Where are the 'In Memoriams' and black-bordered pages for the evocatively named battalions like the 10th West Yorks (620 casualties out of 800–60 per cent

---

ARE YOU A VICTIM TO

OPTIMISM?

—o—o—o—o—

YOU DON'T KNOW?

—o—o—o—o—

THEN ASK YOURSELF THE FOLLOWING QUESTIONS.

—o—o—o—o—

1.—DO YOU SUFFER FROM CHEERFULNESS?
2.—DO YOU WAKE UP IN A MORNING FEELING THAT ALL IS GOING WELL FOR THE ALLIES?
3.—DO YOU SOMETIMES THINK THAT THE WAR WILL END WITHIN THE NEXT TWELVE MONTHS?
4.—DO YOU BELIEVE GOOD NEWS IN PREFERENCE TO BAD?
5.—DO YOU CONSIDER OUR LEADERS ARE COMPETENT TO CONDUCT THE WAR TO A SUCCESSFUL ISSUE?

IF YOUR ANSWER IS "YES" TO ANYONE OF THESE QUESTIONS THEN YOU ARE IN THE CLUTCHES OF THAT DREAD DISEASE.

WE   CAN   CURE   YOU.

TWO DAYS SPENT AT OUR ESTABLISHMENT WILL EFFECTUALLY ERADICATE ALL TRACES OF IT FROM YOUR SYSTEM.
DO NOT HESITATE—APPLY FOR TERMS AT ONCE TO:—

Messrs. Walthorpe, Foxley, Nelmes and Co.

TELEPHONE 72, "GRUMBLESTONES."   TELEGRAMS: "GROUSE."

---

fatal), the Salford Pals and the Tyneside Irish? Roberts' own regiment, the Sherwood Foresters, had six battalions involved in the fighting on July 1st and he must have lost close friends among their 3000-odd casualties. And why no 'Hats off to the Ulsters', the only unit on that terrible day who actually achieved their 2nd line objective beyond the Schwaben Redoubt? Was it because by early afternoon the Ulstermen had advanced into their own artillery barrage and been virtually wiped out? (This incident from the first day on the Somme must surely have been the foundation of the scene from '*Oh What a Lovely War*' when advancing Irish troops try vainly to stop their own artillery from shelling them.)

TO

THE SOLDIERS OF THE SALIENT

AND

THE TRUTH ABOUT THE WAR

Roberts' dedication to *The Wipers Times* compilation published in 1930.

The answer must lie in Roberts' appreciation of morale. He was torn between the recognized need to give soldiers good news even at the expense of truth, and concern amounting to love for his readers which forced him to be honest at all times in his paper. He didn't report victories, as the British press did in July, 1916, because he knew that there hadn't really been any, and he felt himself unable to tell of death, failure and disaster because those yet to be thrown into the battle must be allowed the possibility that things weren't as bad as rumour had them. So he wrote nothing about the battle. He filled his paper with happy trivialities and published as normal, thereby producing the one light-hearted moment in this uniformly tragic month. And that is something that we, the readers of his paper eighty years on, should 'Take Our Hats off To.'

We have examined, so far, the 'factors affecting morale' which were lacking during the First World War. We certainly cannot look to 'good

He made me mad
To see him shine so brisk, and smell so sweet
And talk so like a waiting-gentlewoman
Of guns, and drums, and wounds, – God save the mark!–
And telling me the sovereign'st thing on earth
Was parmaceti for an inward bruise;
And that it was great pity so it was,
This villainous saltpetre should be digg'd
Out of the bowels of the harmless earth,
Which many a good tall fellow had destroy'd
So cowardly; and but for these vile guns,
He would himself have been a soldier.

(Not for nothing I played the 4th Soldier in Geoffrey Crump's Henry IV Part 1.)

Birds of Ill Omen

"There's evidently goin' to be an offensive around 'ere, Bert"

THE DAILY ROUND, THE TRIVIAL TASK.

SCENE I.

—:o:—

COMPANY H.Q. IN FRONT LINE TRENCH.

—:o:—

. Company Commander and Lieutenant sipping rum and smoking: Enter Corporal announcing a General in the offing. "What General?" "Brigadier, sir!." "Which way is he coming?" "From Top end, sir!" "Most of the sentries awake? "Yes, sir, word's been passed down." Captain gets us and makes his way up trench. Meets dapper Brigadier accompanied by C.O. and Brigade Major "Evening, Blearson, how are you?" "Top-hole sir, thanks!" "Your boys fit?" "Never been stronger, sir!". General to his Major aside "Is'nt that splendid, Bobbie." C.O. to Brigadier "Blearson's Coy. has done a lot of work here sir, three dug-outs and two traverses built, and the whole trench drained." Brig.-General to his Major "Is'nt that priceless Bobbie?" "It is, sir." Brig. gets into fire bay next to sentry and peers over no man's land. To sentry: "Seen anything my boy?" Sentry (knowing its the Brigadier but pretending not to recognise him in the dark) "'Oo the 'ell are you?" Brig. coughs slightly. Sentry, "Sorry sir didn't know it was you. C 4 trench number 6 post, wind safe all correct." "Capital"—Brig. gets down and goes along trench till he arrives at another sentry post. Sentry (promptly), "C 4 number 7 pos, wind safe all correct." "Splendid. Seen anything?" "Well, sir! I thought I saw sumthink move about 40 yards 'arf right, so I gives it two rounds, and as I thought I 'eard it groan I asks the sergeant to send up a light, and it was only a tree stump." Brig. to his Major, "Isn't that priceless, Bobbie?" "It is, sir." C.O. aside to Capt., "Ask him into your dug-out, I think he'd like a drink." Capt. does so. "Oh thanks very much old man, but we mustn't stay long, must we, Bobbie?" "No, sir!". They all crowd into Coy. H.Q. and drink whisky and water out of mugs, and have a chin. Brig. about ten minutes later, "Well, come on Bobbie, we must go. Thanks very much Blearson, I'm awfully pleased with the work done, and also to find your stations so alert. . Isn't it perfectly splendid, Bobbie?" "It is, sir." Exeunt Brig., his Major, and the C.O.

—:o:—

SCENE II.

—:o:—

A MUDDY PARADE GROUND IN DIV. RESERVE.

—:o:—

Company formed up. Enter Capt. Coy.-Serg.-Major "Company, Company 'shun." Turns and salutes. Capt. "All right Sergt.-Major stand 'em at ease!" "Stannat ease." Capt. produces copy of Batt. orders and reads as follows :— "The Commanding Officer has pleasure in publishing the following letter for information of all ranks—"To O.C. Umpshires. The Brig. General Commanding desires me to say that he is very pleased with the work done by the Batt. during their last turn of duty. He also wishes me to say that he was much struck by the alertness of the sentries,"—Signed, Robert Commentilouer, Major, Umpieth I.B.

Companys' chests swell two inches "The C.O. has informed me that most o that letter may be specially taken to refer to the Company" (Companys' jackets feeling the strain) "I'll pay the Company at 2.30 p.m. Company! Company, 'shun! Slope hup! Dis-miss!" Turns to Senior Sub. "They can be smart when they like, can't they, it's wonderful what a little praise can do when it comes from the right people." Exeunt omnes.—The war goes on.

ONE OF THE "P.B.I "

ARMA VIRUMQUE CANO.

—o—o—o—

The D.S.O., the M.C. grace my breast ;
My brow is bound with laurels and with
lace ;
I love this war. Perhaps you think that
that
Is strange. Well I am different from the
rest
Of you poor blighters. I live at the Base,
And use the Brain inside my mce, red hat.
                                    C. L. P.

administration, good equipment,' and 'Military Success' as the secret of the Allied troops' remarkable fighting spirit. We should consider also 'Paul the Pimp', mentioned earlier in the Robert Graves quotation, because the acrimonious relations between fighting men and 'Staff' adds to the tally of factors which appear to have adversely affected morale.

Shakespeare might have been at Ypres and based this scene of contemptuous animosity between a fighting man and a visiting staff officer on any such confrontation that took place every day in the trenches.

What is happening in the following sketch '*The Daily Round, The Trivial Task*,' is that the officers in the fighting line, both those who read the paper and those who compose it are disassociating themselves from the inanities of the General Staff. Any infantrymen who read the sketch would recognize immediately the boozy Brigadier General and his half-witted aide. The corporate strength of all fighting men in the Salient, who considered themselves, irrespective of rank, as a band of brothers fighting the whole world, would have been enhanced by this gentle mockery.

I am, at the moment, defeated by the surname of 'Bobbie', the General's aide. 'Commentlouer' is bound to be the encoded name of an actual staff officer but How-torent, the literal translation doesn't seem feasible. (Later … after consideration of an advertisement '*chambres à louer*' the simplicity of the problem embarrasses me. The Major's name was Howlett … Bob Howlett.)

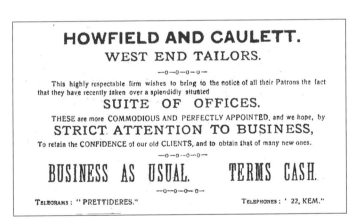

I feel we are solving a real Riddle of Wipers here. The West End Tailors transpose quite simply to Caufield and Howlett and there most probably is Bob again. Telegrams 'Prettideres' would indicate that these men were noticed by their unsullied appearance.

'To be so pester'd with a popinjay.'

And what about God? Did religion play any part in the resilience and determination of men fighting the First World War?

One of the few military campaigns in which infantrymen soldiered on in appalling conditions in a similar way to the PBI of Ypres was the great siege of Malta in 1565. In both wars there was unopposed artillery fire and relentless hand-to-hand fighting. There was disease and privation; unfavourable climate and a stubborn and unmilitary refusal to tolerate strategic withdrawal from untenable positions; Fort Saint Elmo was to la Valette as Hooge was to Haig. But in the 16th century, men could be persuaded to deeds of unimaginable endurance by Faith; Christian against Infidel with the fighters on both sides promised Paradise in exchange for death in battle; and Paradise plus bonuses such as the climax of love lasting a thousand years (for the Turks) if, when they died, they took a few of the enemy with them.

It was not so at Ypres. God is not mentioned on a single one of the 104 pages of the Complete Edition of *The Wipers Times*. Whatever it was that motivated our men it was not Christian religious fervour. Indeed the 'Man who was not a Padre' speaks for most of them when he finds himself doubting the Faith in which he was brought up amidst the horrors of the bombardment of the city.

By a Visitor.

—o—o—o—

If you happen to be a fortunate visitor to Ypres in these energetic times, there is much to see and learn for those who move about with their eyes open. By a fortunate visitor I mean, when you chance to arrive on one of the quiet days —days when the number of shells sent in by the Hun does not exceed 100 per hour (meal times excepted)—you are then able to move about in comparative safety. As a visitor one tries naturally to imagine something of what the historic old town looked like before modern artillery began to destroy the work of hundreds of years, and although one can see all these ruins of buildings, note the terrific effect of shell fire on walls many feet thick, one somehow feels how impossible it is to describe what Ypres looks like, one has to see it to understand the awful dead, forsaken appearance of the place. Then if your visit has brought you up at a time when the old town is lighted up by a full moon, and you happen to be of a somewhat sentimental turn of mind, you will find yourself marvelling at the wondrous beauty of the ruined city, somehow the odd spires, broken towers, fragments of massive walls, fronts of demolished houses all have their rough jagged edges softened by the moonlight, and from these thoughts it is but a step to go on and try to reason out the why and wherefore of these things. One is almost tempted to doubt if there is an over-ruling Power for Good in this world in which we live, and to attempt to reason that no possible good can come out of such appalling misery and desolation ; but surely this is another case of the finite mind coming into contact with the Infinite ? Then listen ! away to the east a faint whistle through the air, then another, coming this way—an explosion, and the guide says—"They're shelling Hell-Fire Corner again,"then quiet again, and later on as you wonder across the Square, you see the motor ambulances wending their way back to Pop. with their loads of mauled humanity, somebody's loved ones, to be looked after and tended by skilled hands—with no effort spared to alleviate pain and repair the damage—and as you travel home you will have many things to remember and think about—after your visit to Ypres,

ONE WHO IS NOT " A PADRE,"

This view is reflected in two quotes, one British and one German, from the *The First Day on the Somme*.

From that moment all my religion died. All my teaching and beliefs in God left me, never to return.

We had 'Gott mit uns' on our belt buckles, but still we lost the war.

There is, however, evidence of a kind of religious motivation in *The Wipers Times* and its successors. The religion is totally unfamiliar in Europe today, but it was probably the sole cohesive spiritual driving-force that uplifted the men of Wipers to the deeds of heroism and endurance which we admire so much today. The religion was Britishism.

Chapter 10

Britishism and Other Morale Raisers

Britishism was probably more of a philosophy than a religion but it was a potent motivating force, especially amongst the junior officers of the British Army fighting the First World War. The position that Britain and her Empire took in international affairs was assumed – by the British – to have divine authority. Britain and her Empire were the greatest military and economic unity in the World. With her power, Britain inherited responsibility and she saw it as her duty to civilize other nations as she thought best. To challenge Britain's authority to govern and oversee was to question a divine right. To doubt the benevolence of her rule was to question the decisions of the Almighty.

The soldiers of the British Army fighting the First World War were convinced that it was their duty to stand and fight for Freedom, and 'Freedom' was but another way of describing the way of life that had evolved in this country and its Empire. They flocked to the colours and sailed for France and Belgium in their thousands with the avowed purpose of – one more time – enforcing civilized behaviour in the British mould, upon their country's enemies.

'Through dread of crying you will laugh instead …'; an appropriate slogan for the whole *Wipers Times* philosophy.

WITH THE USUAL APOLOGIES.
—o—o—o—

If you can drink the beer the Belgians
  sell you,
And pay the price they ask with ne'er a
  grouse,
If you believe the tales that some will
  tell you,
And live in mud with ground sheet for a
  house,
If you can live on bully and a biscuit,
And thank your stars that you've a tot of
  rum,
Dodge whizzbangs with a grin, and as
  you risk it
Talk glibly of the pretty way they hum,
If you can flounder through a C.T. nightly
That's three-parts full of mud and filth
  and slime,
Bite back the oaths and keep your jaw
  shut tightly,
While inwardly you're cursing all the
  time,
If you can crawl through wire and crump-
  holes reeking
With feet of liquid mud, and keep your
  head
Turned always to the place which you
  are seeking,
Through dread of crying you will laugh
  instead,
If you can fight a week in Hell's own
  image,
And at the end just throw you down and
  grin,
When every bone you've got starts on a
  scrimmage,
And for a sleep you'd sell your soul
  within,
If you can clamber up with pick and
  shovel,
And turn your filthy crump hole to a
  trench,
When all inside you makes you itch to
  grovel,
And all you've had to feed on is a stench,
If you can hang on just because you're
  thinking
You haven't got one chance in ten to live,
So you will see it through, no use in
  blinking
And you're not going to take more than
  you give,
If you can grin at last when handing over,
And finish well what you had well begun,
And think a muddy ditch a bed of clover,
You'll be a soldier one day, then, my son.

Rudyard Kipling was the staunchest supporter of Britishism. His poems were widely read in the early part of this century and there are several parodies of his work in the *Wipers Times*;

We can safely assume that the soldier who wrote the parody of *'If'* – by their content he was a Pioneer and probably not an officer – was sufficiently well-read in Kipling's verse to have absorbed the full philosophy of *'For All We Have and Are'* published in 1914:

YOUR COUNTRY NEEDS YOU

FALL IN!

What will you lack, sonny, what will you lack
   When the girls line up the street,
Shouting their love to the lads come back
   From the foe they rushed to beat?
Will you send a strangled cheer to the sky
   And grin till your cheeks are red?
But what will you lack when your mate goes by
   With a girl who cuts you dead?

Where will you look, sonny, where will you look
   When your children yet to be
Clamour to learn of the part you took
   In the war that kept men free?
Will you say it was nought to you if France
   Stood up to her foe or bunked? [glance
But where will you look when they give the
   That tells you they know you funked?

How will you fare, sonny, how will you fare
   In the far-off winter night,
When you sit by the fire in an old man's chair
   And your neighbours talk of the fight?
Will you slink away, as it were from a blow,
   Your old head shamed and bent?
Or say—I was not with the first to go,
   But I went, thank God, I went.

Why do they call, sonny, why do they call
   For men who are brave and strong?
Is it nought to you if your country fall,
   And Right is smashed by Wrong?
Is it football still and the picture show,
   The pub and the betting odds,
When your brothers stand to the tyrant's blow,
   And Britain's call is God's?

     HAROLD BEGBIE.

Reproduced from the London "Daily Chronicle."

Music Copyright, ENOCH & SONS,
14, Great Marlborough Street, W.

For all we have and are,
For all our children's fate,
Stand up and take the war.
The Hun is at the gate!
Our world has passed away
In wantonness o'erthrown.
There's nothing left today
But steel and fire and stone.
   Though all we knew depart,
   The old Commandments stand:
   'In courage keep your heart,
   In strength lift up your hand.'

   ...

No easy hope or lies
Shall bring us to our goal,
But iron sacrifice
Of body, will and soul.
There is but one task for all
One life for each to give.
What stands if Freedom fall?
Who dies if England live?

We can grant Rudyard a little poetic licence and say he meant 'Britain'.

'Remember Belgium' and 'Plucky Little Belgium' are 'Britishist' slogans of 1914. Among the characteristics of our civilization that the Army felt duty-bound to impose on the enemy was an over-developed notion of fair play. If governments might draw the conclusion that the German invasion of Belgium was a dangerous upset to the balance of power and grounds for an ultimatum and declaration of war, our soldiers were more concerned that Belgium was being bullied, that Frightful Fritz wasn't playing fair, that it was their duty to teach the Hun some manners.

A 'Britishist' cigarette box of 1915.

Rubáiyát of William Hohenzollern.

Awake, old Tirpz! Bid Hindenburg
arise,
"Der Tag" has come, I long to hear
the cries
Of Europe! We'll proceed to raise all
Hell,
Let's use our day from dawn. Time
flies! Time flies!

—o—o—o—

Dreaming, it seemed to me the World
was mine,
Waking, I think that the idea is fine ;
We'll wade right in to see what we can
grab,
And glut ourselves with murder, rape
and wine.

—o—o—o—

Come, fill the cup, and don a mask of
pain
That we should have to cleanse the
World again ;
Consider we our cause both pure and
strong,
So first we'll try our hand in old Louvain.

—o—o—o—

Should any doubt my will, or us dispute,
Man, woman, child, don't hesitate to
shoot :
We'll play the policeman, and for
Kultur's sake
My son, young Bill, will pick up all the
loot.

During most of 1916 and 1917 the *Wipers Times* team were simply fighting for survival but occasionally in the paper we can see evidence of Britishism in their dugout philosophy. An example of this can be seen in this quotation from the poem 'War' which appeared in an early edition of *The Wipers Times*.

> Oft we're told 'remember Belgium'
> in the years that are to be;
> Crosses set by all her ditches,
> Are our pledge of memory.

Now we have arrived in pastures new,
Where the Hun's taking lessons that
once he gave.
Here's the best of good luck to all of you
In the teaching of blackguards how to
behave.

Hauptmann Van Horner,
In trench traverse corner,
Once heard what he thought
                was a " goer " ;
But he was mistaken
Said Fritz Carl Von Haken,
" I'll write to his widow, I know
                her."

Careful examination of this nursery rhyme parody reveals another example of Britishism.

Descriptions of the epic siege of Khe San, the American base in Vietnam and its heroic defence by the U.S. Marines will remind readers of a skill that is rapidly acquired by soldiers under fire. They identify shells as friendly or hostile simply by the sound they make while in flight. This gives experienced men time to shout a warning when they identify a projectile coming their way and to give their comrades a fraction of a second to take cover. In Vietnam the warning shout was 'Incoming!!!' In the Great War a 'Goer' posed no problem but you ran for your life from an 'Incomer'.

The story in those four lines of doggerel is that of David and Bathsheba with Hauptman van Horner in the role of Uriah the Hittite. David arranged for Uriah to be posted to the hottest part of a biblical battlefront so that Uriah's wife would be soon widowed and thus become available to David who had already cast a lustful eye upon her. Such behaviour, although apparently sanctified by biblical precedent, was anathema to the British Army. Our soldiers simply did not behave like that and even now, some eighty years after *The Wipers Times*, a British service unit will act in a conspicuously honourable manner towards wives and families of men killed on active service. Although the poem is a parody of a nursery rhyme as British as they come, it could never have found its way into print unless the perpetrators of such blackguardly behaviour had been transposed to the German side of the Line.

The two remaining 'Factors Affecting Morale', to which the British Army in the Great War can look to for its survival and ultimate Victory were 'esprit de corps' and 'good leadership'.

'Esprit de corps' is interpreted as the force which convinces a fighting soldier that to let down his comrades and the unit in which he is serving is, simply, unthinkable. This spirit was grounded in the British Army by the accident of territorial recruitment in the Middle Ages. It was then deliberately fostered by military commanders over two or three centuries of war. Traditions and a regiment's behaviour under fire were chronicled and embellished and force-fed to recruits. Glory was added and many quite inexplicable military traditions perpetuated as though they were, in themselves, the makings of a unit's victorious military past.

'Why,' people ask, 'do you have a goat on parade with a Goat-Major to look after him? Why do you wear a cap badge at the back of your beret?

1929 The Second Battalion, The Royal Welch Fusiliers.

Why do you force young men to eat raw leeks? Why do you go to war with an ancient Nepalese hunting knife at your waist? Why do you wear skirts?'

The answer from the regiments of the British Army is always the same:

'Because we have done things this way for the last three hundred-odd years and, if you would care to glance at the regimental battle honours, you must admit we have served the country well. Ousiders must allow us our traditions. We believe that they contibute materially to our success in battle.'

Some outsiders believe that the British Army of the Great War over-emphasized tradition and ritual behaviour to the point of inhumanity. Today more care is taken to ensure that military rituals are not used to impose the 'Duty of Obedience' at the expense of a twentieth-century conception of human rights.

There are many examples of 'esprit de corps', and practically nothing else, driving men to deeds of unbelievable heroism in the Salient. Most chroniclers initially describe these moments of glory as deeds carried out by battalions or perhaps regiments and only later, almost as an afterthought, are descriptions of individual actions included. Look once again to Robert Graves for an unexpected view of the connection between 'esprit de corps', morale and military well-being. The Second Royal Welch Fusiliers were a spit-and-polish regular army infantry battalion posted to the Western Front from India in 1916. In the following excerpt a subaltern warns the newly posted Robert Graves of the regimental 'Riding School' to which tradition demanded that subalterns were subjected.

'Subalterns who can't ride like angels have to attend riding school every afternoon while we're in billets. They give us Hell too. They keep us trotting round the field, with crossed stirrups most of the time, and on pack saddles instead of riding saddles. That reminds me, you notice everybody's wearing shorts? It's a regimental order. The battalion still thinks it's in India. Well what with a greasy pack saddle, bare knees, crossed stirrups, and a wild new transport pony pinched from the French, I got a pretty thin time. The Colonel, the Adjutant, the Second – in – Command, and the transport officer stood at the four corners of the ring and slogged at the ponies every time I came round. I fell off twice. The funny thing is they don't realise how badly they're treating you, it's such an honour to be serving with the regiment.'

Graves protested:

'But all this is childish. Is there a war on here or isn't there?'

'The Royal Welch don't recognize it socially; still, in the trenches I'd rather be with this battalion than any other I have met.'

And in the following quotation we can see how 'esprit de corps' built on such traditional disciplines and gave practical benefits to the battalion's fighting effectiveness.

A soldier could go to sleep with cold, wet feet and find that they had swelled slightly owing to the pressure of his boots and puttees; but 'Trench Foot' (the disabling fungal infection of feet and ankles) came only if he didn't mind getting 'Trench Foot' or anything else – because his battalion had lost the power of sticking things out. At Bouchavesnes, on the Somme, in the winter of 1916–17, a battalion of dismounted cavalry lost half its strength in two days from 'Trench Foot'; our Second Battalion (Royal Welch Fusiliers) had just completed ten days in the same trenches with no cases at all.

With a little explanation, the article 'As of Old' from a late edition of the paper – *The BEF Times* of December 25, 1917 – tells a similar story. It is a little piece of inter-unit one up-manship. The Royal Engineers or 'Sappers' considered themselves superior to the Pioneers; they were the brains of the digging and building branch of the Army, while the Pioneers, who actually masterminded the composition of *The Wipers Times*, were supposed to supply only the brawn.

So, when a Sapper tried unsuccessfully to 'Swing the Lead' or otherwise engineer an escape from front-line duty by feigning illness, the story was repeated with some glee by a Pioneer rival who wrote the pseudo-biblical column in the paper.

'NYD' was the Medical Officers' inconclusive finding 'Not Yet Diagnosed'. The Sapper's Commanding Officer had no such doubts. We should note that the 'Crucifixion' punishment (Field Punishment Number One) was still in force at this late date in the war. There wasn't much Christmas Spirit about that year either.

The military manuals concerned with the morale of fighting men devote many pages to 'Leadership', the mysterious influence by which men are united in a common cause and persuaded willingly to follow a frightening and hazardous road towards victory. Good leadership is pronounced to be the single most vital constituent of high morale, and all officers, both commissioned and non-commissioned, are constantly assessed for their ability and potential to be good leaders.

There can be few more extreme examples of persuasive military leadership than that revealed by examination of the role of the infantry subaltern in the murderous military stalemates of the First World War. This relationship is reflected in the cartoons of the day and in the poems, articles and advertisements of *The Wipers Times*. As an example let us consider in some detail the question of 'Offensive Thinking.'

Imagine the situation at nightfall in a front line trench somewhere in the Salient. It is January and a light rain is solidifying into sleet as the temperature drops. At intervals along the trench sentries peer out into the darkness so black that they can't see their own barbed wire, let alone the

Ne'er be peaceful, quiet, or pensive,
" Do your best to be offensive,"
His success shall greatest be,
Who regards this homily.
In the future day and night be
" As offensive as you might be."

AS OF OLD.

— o — o — o —

AND it came to pass that divers men were needed to labour in the land, so that the King's hosts might journey to the Land of the Amalekites. And they sent for those skilled in the art of digging and delving, and said unto them "Go ye and prepare the way for us." And men to the number of fifty girded up their loins, and they took spades and weapons, and tin hats they took also. And one of them, by name SAPPA, the son of ARREE, did quake exceedingly when he heard the tumult that there was in the place, for the Amalekites did have an up-wind, and raged furiously. And it came to pass that SAPPA, the son of ARREE did say to his Captain "Lo, I am not afraid, but I am suffering from a palsy." And the Captain said unto him "Get thee back, and tell the leech what thou hast told me, and peradventure he will give thee a potion, which will drive out the palsy." And he went. And when he had come unto Rap, where the leech dwelt, he went in unto him and made much lamentation, and said, "Lo, thy servant is stricken with a palsy, and the blood is like water in my veins." And the leech said unto him "Beware, oh SAPPA, that thou deceivest me not." And SAPPA answered him and said "Lo, my speech is as the speech of babes and sucklings, and there is no guile in my tongue." Then did the leech make much examination, and he went away and thought for a space. And when he had come back he did write on the parchment N.Y.D., which being interpreted means "No you don't." and he gave unto SAPPA a potion of Kasteroil. And he sent a messenger to the Captain, and he said "Lo the feet of SAPPA are cold, and it behoveth him to labour like Tumen, and peradventure he will not again suffer with a palsy. And the Captain tied SAPPA to the wheels of his chariot, and left him for a space. And then he said unto him, "Thou wilt now labour like Tumen, lest a worse thing befall thee." And SAPPA did as he was bid, and the palsy left him, and he was cured. And the fame of it went right through the King's hosts, as is written in the Second Book of Battorders.

Annotations (right margin):

- The Germans.
- Sapper. RE – Royal Engineer
- Leech – The MO
- RAP Regimental Aid Post
- Not Yet Diagnosed
- Caster Oil — a laxative
- Battalion Orders.

enemy's, some thirty yards distant. Mittened fingers clench and re-clench against the ice cold of rifle actions, and feet in sodden socks tread the muddy duckboards to keep warm. Conditions are scarcely better in the candlelit dugouts where the first reserves huddle together for warmth and try to snatch a few minutes sleep before stand-to or their turn for duty. No fire can be lit, no cigarette smoked; there are no rations and the rum's gone astray. This particular unit of the British Army are doing what they have done so well for many months in the Ypres Salient. They are enduring and surviving, denying by their muddy and indomitable presence this particular trench to the enemy.

A routine has been established in this terrible environment which is based on the understanding that soldiers, whomsoever they are fighting for, will always tend towards self preservation. A sort of peace is established, an unstated agreement with the Germans not to attack or patrol or fire fixed-arc machine guns. Maybe there might be a wire repair patrol later in the night after the rum issue – if there's a rum issue; maybe a burial party; maybe a sniper'll go out at dawn; maybe.... And suddenly,

'Smarten up lads – show a leg – wake up Chalkie – officer approaching.'

Muddy and slighly breathless with his head full of a briefing from his battalion commander that included several repetitions of the exhortation 'Think Offensive', appears a Lieutenant of His Majesty's Infantry. It is now that we see 'Leadership' at work. The manuals never explain exactly how a 19-year-old Lieutenant one year out of school, six months out of military academy and three months on the Western Front, should set about inspiring his company of half-frozen and apathetic soldiers into offensive action that will shatter the comparative peace of the night, that will lead inevitably to casualties and that will destroy the fragile security that his men have built up around themselves. Some chose to lead by example and inspired their men by their own displays of almost reckless courage.

Robert Graves again:

The first night I was in the trenches my company commander asked me to go out on patrol; it was the regimental custom to test new officers this way ... There was not a night at Lavantie that a message did not come down the line from sentry to sentry; 'Pass the word; officer's patrol going out.' My orders for this patrol were to see whether a German sap-head was occupied by night or not.

I went out from 'Red Lamp Corner' with Sergeant Townsend at about ten o'clock. We both had revolvers. We pulled socks, with the toes cut off, over our bare knees, (remember the Regiment still thought it was in India) to prevent them showing up in the dark and to make crawling easier. We went ten yards at a time, slowly, not on all fours, but wriggling flat along the ground. We crawled through our own wire entanglements and along a dry ditch; ripping our clothes on the barbed wire, glaring into the darkness till it began turning round and round (Once I snatched my fingers in horror from where I had planted them on the slimy body of an old corpse), nudging each other with rapidly beating hearts at the slightest noise or suspicion, crawling, watching, crawling, shamming dead under the blinding light of enemy flares and again crawling, watching, crawling …

After this I went out fairly often. I found that the only thing the regiment respected in young officers was personal courage.

The Raid
" Bert! It's our officer !"

There was a strong bond of love that existed between junior officer and soldier. Bairnsfather thoroughly understoond this. 'I love those old work-evading, tricky, self-contained slackers – old soldiers! They are the cutest set of old rogues imaginable, yet with it all there is such a humorous child-like simplicity'.

Sometimes the subalterns led by a mixture of friendliness and a shameless façade of taking the side of the soldiers against the tyranny of the General Staff. Sometimes it was with a smile and a kind word, sometimes by sheer strength of personality. In whatever way it was achieved, their leadership was one of the cornerstones of the British Army at war and without doubt it was the single most powerful force that sustained British morale in the trenches.

There is no pretence in this dramatic and beautifully written record of a soldier's thoughts before going 'over the top'. There is no sycophancy in his praise for the cool-headed officer and, if questioned in those few moments before zero hour, the writer would have loyally stated that 'He would follow Lt. So-and-So, the officer I/C B. Company … anywhere.' This particular phrase, used often as a military accolade for a good leader, occurs frequently in reports and citations.

FIVE MINUTES.

—o—o—o—

ZERO MINUS FIVE.—Two hours, we've been lying on the tape. Blondin's on a wire ; and Niagara, the No Man's Land, we have to cross at Dawn. Our guns are busier than ever they have been before. See :—gigantic flashes of light ; gigantic flashes of sound ; a hundred hundred gigantic, jewelled hands rapidly running over the whole horizon, playing concerted Hell on the Harpsichord of Hate to an audience of terrified Teutons.

That is good. I must remember it, if I get out of this alive.

—o—o—o—

ZERO MINUS FOUR.—The music goes on. Starting off staccato, it has become forte, fortissimo, crescendo. I didn't think I could be sorry for those Huns. Not since they got my mate at Vimy. Well, Jim, old man, the Twenty-fourth is getting a bit of its own back to-day.

—o—o—o—

ZERO MINUS THREE.—That was a short one. Wonder why these Artillery blokes don't scrap their worn-out eighteen-pounders. God ! There's another. Shrapnel too. Why, it's all along the line.

A big dump's been put up, somewhere back of Gheluvelt. Just in that dip, beyond the rise. Red fingers of flame, reflected in the window of the sky. There, chum, there—just below those shrapnel bursts. Look, straight where I am pointing.

—o—o—o—

ZERO MINUS TWO —My mistake. It's the sun coming up. Phœbus they call it. And he'll be shining on Mary Matthews in her little cottage at home. What silly ideas to come into my head at a time like this !

ZERO MINUS ONE.—Here's the sergeant coming along. And the orficer, with him ; a cool one he is, and the best one we've ever had in Beer Coy. Yes, sir, it is a bit cold this morning. What's that, serg'int ?—Give them muckin' Fritzes, 'ell ?—You bet, WE WILL !—

A book of Remembrance to commemorate the 1400 Old Boys of Rugby School who died in the Great War makes an interesting study in Leadership. Ninety per cent of them were officers, seventy-five per cent were infantry subalterns aged between nineteen and twenty-two and few of them had more than six weeks' service on the Western Front. In almost every case where a letter of condolence from a commanding officer was quoted, the same phrase occurred: 'he was adored by his men who would have followed him anywhere.' This was cold comfort for grieving relatives, but the highest praise that could be bestowed on young men cut down in the prime of life while loyally leading their men to a futile battle in a foreign land.

We must think of the leadership exerted by the infantry subalterns as one of the priceless advantages that the British High Command possessed in the First World War. The armies of France, Italy, Russia and Germany all suffered mutinies in which soldiers declined to follow their infantry commanders into the front line, usually after periods of rest. It was not so in the British Army. Researchers into the campaigns on the Western Front are of the opinion that this powerful link in our military chain of command was wickedly and cynically abused by those who were running the War.

Consider for a moment the catalogue of 'Duties' that weighed down on a young company commander, perhaps one of the 1400 old Rugbeians, at dawn on 1 July, 1916 – The first day of the Somme. 'Don't let the School down,' his old headmaster had said. 'The Hamilton-Brownes (or some such 'Public School' name) are proud of you,' from his father. 'Your Country needs you,' said Lord Kitchener. 'You have a duty to

ACHTUNG!

The day will come when even Mars is tired,
When obus slumber and no shot is fired,
When unashamed we'll don our bowler hats
And men shall dress complete, yea down
    to spats,
Then " what about it " you who find it hard
To hear unfettered comment from the bard.

The stars on this poetic sleeve are three,
That they're as many is *bonne chance* for me
Numbers there are who starred and likewise
    crowned,
Do tread the grateful and subservient ground
Some who by prowess lately proved in war,
May sport red 'tabs' and ribboned breasts
    galore.

—:0:—

When back returns the poise of other days,
When we shall tread the old, civilian ways,
Maybe we'll find that other honours count
Besides the ones with warfare for their fount
This bard may rise ere Phoebus rents the
    dark,.
To do the bidding of his whilem clerk !

—:0:—

All men shall reckon, when reigns common-
    sense,
That crowns and stars don't mean omni-
    science.
That somehow there are lots of things in
    life
Quite as important as the battle's strife
Consider, bard, the men you thus contemn,
How shall we e'er gain peace— except
    through them ?

THE LECTURE.

If at any time you happen to be at all depressed—though of course this is extremely unlikely out here where there is so much to interest and delight one—find out whether there is a lecture on anywhere, given by the G.S.O. first or second of a Division about to be relieved, to the officers of the relieving Division, and go to it at once. It will make you realise that war is worth while. Roughly speaking, the show will be as follows :— The room is packed with an expectant but nervous conglomeration of officers, of whom certainly not more than the first two rows will hear a word of the glad tidings. That doesn't matter, however, there is a screen and a magic lantern which you may be deluded into thinking is going to show you a reasonably clear picture of the trenches—don't be had by it—it's only a trap. Well, eventually a Staff Officer mounts the platform, and you gather from his opening remarks that he has been deputed to give the lecture, that he is not much of a hand at the job, and that you must forgive him. This is greeted with sympathetic noises —the audience apparently attempting to ingratiate themselves into his good offices thereby, and hoping that if they are successful in this he'll let 'em down with a minimum of forgetfulness. The Staff Officer is not moved in the least. He proceeds as follows :—"As a matter of fact I haven't been up to the front line for—er—some time (the audience appear incredible) but when I was last up, A 1 had fallen in, and of course most of the communication trenches had been—er— crumped in." The audience seem to appreciate the fact that there are still a few trenches extant " I will now show you some photographs of the craters." The operator having woken up, the lantern is lit, and a beautiful bright light, accompanied by a very realistic imitation of the odours encountered at Hooge is given. Unfortunately the lighting effects are poor, but anyway you have a quiet ten minutes in which to give your pal instructions what to do with your corpse. Eventually a picture is shown, which may remind you of your late Uncle Bill, who used to suffer severely from warts. As the lecturer invariably holds his pointer at least one foot from the screen, you will naturally look at the wart indicated by the shadow, but that always adds to the amusement, and you can run a book as to which smudge is the crater. The grand finale is always worth paying attention to. " The enemy shoot at you from three and a half sides, some officers make it three and three quarters, though personally I incline to the latter view." The Staff Officer then tells you that he doesn't think he has anything more to say, and though everyone seems grieved to hear it, he subsides into a chair next to the G.O.C. The best part of the lecture is, of course, that it leaves you with a magnificent thirst.

                P.B.I.

protect us,' said the white-feather women; 'a Christian duty' from someone or other. Later when he joined the Army the litany continued: duty to the Regiment, duty to the men, a duty to lead and, most important of all, a duty to obey the orders of those set in authority over him without delay and without question. So what did a subaltern do when orders were, as they clearly were on the first day of the Somme, simply suicidal? How could a young man equate his duty to his men who, you will remember, 'trusted him and would follow him anywhere', with an order that had all the military prescience of an instruction to take them out and lead them over a cliff? The answer must be that he lied. He lied to his men whose trust and confidence he had carefully built up under the military guise of 'Good Leadership'. Robert Graves lied to his men when he had to lead them on 'Paul the Pimp's' suicidal mission that we read of earlier, and as they waited at the departure line tapes for the sun to rise on that disastrous First of July the company commanders were lying again:

> Our barrage will kill all the enemy in the opposing trenches – intelligence reports all enemy machine guns destroyed – walk forwards in line, there is no need to run. Our guns have blasted gaps in the wire a hundred yards wide. We'll have a brew of tea when we stop for a rest at the Schwaben Redoubt.

Lies in the process of leadership and in the cause of high morale are possibly excusable as part of the dehumanization of war. Nothing that took place in those terrible times should belittle our admiration for the nineteen-year-olds, briefly attired as officers, who somehow persuaded one hundred thousand men of the New Armies to follow them up and over the top to almost certain death. However, there should be little sympathy for the War Council and the generals who forced through their hopelessly flawed battle-plan sustained only by the leadership of the same junior officers many of whom must have understood the magnitude of the disaster that was about to unfold.

The duty of obedience is no longer present in our young men. Quite rightly the nineteen-year-olds of today want hard evidence that their own personal interests will be well served before *any* authority can tell them what to do. If the circumstances of 1916 were transferred to the 1990s every military order would be tested by hard-headed young men who would for ever want to know *'Why?'*

Before we conclude that the tendency to question orders is destructive of our national strength, one fact should be stressed. If every junior commander who had doubts about the anticipated results of the battle had questioned his orders instead of blindly obeying them maybe the generals

THE GREAT ARMY PEACE MOVEMENT.

ENROL TO-DAY!!!

WE WANT PEACE!!!

ENROL TO-DAY!!!

—o—o—o—o—

THE SOCIETY has been formed with the object of insisting on PEACE at the EARLIEST POSSIBLE MOMENT.

—o—o—o—o—

YOU ARE ASKED TO HELP!

BIG ADVANCES IN THE CAUSE HAVE BEEN MADE THIS YEAR and we are holding a GREAT ANTI-WAR DEMONSTRATION at PASSCHENDAELE. All are welcome.

—o—o—o—o—

PRESIDENT:

D. HAIG, Esq.

—o—o—o—o—

SPEAKERS:

R. TILLERY and T. ATKINS.

Lancashire Fusiliers advance across Passchendaele ridge. Photo; IWM

could have been prevented from sending four hundred and fifty thousand British soldiers to become casualties in the killing fields of the Somme.

The 'Duty of Obedience' forced Roberts, himself a battalion commander, to reject any blatant insubordinations that were offered for publication in the paper. However, the message of 'The Lecture' is of a Line Officer questioning the competence of those who give him his orders and in *'Achtung'* we see the beginnings of revolt against military top brass who have been sustained in their positions by rank and not by merit. The latter article appeared in the Armistice edition of the paper.

It is surprising that Roberts got away with the 'Great Army Peace Movement' advertisement which appeared in August, 1917. In less tormented times a 'Special Branch' investigation would probably have followed such an apparent call for a cessation of hostilities. D. Haig Esq. had within the last month overseen the horror of Passchendaele.

Alan Brooke, an 'R. Tillery' Staff Officer at Headquarters Canadian Corps, who had observed closely the fighting at Passchendaele, wrote the following words about the battle;

> At a conference addressed by Haig I could hardly believe my ears were not deceiving me! He spoke in the rosiest terms of our chances of breaking through. I had been all over the ground and to my mind such an eventuality was quite impossible. I am certain he was misinformed and had never seen the ground for himself.

Part Three

The Correspondents

Chapter 11

The Riddle of Teech Bomas

I travelled by train to the British Newspaper Library at Colindale. The object of my journey was to find out if the library held copies of The Wipers Times; to establish whether Roberts, the editor, had any sort of career in post-war journalism, and to identify the actual war correspondent on which the outrageous reports of Teech Bomas were based. Serendipity gave me my first clue in the pages of Gilbert Frankau's biography, which I was reading as we

Mr. Teech Bomas.

—o—o—o—

We regret to inform our readers that as Mr. TEECH BOMAS has left for his usual winter trip to warmer climes, all proceedings will be stopped meanwhile. The battle will be resumed immediately on his return, when we hope to have further graphic articles from his pen. —ED.

clattered up to Euston. The author describes this book as a 'Novel of his Own Life'. It is a difficult work on which to base research. Much of the drama comes from brief pen sketches of the innumerable famous people that Frankau met in his varied and interesting life. The narrative is irregular and the story often difficult to follow as he diverges abruptly in order to encompass yet another unexpected meeting or to introduce another well-known character of the day. The names were now mainly forgotten but my mind was attuned to any reference to Roberts and The Wipers Times. I was also looking for any name that might be bowdlerised, spoonerised, rhyming-slanged or otherwise simply encoded into 'Teech Bomas' or 'Cockles Tumley'. 'Self Portrait' by Gilbert Frankau, I regret to say, has no index.

The train stopped and I focused more easily on the close-printed page. Frankau, already suffering from combat fatigue if not actual shellshock after eighteen months active service in the Ypres Salient, has been sent, possibly by a sympathetic CO, on an anti-aircraft artillery course behind the lines at Montauban. He has completed the course and is now pulling all available strings to get himself transferred to a special task; that of making and releasing cinema films about the war for propaganda purposes in Italy. In everyone's opinion he has done more than his share of active fighting, but his guilt at actually engineering his posting away from the front and his comrades is plain to see. I sympathized and read on:

I returned to Montauban via Amiens, being hospitably entertained there by Philip Gibbs, Beach Thomas, Russell and others of my present craft at War Correspondents' headquarters. There followed a few more safeish days with Kingscote, my one and only lunch at the famous 'Restaurant Godbert' in Amiens, more drillings by a Canadian dentist, and a second visit to Querrieux where I found Edric Weldon with the Eighth Hussars.

Teech Bomas, Beach Thomas; a straightforward spoonerism with an e / a substitution. 'Elementary my Dear Watson' … there was, a section in The Wipers Times *devoted to the adventures of a great detective, Herlock Shomes.*

Searching for the work of a correspondent that you know by name only is not easy in a newspaper library. The whole complicated system of indexes, porters, trollies, micro-film and antiquated lifts to and from the basement is geared to locating an actual copy or facsimile of every issue of every newspaper that has ever been published in this country. But if you don't know what issue of what paper you are looking for it is needle and haystack time. The kind lady at the desk said, ' Try *The Times*; Beach Thomas sounds like a Times sort of name and there is an index of every name that appears in every issue of that paper.' It took me half an hour to discover that B-T didn't write for *The Times*, or if he did it was never under that name. However, I was encouraged by a chance encounter with a friend. The Times Index for 1916 fell open at the page recording the award of the DSO to Colonel G.E.H. Sim, a friend of my father's and a revered godparent. Bill Sim lost an arm on the Somme and in retirement became highly skilled as a carpenter and wood worker. He fashioned jig-saw puzzles of devilish cunning out of the prints of famous Victorian paintings once used to advertise Pears soap. My father delighted in Sim's puzzles and if my memory serves me he finally completed the umpteenth re-construction of 'Bubbles' just a few hours before he died.

I summoned up, as a shot in the dark, copies of *The Daily Mail* for the first three months of 1916. An hour-and-a-half later I was presented with a micro-film in a brown cardboard box. This was disappointing as I had much admired the full-sized leather-bound volumes that were wheeled out and man-handled onto the generous floodlit reading desks surrounding the reading room of the British Newspaper Library. However, full-size and leather bindings are for lesser-known, provincial papers. The Dailies come on microfilm. All anti-climax disappeared once I threaded the film into one of the viewing machines provided. *The Daily Mail* for Saturday 12 February, 1916, the day the first *Wipers Times* appeared in the Salient, swam into focus. There is no time transporter like a newspaper. Here were front page views of battle, wills and litigation, casualty figures and football scores. My eye was caught by corset advertisements and Gold Flake, road-test reports on long forgotten motor cars and pompous letters to the editor airing displeasure at imagined erosions of liberty. Like a reader of fish and chip wrappings or the linings of old drawers, I was transported back in time from 1993 Colindale to mid-First World War London; and an hour later, with aching eyes, I found an article, 'From Our Special Correspondent,' over the byline 'William Beach Thomas'.

The Daily Mail, June, 1916:

> One officer, after using up all the clips of cartridges which he had taken for his revolver, seized a German rifle, rushed on a group of Germans behind a traverse and bayonetted 3. He himself escaped scot free. All the bombs were spent in a few moments, some thrown high into the trench, some along it and some into dug-outs. A short, sharp time limit had been set to this venture.
>
> > Sound, sound the clarion, fill the fife
> > To all the several world proclaim,
> > One crowded hour of glorious life,
> > Is worth an age without a name.

And I could imagine every fighting man in every trench and shell-hole on the Western Front making lavatory-flushing gestures and chorussing 'Bollocks' in angry unison.

You don't have to have been on active service to know that the construction of a revolver makes it impossible to load it from any sort of clip. Clips are for .303 Lee-Enfield rifles, the infantryman's trusted weapon. It was such an error of technical knowledge that made it clear that Beach Thomas had never seen, fired or handled a revolver in his life and the readers of *The Wipers Times* will have drawn the obvious conclusion that he had never been near a trench either. Can they be blamed for imagining that Beach Thomas's despatches came from no nearer the war than Correspondent's Headquarters in Amiens and the greatest danger he faced was the chance consumption of an unhealthy oyster in the Restaurant Godbert.

The Wipers Times allows its readers to work off some of their anger at the untruths of War Correspondents by laughing at the the outrageous writings of their own 'Special Correspondent.'

HOW THE TANKS WENT OVER.

—:o:—

BY OUR SPECIAL CORRESPONDENT,

Mr. TEECH BOMAS.

—:o:—

In the grey and purple light of a September morn they went over. Like great prehistoric monsters they leapt and skipped with joy when the signal came. It was my great good fortune to be a passenger on one of them   How can I clearly relate what happened ? All is one chaotic mingling of joy and noise   No fear ! How could one fear anything in the belly of a perambulating peripatetic progolodymythorus. Wonderful, epic, on we went, whilst twice a minute the 17in. gun on the roof barked out its message of defiance. At last we were fairly in amongst the Huns. They were round us in millions and in millions they died. Every wag of our creatures tail threw a bomb with deadly precision, and the mad, muddled, murderers melted. How describe the joy with which our men joined the procession until at last we had a train ten miles long. Our creature then became in festive mood and, jumping two villages, came to rest. in a crump-hole. After surveying the surrounding country from there we started rounding up the prisoners. Then with a wag of our tail (which accounted for 20 Huns) and some flaps with our fins on we went. With a triumphant snort we went through Bapaume pushing over the church in a playful moment and then steering a course for home, feeling that our perspiring panting proglodomyte had thoroughly enjoyed its run over the disgruntled, discomfited, disembowelled earth. And so to rest in its lair ready for the morrow and what that morrow might hold. I must get back to the battle   TEECH BOMAS.

WE ATTACK AT DAWN.

—:o:—

BY OUR SPECIAL CORRESPONDENT

Mr. Teech Bomas.

—:o:—

All was still as the first flush of dawn lit the sky. Then suddenly the atmosphere was riven by the crescendo chorus which leapt to meet the light as a bridegroom to his bride. The delicate mauve and claret of the dawning day was displaced by a frothy and furious fandango of fire. The giant trogolythic ichnyosaurus crept fawning from their lairs, and gambolled their way to the line oblivions of anything that barred their passage. The disgruntled bosom of mother earth heaved with spasmodic writhings as the terrible tornado tore the trees. I was picking wallflowers in Glencorse Wood when all this happened, and even now the memory of that zero hour is with me. Having passed through several liberated villages, I stood on that historic spot and waited to put my watch right by the barrage. It came, and the world wilted. Then on came the gallant Esquimaux and Peruvians (I musn't mention anything English, it isn't " done,") and with a wild rush shattered Germany's grey-clad hosts. The while the guns thundered and boomed in hellish chorus across the riven bosom of Belgium, the wild flowers grew and the birds sang, revelling in hectic competition with their human rivals who figured in fantastic feats turning many a lark green with envy. Even the tanks, catching the atmosphere of excitement, threw cartwheels in an earnest endeavour to camouflage their real nature. Many parties of Huns were so surprised at their appearance that they offered them bird seed. In fact we attacked at dawn.

TEECH BOMAS.

33: ZILLEBEKE - VUE D'ENSEMBLE DU CIMETIERE DES TANKS
GENERAL VIEW OF CIMETERY OF TANKS

The Tanks; reality and propaganda.

THE IRRESISTIBLE TANKS

In Nigel Cave's book on Beaumont Hamel there is a more realistic report of the return from a raid by a genuine fighting man. His thoughts also turned to the insistent sounds of military music.

> Trumpeter what are you sounding now?...
> I am calling them home, 'Come home, come home'
> Tread lightly o'er the dead in the valley
> They are lying around face down to the ground
> And can't hear me sound the rally.

There was just time for me to make a few notes before I had to return the micro-film. I also skimmed through every dictionary of journalistic biography that the library offered. Beach Thomas was knighted for services as a war correspondent after the end of the war and lived in respected and honourable retirement until his death in 1957. Of Roberts and *The Wipers Times* I could find no mention. As I left Colindale and rode back to Euston on the underground I reflected on the relative success of the two men. 'Tell your readers what they want to hear' could have been the philosophy of both, but Roberts had fewer readers and was more concerned with the truth. Did B-T deserve his knighthood anymore than Roberts deserved obscurity? Is a war correspondent's duty as much to maintain public morale as to report reality? What about censorship? Was either man allowed to write without restriction? 'I am not permitted to say if we lost any aircraft, but I counted them all out ...' Damn it – that was Euston.

Chapter 12

Cockles Tumley and Other Correspondents

The war correspondent, Cockles Tumley, was a regular contributor to *The Wipers Times*. His column was a parody of one that a real correspondent wrote for a national newspaper. These pieces were apparently exaggerated and untruthful and the staff of the trench journal and its readers had a withering contempt for the writer. This animosity of fighting men towards those who write about war is not unusual and soldiers who saw action in The Falklands, The Gulf and in the wreckage of Yugoslavia no doubt carry on the tradition. A war correspondent usually likes to surround himself with an aura of bravery in action which the fighting men know to be bogus. Hence the flak jacket and the carefully contrived distant burst of gunfire that appear to be mandatory in all television reports from the 'front'. With certain honourable and notable exceptions war correspondents are not usually around when the real bullets are flying.

Journalists also seem to be compelled to embroider reality. There was enough drama in the daily life of a man in the Ypres salient to fill a hundred copies of *The Daily News*. Why did journalists, who only paid Belgium a fleeting visit, if they ever got that close to the front, have to exaggerate and improve on stories? The argument that a journalist knows what the public wants to hear was as specious then as it was in Tiananmen Square when Chinese Government tank commanders were invited by TV reporters to burst through a barricade for a second time because the cameras had apparently missed their first appearance.

The original correspondent on whom the inanities of H. Cockles Tumley are based can only by derived by guesswork. However, there was a clue in some memories from the British reaction to the Rhodesian rebellion of the 1960s. A squadron of Javelin all-weather fighters was briefly stationed in neighbouring Zambia as some kind of sabre-rattling excercise. The detachment was visited by Mr Arthur Bottomley, Colonial Secretary in the Harold Wilson government. Mr Bottomley did not endear himself to the aircrews, and two stories, probably apocryphal, underline this hostility.

NEWS FROM THE RATION DUMP

The Czar of Russia has antiquated.

Horatio Bottomley has accepted the Turkish throne on condition they make a separate peace.

A party of A.S.C. were seen working in the reserve line.

40,000 Huns have surrendered. They were so thin that they walked down one of our C.T.'s in fours.

The German fleet has bombarded Wapping Old Stairs, and ruined the carpet.

Leave is about to re open on the Western front.

Patrols of British and French cavalry swam the Rhine last night near Cologne, and are now meeting with sharp resistance in the suburbs of Berlin.

[The EDITOR takes no responsibility for the truth of the above statements.]

The first is that he referred to the country in which he found himself as 'Gambia', a geographical error as wide as the whole African continent; and the second, that he farted hugely within the overheated confines of a radar caravan, causing a hurried evacuation by the operators and a temporary breakdown in the radar surveillance across the Zambesi. Small wonder he was nicknamed 'Bumley'.

The men in the Ypres front-line might well have referred verbally to a man as 'Bumley', but Victorian sensibilities would have insisted that they never wrote the word. It was the long-forgotten notion that 'rude' words somehow isulted women that gave rise to asterisks in prose and rhyming slang in everyday speech. Words that were thus disguised were usually swear-words or ones that carried some lavatorial or sexual connotation. Hence D**n, Bu**er, H**l, and Bristols, Hamptons, Berkeley Hunts and, of course, Tumley for Bumley.

So, if Tumley is rhyming slang for Bumley, who is the Mr Bottomley who wrote articles for the Press and to whom the Wipers men took such objection? A check of the Bottomleys in a biographical dictionary indicates that Horatio was the guilty man. Someone on *The Wipers Times* staff knew enough of the Classics to

SOMEWHERE IN—WIPERS.

—o—o—o—

By COCKLES TUMLEY.

—o—o—

(Our representative, Mr. COCKLES TUMLEY, has just paid a visit to the Front, and here describes his experiences in his inimitable manner.)

—o—

YOU can't imagine what I've seen. Neither can I! Stay, I will tell you. I've worn a tin hat!

I've eaten a tin of bully beef!

I've talked with a general!

I won't tell you what he said, but you can take it from me THE WAR IS OVER.

I've been in the support line, which is much more dangerous than the first.

I've been in the reserve line, which is much more dangerous than the support.

I have been in Div. H.Q., which is more dangerous still.

And I have even been back to G.H.Q.

I have discussed the situation with the soldiers themselves. I can't tell you what they thought of it.

AND NOW FOR WHAT I HAVE LEARNT.

I have learnt that there's a lot of meat in a tin of bully. I have learnt that an army biscuit is a hard nut to crack. I have learnt that a tipping duckboard needs no push. I have learnt that Belgian beer wants a good deal of bush.

Every German prisoner I spoke to said the same thing. I can't tell you what it was, but THE WAR IS WON. To use one of our familiar slogans, I say "Watch the Q.M." I was having a talk with one of the Tommies who had answered the call of King and Country, and I asked him what he thought of it all. I can't tell you his answer, but it impressed me wonderfully. Well, I will write more next week when my head is clearer. I must go now and have my photo taken in a gas-bag and tin hat,

COCKLES TUMLEY.

remember that Cocles was the surname of Horatius – he who 'kept the Bridge in the brave days of old.'

Not much is written about Horatio Bottomley because he was in fact a charlatan, fraudster and confidence trickster who died in obscurity. His career was one of spectacular peaks and troughs. He was born in an orphanage and became successively an errand boy, a solicitor's clerk and a shorthand writer in the supreme court. He started a newspaper, the *Hackney Hansard* and was by all accounts a brilliant speaker and journalist. At one time before the First World War he had set up about fifty separate companies with £20,000,000 of share capital. Sixty-seven bankruptcy writs and petitions were filed against him. He was MP for South Hackney but resigned after one of his many bankruptcies. During the war he floated enterprises supposedly for the benefit of the fighting men and wrote nonsensical articles for *The Sunday Pictorial* on military matters. These were avidly read at home and greeted with derision on the Western Front.

'Belary Helloc'

Hilaire Belloc was already a celebrity at the outbreak of the First World War, when poets and writers were accorded a great deal more respect than nowadays. It appears that the reputations of men like Kipling and Belloc assured them of the opportunity to write articles in the popular press, and the readership took note of their opinions. This, unfortunately, led the great literary figures of the day to make fools of themselves in the eyes of the soldiers every time they delivered, from ignorance, stern pronouncements on how to win the War. The British public at home simply could not understand why we were not winning. For over one hundred years the British had won a series of small wars often by sheer weight of numbers and fire power. Even in the Second Boer War, where they took a severe beating from the Boers at the outset,

HOW TO WIN THE WAR.

By BELARY HELLOC.

HAVING very little time at my disposal this week I only intend to roughly outline my plan for ending the war satisfactorily and quickly.   Briefly then to do this we must reduce the war to a man to man encounter.   Take things like this.   The line held on all fronts is 1:500 miles (circa).   That is 2,640,000 yards.   Now we must get that number of our troops and allot one yard per man.   Give each man a bomb, and at a given signal let them all go over and each to account for his own particular opponent.   This would account for 2,000,000 of the enemy (that is giving the generous allowance of 640,000 failures), besides putting him to much inconvenience.   Each time the enemy brings up reinforcements and re-establishes his line then repeat the performance.   I think I may safely say that, after the tenth or eleventh attack, the enemy would be ready to consider the advisability of making terms rather than continue the war.   This is merely a rough outline of my plans, and super-ficially it may seem that there are objections. . However, I think these may well be dealt with as they arise.

BELARY HELLOC.

People We Take Our Hats off To.

——:o:——

Mr. Asquith, for at last making up his mind.

THE WAR IN THE EAST.

—:o:—

Major Taude, B.C.

—:o:—

Of course all the tactics employed in this campaign are wrong. I have studied the whole affair carefully (from maps and the histories of previous wars) and I find them absolutely contrary to all the rules laid down by Julius Caesar and Hannibal. I well remember the excellent results obtained by my adoption of the tactics used by Bruce at Bannockburn, and I consider that it was due to these that I obtained the splendid moral victory over the Church Lads' Brigade, at Shepherd's Bush, in 1870. I have proved time and again in my articles that the opposing force can only hope for success so long as it beats the defending force, and that, once the positions are reversed, then the defending force will become the attacking force. War and tactics have been my constant study, and I feel sure that a more careful scrutiny of my works would lead to an earlier successful termination of the war. There was that successful little affair of mine at Clapham Common which might be emulated with advantage by Sir Douglas Haig in his Western campaign. Verb. sap.

To the Editor,
Wipers Times."
Sir,
As the father of a large family, and having two sons serving in the Tooting Bec Citizens' Brigade, may I draw your attention to the danger from Zeppelins. Cannot our authorities deal with this menace in a more workmanlike way. My boys, who are well versed in military affairs, suggest a high barbed wire entanglement being erected round the British Isles. Surely something can be done :—

PATER FAMILIAS.

the war was finally won by their ability to overwhelm their enemy and flood the country with troops.

Hilaire Belloc expanded on this theme in his articles in the Press. 'Statistically the armies of Britain and her Empire should be able to overcome the forces of Germany; what is the the reason for the delay?' It seems that no one had explained to him about the machine gun. Belloc was, for a time, MP for Salford. Perhaps he began to appreciate the weakness of the statistical theory of military superiority when four-fifths of the 15th Battalion the Lancashire Fusiliers (The Salford Pals) were wiped out on the First Day of The Somme.

'Major Taude' and 'Pater Familias' are typical of the retired military men who constantly write to the papers when the country is at war. Such correspondents seem unable to grasp the fact that strategies which were successful in previous campaigns are no guarantee of victory in the current one. Military staff have been guilty of making the same mistake.

Most probably the articles by all these imaginary writers were the work of F. J. Roberts. Of Roberts himself so little is known that it appears that his trail has been deliberately blurred. Patrick Beaver's book '*The Wipers Times*' includes the following biographical notes, along with an acknowledgement to Marcus Roberts, the editor's son, for providing them.

Lt Col F J Roberts, MC, founder and editor of *The Wipers Times*, was born in London in 1882. As a young man he became a mining engineer and claimed to be the first European to trek across North Borneo. He also adventured and prospected in the diamond fields of South Africa. In 1914 he returned to England and joined up with the 12th Battalion Sherwood Foresters. In August 1915 the Battalion was sent to the Western Front with the newly formed 24th Division. Roberts started *The Wipers Times* the following February and edited it until 1918. He was twice mentioned in dispatches and won his MC on the Somme front in 1916. He returned to prospecting after the war and died in Canada in 1964.

Roberts' name does not appear in the Army List indexes for 1914 to 1918 and his MC award was published without citation in an Honours Gazette. After the war he apparently had difficulty in re-adjusting to civilian life and seems to have found no future in writing or journalism. He kept contact with Gilbert Frankau who mentions that, in 1929, Roberts was working as a compiler of crosswords for the Daily News. This appears to have been only a part-time occupation and Frankau notes that his former editor was mentally swamped by the requirement to produce, at short notice, a clutch of crosswords for a national competition.

The last known writing of F. J. Roberts was the introduction to the 1930 facsimile reproduction of the complete *Wipers Times* published by Eveleigh Nash and Grayson in London. The introduction ends, with a trace of the disillusionment that was so widespread in that depression year, as follows;

> The sub-editor and myself would like to take this opportunity of sending our best wishes to all old friends of those far-off days. Talking things over two or three months ago, we came to the conclusion that Peace of the 1929 vintage is nothing to write books about. In the days of *The Wipers Times* we had some bad times, but – well! we had some good ones too. Thank Heaven that friendships made in those days have held in these after years.
>
> When you get fed up with the joys of peace, grab your *Wipers Times* and you'll soon be longing to be on a 'working party' again. 'Over the top and the best of luck' to all of you.

In an attempt to unearth further biographical information on the editor of *The Wipers Times* whose work I had come to admire so absolutely, I endeavoured to contact any of his family and spoke to the Sherwood Forester historical branch in Nottingham. I was completely unsuccessful. Roberts has disappeared without trace. I did obtain from Patrick Beaver a suggestion that

The Editor of *The Wipers Times*.

MORE MUD THAN GLORY.

—o —o—o—

Scene—Regent Street Tunnel. C.O. and Adjutant discovered sitting in recess.
C.O.—"Gawd ! How this filthy place stinks." Adj. (trying to write)— 'Yes, sir." C.O —"Damn this water ! It'll be over the tops of my boots directly." Adj.—"And I'm sure we shall all be getting trench feet." (Enter orderly hurriedly, perspiring and breathless.) Ord.—"Tunnel's just been blown in, sir, and the water's pouring in the hole." C.O.—"So that's it, is it ?" Ord.—"Yes, sir." Adj.—" I'd better send for the Tunneller." (Shouts out some instructions.) (Exit Orderly.)
C.O.—"Some life, isn't it ?" Adj.—"B- - - - -y." (Enter Bombing Officer very noisily and perspiring at every pore.) B.O.—"Have you heard the nooze ?" C.O.—"What news you fool ?" B.O.—"Why, the Germans have no shells ! " C.O.—"What, no shells ! " (Heard on the roof) Zip bang ! Zip-bang ! Zip bang! B.O. (humming to himself)—"La ta ta ta ta-" C.O.—"Shur·r·r-rup that blinking noise ! " B.O.—Yes sir, shall I – " (Shouts of "gas" in the passages.) C.O.—"Where's my ruddy respirator ?" Adj.—"Dammed if I know where mine is either!" (After much searching respirators are adjusted. After 5 minutes it is found to be a false alarm, and they are taken off again.) C.O.—"I can't stand these d- - - -d gas-hats ! " Adj.—"Nor can I." C.O.—"My nose is quite sore where the d- - - -d thing pinches." Adj.—"And I've got a beastly headache !" C.O. (turning to B.O.) ' Just fetch the I.O., will you?" B.O.—"Yes sir." (Exit B.O., returning 2 minutes later with I.O.) C.O. (to I.O.) —"About this relief. Are you quite sure all the guides know their way and there will be no hitch ?" I.O.—"Quite sure sir. They've all been over the course at least a dozen times." (At that moment the first relieving company is reported arriving.) I.O. (saluting)—"I'll go and see about the guides sir. It's now 8 p.m." C.O.—' And now for goodness sake let's have a glass of port or something. B.O.—"No port sir ! " C.O.—"Well, some whisky ? " B.O.—" No whisky, sir ! " C.O.—"Well, what the devil have we got ?" B.O.—"There's only well water left sir." C.O.—"Hell ! "

JOURNEY'S END. THE SCENE.
A dug-out in the British trenches before St Quentin. A few rough steps lead into the trench above, through a low doorway. Gloomy tunnels lead out of the dug-out to left and right. Earth walls deaden the sounds of war, making them faint and far away, although the front line is only fifty yards ahead.

HARDY Hullo Osborne! Your fellows arriving?
OSBORNE: *(Hitching off his pack and dropping it in a corner):*
Yes. They're just coming in.
HARDY: Splendid! Have a drink.
OSBORNE: Thanks.
HARDY: *(Passing the whisky and a mug):* Don't have too much water. It's rather strong today.
OSBORNE: *(Slowly mixing a drink);* I wonder what it is they put in the water.
HARDY: Some sort of disinfectant, I suppose.
OSBORNE: I'd rather have the microbes, wouldn't you?
HARDY: I would - yes -
OSBORNE: Well cheero.
HARDY: Cheero. Excuse my sock won't you?

---

his family wished that no further details of his life should be made public.

To end this section on the correspondents of *The Wipers Times* we should consider the possibility that R.C. Sherriff, the immensely successful playwright who achieved fame through the publication of *Journey's End*, once wrote for the paper. In the introduction to the 1930 edition of *The Wipers Times*, Roberts stated, with perhaps an excess of modesty, that it seemed all wrong that he should write the Preface when his Division had literary stars of such magnitude as Gilbert Frankau and R.C. Sherriff, even though Sherriff's name never appeared in the Paper.

Journey's End, with Olivier in the leading role of Stanhope, the whisky-sodden Company Commander, was first produced in December, 1928. Publicity for the play suggested that it was a remarkable story by a war survivor who had *never written anything before*. In his biography Sherriff admits that this wasn't strictly true but he states that his previous works

" Dear ———. At present we are staying at a farm. . . ."

Note the familiar allusion to 'Dead Cow Farm'.

had been one-act plays produced for amateur performance at the Rowing Club. He makes no mention of *The Wipers Times*. Stage Directions and early dialogue for *Journey's End* are very similar to a sketch 'More Mud than Glory' that appeared in the *BEF Times* of 15 August, 1917.

There is both irony and tragedy in the story of *The Wipers Times* correspondents. The literary reputations of the writers who were lampooned in the paper were undamaged, even though Roberts and the men of Wipers were not alone in realizing that their columns were filled with dangerous nonsense. In the nineteen-twenties Sherriff, Frankau and Bairnsfather drew on their wartime experiences to earn fame and fortune; but Roberts, who was undoubtedly as talented as the rest of them, could make no progress in literature or journalism after the war and died unsung and unrecognized in the seedy world of get-rich-quick mining in Canada.

> ...the enemy attacked at 4 'ack emma' or thereabouts. I have heard that a few shells fell in other parts of the line, but I can not credit this as I am morally certain they <u>all</u> fell on or near the editorial sanctum. The Sub-Editor supports me in this statement. Hastily taking two aspirin and placing helmet, gas, in position, I looked out of the door only to find the beautiful March morning obscured by what seemed to be one of London's best old-style November fogs. Shouting for batman, Adjutant, Sergeant-Major and the Mess-waiter, I emerged into the chilly air, which was being torn and rent in a most alarming way. All was <u>not</u> Quiet on the Western Front; the Sub-Editor and I drank a case of whiskey, shot the Padre for cowardice and said 'Goodbye to All That.' (The influence of these modern war books is most insidious.)
>
> The printing works were a matter of 50 yards or so down the road, and there was an issue of the Paper nearly finished. We did not stay to finish it.

Roberts describes, in his own particular style, the Battle of Villescholles near St Quentin in which the editorial staff had to run for their lives before the German thrust that was the beginning of the end of the War.

Part Four

Then and Now

Chapter 13

The City Revisited

By the time I made my first visit to Ypres and the Salient in October, 1994, I had studied *The Wipers Times* and its successors so intently that I could recite pages by heart and quote verbatim many of the articles and advertisements. On my journey to Belgium I carried a 1917 map of the Front Line, a Michelin Guide and a complete *Wipers Times*. I also had a tentative booking for one night at Talbot House in Poperinghe. About an hour and a half's drive from Calais names began to leap out from sign posts and jangle bells in my memory.

Bailleul 8 kms

> Oh! to be in Flanders in a gas alert.
> How I love a 'stand to' in a little shirt
> When the winds erratic, and you're dining in Berloo,
> Don't forget your PHG and take it in with you.

Bailleul, a very ordinary little town that came and went almost before I realized it, was for the most part of the War far enough away from the front for soldiers at 'Rest' to visit an estaminet and enjoy something like a restaurant meal. Enjoy it, that is, unless an evil cloud of poisoned gas came rolling over the low hills on a light wind from the East to choke them to death before they finished the soup.

There was no signpost to 'Gertie wears Velvet'. Alone in my car I smiled as I caught sight of the name on the outskirts of a poplar-lined Belgian village. Rain was slashing from angry grey storm clouds when I made my first mental contact with Roberts, at 'Gertie'. His battalion of the Sherwood Foresters bivouacked here en route from Locrehof – of the absurd cricket match – to Morlacourt where the first *Somme Times* was written. There are Sherwood Foresters buried in the cemetery at Goderwaersvelde. By the regimentally-aligned graves I tipped my sodden hat to the memory of men who might actually have worked on *The Wipers Times* and I imagined

Roberts, the battalion commander, penning letters of condolence to their next-of-kin before he began work on his latest editorial.

I needed to go to Poperinghe simply because during the Great War everyone went there on the way to Ypres. There were quotes again to jog my memory as the kilometres reduced on the signposts.

AGONY COLUMN.
'... meet us at the clock, Poperinghe Station at 6pm. Wear red carnations ...'

ANSWERS TO CORRESPONDENTS.
'Motorist (Poperinghe) – Yes we have had other complaints of the suspected police speed trap on the Menin Road ...'

THINGS WE WANT TO KNOW.
'The name of the MGO who has come to the conclusion that the only reason the Hun planes visit Pop. is to bomb his camp'.

THE RATION CARRIERS.
On the road from Pop. to Boesinghe
And from Boesinghe down to Ypres
Where the Pavé's rent with Johnson
And the mud is ankle deep.

GILBERT FRANKAU BIOGRAPHY.
... Tubby Clayton, whose predecessor in office once gave me a bed at the original Talbot House in Poperinghe.

As I drew into Pop, the rain was still falling and dragging down the last golden leaves from the poplars. I thought about what *they* were thinking about as the train slowed to a halt at Poperinghe station.

Pop. was a watershed, a demarcation point between civilization and anarchy, between Home and the War, between the creature comforts of the early twentieth century and a struggle for survival that belonged to the dark ages. In perhaps the most simplistic example of this dichotomy we should consider the basic problem of killing people. West of Poperinghe a soldier bound for the Ypres Salient, be he a New Army recruit coming to the war zone for the first time or a young officer on his unwilling way back from leave, was bound by the British code of law. He could be hanged for murder and locked up almost indefinitely for inflicting Grevious Bodily Harm. East of Pop., the more a man killed the better he was perceived to be doing his duty and if he happened to ram the pig-sticker bayonet that hung so jauntily from his belt into the recumbent bodies of a few Huns; someone might give him the Victoria Cross or the 'Don C Emma.'

Consider the habit of cigarette smoking which, by 1916, was almost universal among the Allied soldiers; in the requisitioned coaches of the Poperinghe train no doubt there were areas designated for non-smokers. For smoking in a no-smoking area in Britain and free Europe a soldier could be fined the equivalent of a pound. East of Poperinghe a glowing cigarette end could be a death warrant.

> Where you darsn't light a fag up
> 'cos the Boche's eyes are skinned,
> Ah that's the place to be boys
> If you want to raise a wind.

The superstition that one should not light three cigarettes from one match extended, to my knowledge, into RAF crewrooms in the 1960s and 70s. The first, it was suggested, would catch a sniper's eye, the second was aimed at, and a high velocity bullet could be expected to extinguish smoker and flame before the third was properly lit.

Shortly after the First World War 'Tubby' Clayton, the Talbot House Padre and founder of Toc H, wrote that for the previous five years Great Britain had been moderately successful in turning civilians into soldiers. The problem now would be to turn soldiers back into civilians. This fundamental change in patterns of behaviour – almost from human being to beast and back again – was mirrored in the transition at Poperinghe and it was for the benefit of the confused young men inbound or outbound on the train that Talbot House was acquired and opened as a refuge in the centre of the town.

Having photographed the railway station, I metaphorically shouldered my kit-bag and set out to walk the mile or so of cobbled streets to the original Talbot House in Poperinghe. As I strode along with my imagination running free I was disappointed and yet relieved to see no reminders of the War apart from an already familiar

Talbot House.

The Outs and the Ins

British War Graves cemetery. There were no craters, no bomb damage, no bullet-pocked walls and no mud, only a typically dramatic continental war memorial with helmeted 'Poilu' cresting a small hill with a banner, while women and children, frozen in attitudes of supplicant gratitude, gazed upwards at him from the four corners of the granite plinth.

What was the secret of the popularity of *The Wipers Times*? What was its connection with Toc H and this town? Why, as a devoted student of the Paper, did I feel such an affinity with its writers and readers as I entered Gasthuisstraat and caught my first glimpse of the magnificent wrought iron doors of Number 43?

The answer is that both were, reminders, lifelines between the comforts and security of home and the anarchic bedlam of the Salient. Whether inbound or outbound from Ypres, at Poperinghe the transient soldier was helped to adjust by the kindly, understanding people he met at the House. Later, as he cringed in his muddy dugout and hoped that the next whizz-bang didn't have his name on it, as he listened in dread to orders for yet another suicidal offensive, he might recall the atmosphere of Talbot House and maybe there would be a copy of *The Wipers Times* to remind him that his removal to the world of the insane was not total and permanent. There was still British intellect, British humour, British understanding and British civilization in the world and, even if the unfortunate soldiers of the day might not survive to see it, that was what they were fighting for.

I was not yet ready to take up my booking at Talbot House so I made sure that there would be a bed for me and then set off down the 'Ration Carriers' road from Poperinghe to Ypres via Boesinghe. Only in one's mind's eye could the dangers of this northerly approach to Ypres be assessed. The road wasn't 'rent with Johnson' and although one can pinpoint 'Dawson's Corner', there was no sign that it had ever been shelled with 'Shrapnel' or with 'Crump'; and, in spite of the steady rain, there was no mud.

'Where has all the mud gone?' may seem a strange riddle for a pilgrim to Ypres to concern himself with, but mud plays such a universal part in the images of the war-torn Salient that I imagined it could never have been cleared up and dried out. The mud was once 'ankle-deep' on every step of the Ration Carriers' route that I was now driving along. Further east in the Salient men could drown in bottomless mud if they slipped or were blasted from the precarious walkways and duckboards. To the south, guns, tanks and battalions were lost in the mud and I remembered a picture of an ammunition mule, weighed down with a load of shells, sinking, with panic in its eyes, into the mire.

Belgium, like the Netherlands and Northern France, is a country with a water table not far below the low-lying, mainly agricultural land. The soil is only workable by reason of meticulous and ingenious drainage systems. Around Ypres every field has its ditches which run with clear water all year round. The ditches run into Becs, rivers and canals, and into the lakes of Bellewarde and Zillebeke. Although the soldiers fighting in this area considered every shell that didn't land in a trench and kill people as a harmless 'miss' the damage that they did was, in fact, enormous. The carefully constructed banks of rivers and canals were broken down, water courses were disrupted, dams were destroyed and the trenches themselves, the lifelines of an army living below ground level, became rivers of mud. By 1916 the Salient reverted to primordial slime. The achievement of the Belgian water-engineers who, over seventy years, have rebuilt the drainage system is probably as great as that of the builders who have remade the city of Ypres. However, as I pondered on the absence of mud while rounding 'Dawson's Corner' and heading for 'Wipers', I was aware for the first time of an awakening anger. I had been sad before, and on occasion full of admiration, inspired by the sacrifices that my studies had led me to, but the memory of the mud made me angry.

It is a principal rule of war, so simple that it sounds facile to repeat it, so basic that all generals from Mark Antony to Norman Schwartzkopf have remembered it to their gain and disregarded it at their peril; it is so universal that military instructors, wherever tactics are taught and battles are rehearsed, repeat it until they need only to say the first word and the class will shout the completion in chorus as children used to recite the five times table;

'Never – unless you are fighting for survival – engage the enemy *without terrain advantage.*'

Can those who were running the War in England have known nothing of the mud? Did they imagine that there could be any possible future in asking British infantry, who would not be fighting for British national survival until the Hun was across the channel and advancing up the road from Dover, to hurl themselves against entrenched Germans on the drier, higher ground around Ypres? Why are all the names of the bloodiest battlefields of the Salient, Hills and Ridges? Why did *The Wipers Times* define Hell as 'Hooge' and Hooge as 'Hell'? and why were there twenty thousand Canadian casualties in one of the battles for Hill 60? In essence because they were fighting without terrain advantage, struggling uphill through the bloody mud.

In a book called 'The First Day of the Somme,' I read of a staff officer, more courageous than most, who came forward to view the progress of the battle on that dreadful day and saw only mud. 'How can we have expected our men to advance through this?' he is reported to have said before breaking down. 'Too late' I thought; 'the work of the staff is to plan and anticipate.'

There can be no doubt that, if the British High Command had the strategical sense to retire, the mud of Flanders could have been as successful as a barrier to further German advance as the 'Scorched Earth' of Russia and the shifting sands around Alamein. If this seemed so obvious to me eighty years after the event when the countryside was peaceful and the ditches and streams gurgled gently beside the fields as though nothing had ever

> The fishing in the Moat and Zillebeke Lake is falling off, as the fish is getting shy.

churned the land into a morass of death, when contented fishermen cast hopeful lines into the Ieper canal and the Zillebeke lake, what can have been the thoughts of the soldiers of 1916 as they slogged up this very road and felt for the first time the mud seeping over the tops of their boots to saturate the last pair of clean socks from home?

Note how the editor suggests that the number of fish available for sportsmen in the shell-torn waterways of the Salient has been so reduced as to justify a singular verb.

The illustration shows a battered, leaky spirit flask presented by one member of 36 RFA to a colleague in celebration of their survival of every battle and skirmish that took place in the Ypres Salient.

Field guns needed to be constantly on the move in order to survive. Once they fired, their position was revealed to the enemy and they had to limber up and move on before the hostile barrage ranged in on them. In the Salient they were not safe when on the move because of the mud. The guns could only move along laboriously prepared timber roadways across the hostile terrain and thus their position and destination were constantly visible to enemy observers. The picture of frantic, galloping Horse Artillerymen is familiar. So is the dead horse sinking in the mud and the damaged gun amongst the wreckage.

It is only as you approach the city and fix in the mind's eye the orientation of the front and the positions occupied by the opposing armies in the stand-off around Ypres that you begin to realize that the Salient itself was militarily indefensible. The line along which the Allied armies were entrenched ran on a bearing 340/160 degrees, except at Ypres, where it bulged. North and south of the City the lines were briefly due east and west and they curved round to meet in the Zonnebeke – Polygon Wood area three to four miles due east of the Menin Gate. Thus a simple man's glance at the map confirmed that the city itself could be fired upon from north, south and east, while soldiers in the trenches in forward areas could be shelled and shot at from an arc of 270 degrees. Can we be surprised that not a single building in the city remained standing at the end of the war; that on Armistice Day in 1918 enemy shells were still falling indescriminately into Ypres and British soldiers were killed in the dying minutes of the war. With 'cannon to left of them and cannon to right of them', things were bad enough for the troopers of the Light Brigade. For the PBI trying to hold the outposts of Hooge and Sanctuary Wood there was the additional problem of cannon behind them.

'Salient' is a word from mediaeval siege warfare; so is 'enfilade'. 'Enfilading' is the process wherby gunners can fire along an opponents defences rather than at right angles to them. This gives many advantages. A projectile can cause mayhem over a much greater area; 'undershoots' and 'overshoots' remain lethal provided the line is right, and the enemy's frontal barricades are rendered ineffective. Enfilading fire is particularly lethal when the enemy is entrenched. In other words a machine gun can fire directly at the sandbag parapet in front of an opposing trench and probably only frighten the occupants; put the gun in a position to fire along the trench and a few bursts will satisfactorily kill a battalion.

When trying to defend a Salient there is always someone in a position to put enfilading fire along your trenches. Also, when poisoned gas is introduced into the battle, there are few wind directions which can be considered 'Safe' It is not my purpose to add to to the volume of words already written on the strategies of the First World War. Apologists for the British High Command have for many years endeavoured to explain why 200,000 allied casualties were sacrificed in the defence of the indefensible around Ypres. It has been suggested that Allied morale and public support at home made it vital that Ypres didn't fall. To my eye the prolonged defence of the city was criminal lunacy.

As always, I tried to put myself in the minds of the soldiers whose steps I was tracing as I finally entered the City of Ypres seventy-eight years after The Wipers Times was printed. The riddle that concerned me most as I caught my first glimpse of the stern, Gothic spires of the Cloth Hall and St Martin's Cathedral was 'Did they believe Ypres must be held at all costs, and glory in the part they were playing in a vital battle; or did they realize, as I had done simply by looking at a map, that they were out on a limb, fighting for a lost cause, doomed pawns in a playground squabble between big bully Wilhelm and plucky boy Haig?'

Roberts was an intelligent man, a graduate and a qualified mining engineer. He must have realized that the defence of the Salient was madness, so, having found himself unexpectedly with the power of an uncensored newspaper editor, how did he refrain from making any authoratitive comment on the conduct of the war around Ypres? Why was there not an 'Advice for our Generals' column in which some anonymous 'Expert' could float the suggestion that the British pulled out of the Salient, straightened the line, gave the mud over to the

For Exchange.

FOR EXCHANGE.—A SALIENT, in good condition. Will exchange for a PAIR of PIGEONS, or a CANARY. —Apply Lonely Soldier, Hooge.

Germans and concentrated on winning the War worldwide? The answer is that Roberts was also a typically well-trained and well-disciplined British soldier who had absorbed totally the religion that wars can only be won if orders are obeyed unquestioningly and that soldiers, even battalion commanders, shouldn't think too much. But he couldn't resist completely the opportunity to put forward a suggestion that the Salient wasn't worth the trouble of defending it.

Canaries were used in forward areas and in underground mines to detect small accumulations of poisoned gas. Typically they often became the beloved pets of their handlers and there are stories of soldiers risking their lives in a gas attack by using their gasmasks to protect the birds.

Within the ancient city of Ypres at last, I went straight to the museum to seek help in pinpointing exactly where The Wipers Times was composed and printed. Once again I had quotations to help me.

'To get an idea of the birth of the paper one has to try to visualize Wipers in those early days of 1916. We lived in rat-infested, water-logged cellars by day and at Hooge by night ... The editorial den was in a casemate under the old ramparts built by Vauban – heaven alone knows when!

FOR SALE.
THE SALIENT ESTATE.
COMPLETE IN EVERY DETAIL.
INTENDING PURCHASERS WILL BE SHOWN ROUND ANYTIME DAY OR NIGHT
UNDERGROUND RESIDENCES READY FOR HABITATION.
—o—o—o—o—
**Splendid Motoring Estate! Shooting Perfect!!
Fishing Good!!!**
—o—o—o—o—
NOW'S THE TIME.   HAVE A STAKE IN THE COUNTRY.
NO REASONABLE OFFER REFUSED.
DO FOR HOME FOR INEBRIATES OR OTHER CHARITABLE INSTITUTION.
Delay is dangerous!   You might miss it!!
—o—o—o—o—
Apply for particulars, etc., to
**Thomas, Atkins, Sapper & Co., Zillebeke
and Hooge.**
HOUSEBREAKERS: WOOLEY, BEAR, CRUMP & CO.   TELEGRAMS: "ADSUM, WIPERS."

On February 30th,

Sale

Sale

Sale

A Large Quantity of SECOND-HAND FURNITURE
SLIGHTLY DAMAGED.   HARDWARE.

Tell your friends about it.

9, RUE D'MENIN.   Telephone : 14, RUINS.

'Numbers one and two of *The Wipers Times* ... were produced on the original press up by the Cloth Hall in the days when the air was generally full of shells ... So when the page was put up in our casemate the Sergeant and his 'Devils' would go to the door and look at the atmosphere. If all was moderately quiet they would make a dash for the 'works' and stay till Fritz got too near to be pleasant.'

I had been carefully studying the 'Sale Sale Sale' advertisement from an early edition of *The Wipers Times*. What was the significance of the spurious date? Assuming that the apostrophe once again signified nothing other than a shortage of Es, could I deduce anything from the unusually exact location given as the advertiser's address?

As I walked round the museum my eye was caught by a wooden door with unusual arched top. The faded writing on the door was in English and one could see the word 'Headquarters' and faintly make out 'Brigadier' and 'Plumer'. A notice beside the door explained that it was a wooden door from General Plumer's headquarters in the Ramparts of the old city. The General had for a while masterminded the underground tunnelling campaign in the Salient. Could he have been a later occupant of the palatial and relatively secure 'Hotel des Ramparts' where Roberts once had his editorial den?

I was allocated a guide and escorted to what had once been General Plumer's rampart Headquarters by the Lille Gate. It was dry and airy like a well-built cellar. Light came from windows beside the door on the town side and from an archer's slit window which overlooked the moat that surrounds two sides of the city of Ypres. The high vaulted roof impressed me. Like a cathedral crypt, the Gothic arches were elegant and symmetrical. The construction was of mortar and small bricks which gave the whole casemate a warm and permanent atmosphere like the entrance hall of an inhabited

EUROPEAN THEATRE OF VARIETIES.

THIS WEEK AND FOR ONE WEEK ONLY.

PLUMER AND CO,
IN THEIR SPECTACULAR DRAMA,
"THE CROSSING."
MAGNIFICENT SCENIC EFFECTS.
NO EXPENSE HAS BEEN SPARED TO ENABLE THIS PLAY TO BE STAGED.

castle. It was the archer's slit that convinced me that this was not Roberts' editorial den. The rampart that I was now standing in, with a diagram of Plumer's tunnellings on the wall, must have pre-dated Vauban, the builder of Roberts' grape-shot-proof casemate, by some two hundred years. My guide confirmed that Vauban had indeed improved the defences of the city in the early eighteenth century, but Plumer's erstwhile headquarters had been built nearer the time of Crécy and Agincourt when the main anti-personnel weapon was the long-bow. Roberts was himself a mining engineer and historian and it was unlikely that he could have ascribed the construction of his rampart casemate incorrectly to Vauban even if there was some confusion over the spelling of the name.

General Plumer was still serving at the end of the War. The successor to *The Wipers Times* that recorded the Armistice in 1918 reminds readers that he commanded the first troops to cross the Rhine and actually invade Germany.

I walked from Plumer's headquarters across the city to No. 9, the Menin Road, because I was fairly sure that this was where *The Wipers Times* was first printed. Number 9 is now a green- grocer's shop but, as it had clearly been rebuilt in the old Flemish style, it was undoubtedly a 'Pre-bombardment' location. The Ypres Museum confirmed that the building originally housed a printing school which had a press in the cellar. *The Wipers Times* must be the only paper in history that came into being because some one found a press and needed something to print on it. When scrounging among the bombed cellars of Ypres for timber and furniture to use in the trenches of the Salient, a Sherwood Forester Pioneer stumbled on this press and reported its location to his commanding officer just round the corner in the rampart dugout. Roberts' fertile brain took care of the rest.

Farewell Yperen! Yperen farewell!
Long have I known thee, and known thee well!
Thy stoney streets, thy shell-pitted square,
Looted thy houses for dug-out ware,
Looking for cellar cool and deep,
With a shell proof roof where I could sleep.

The press, 'Just off the square at Wipers,'– the 9 Menin Road address complies with this description – printed the first two editions of The Wipers Times. The ruins of the building then received a direct hit from a '5.9' and the press, the remaining furniture and most of the type were destroyed. Using Roberts' introduction again, we see that this disaster occurred shortly after issue No. 2 which is dated 26 February, 1916. I feel it is not too great an assumption that this event was the origin of the 'Sale, Sale, Sale,' advertisement for the '30th' February at No 9 Rue d' Menin.

It was a simple matter to follow the printer's route back to the editorial office. I walked about a hundred metres down the Menin Road and turned right at the Memorial Gate, following a minor path and road along the inside of the rampart walls. To my right were the old Ypres houses which in 1916 were already largely reduced to rubble by the German bombardment. Their cellars still offered precarious underground security and were used as billets and daytime refuge for the night workers of the Salient. Here the printer's devils of *The Wipers Times* could scuttle for safety from an unexpected

Ruines d'Ypres 1914-18 Les Remparts

'Incoming' as they made their hazardous way, clutching pages still wet from the Press, from Works to Office where the paper was made up. Thus I arrived at *The Wipers Times* casemate. It is well restored now with arched doors and glazed windows. Inside there is the same vaulted roof and, although the only way in is now from the town side, one can see evidence of an earlier moat-side entrance where the Pioneers once set out on their nightly journeys to Hooge and the Front Line, weighed down with dugout repair equipment, rifle and pack, spades and hammers and the first distribution of *The Wipers Times*.

Copies were also sold outside the entrance on the town side of the ramparts by subalterns of the editorial staff. The following quotation from *The Ypres Times*, journal of the Ypres League, first published in 1922, records the moment in February, 1916 when the first edition went on the streets.

''ere y'are; piper, piper; all the winners! sensytion! full account of the big fight; read all abaht it; piper!'

The irrepressible young subaltern at the door of the Mess beneath the ramparts did it beautifully; he did it to the manner born and, most miraculous of all, he was actually displaying a newspaper.

Orientation by the remains of the Cloth Hall clock tower on the skyline of the 1914/1918 postcard enabled me to establish that the darkened entrances to the right of centre were the moat-side portals of the *Wipers Times* casemate. The other photos show the city-side entrance where the vocal subaltern first offered *The Wipers Times* for sale.

As I walked around the restored vault beneath the walls of the city I tried hard to imagine it as Roberts had known it in 1916 when The Wipers Times was born at this exact location.

Our casemate will always be vividly remembered by those who knew it. We had a piano – loot from a neighbouring cellar where it had been propping up the remains of a house – a gramophone and a lot of subalterns. Can anyone wonder that we are but shadows of our former selves? When Fritz's love tokens arrived with greater frequency and precision than we altogether relished we would turn our whole outfit on together. The effect of 'Pantomime Hits' on the piano, 'Dance With Me' on the gramophone, a number of subalterns, and 5.9s and 4.2s on the roof had to be heard to be realised.

That night I was the only guest at Talbot House. They gave me the General's room. Everywhere notices were displayed which at first gave the impression of a seaside boarding house with a particularly repressive landlady.

The Editorial Sanctum
Above: 1994
Right: 1916

However, on careful examination they contributed much to the light-hearted atmosphere of the place and many were unchanged since the days of Tubby Clayton's chaplaincy. They reflected much of the humour of The Wipers Times.

'Abandon Rank All Ye Who Enter Here'; *on the Chaplain's door.*

'The wastepaper baskets are purely ornamental'

'Remember Belgium? - Remember *Us*'

'What idiot called the place *Sanctuary* Wood.'

There were two notices on the door of my room.

The General's Bedroom.
Originally this room contained a bed with one sheet (the other in the wash) and was therefore reserved for Generals, Subalterns and others of high degree.

From each officer five francs were demanded for board and lodging on the Robin Hood principle of taking from the rich to give to the poor. For this sum the officers secured on arrival from the leave train at 1 am, cocoa and Bath Oliver biscuit, or before departure at 5 am, a cold meat breakfast. The bedrooms were communal, save for the dressing room which we turned ambitiously into the General's Bedroom on account of a bed with real sheets.

If I was ever to encounter any ghosts from 1916 surely it would be here as I wearily unpacked my bag and turned down the sheets, now thankfully a full set, in the narrow confines of 'The General's Room'. What youthful heads had lain here trying vainly to sleep through the last hours before returning to the Salient and all its horrors? What doubts were encompassed in the four walls of this coffin-sized bedroom little bigger than most dugouts? 'Will I be killed tomorrow? Will there be gas again? Will I let the men down? Will I have to go over the top ? Will I be buried alive? Will I go mad? …'

But there were no ghosts; maybe they were tougher than me and not so plagued with vivid imagination. Maybe the earlier occupants of this room managed to fortify themselves with biscuits and cocoa, whisky from tin mugs, a sing-song round the piano and the comradeship of adversity shared. Perhaps they defiantly let tomorrow take care of itself and slept like babies. Anyhow, for whatever reason, none of them came back to haunt me and I slept soundly, lulled to unconsciousness by a tune that went round in my head like the sails of a windmill.

'They'll never believe me, no they'll never believe me …'

My Uncle Tony, a Sapper subaltern at Ypres, used to play 'They'll never believe me' on the piano. He was one of a fortunate few young men who could play anything by ear. They could count on instant popularity in Mess or canteen and in the ballrooms of commandeered châteaux by reason of their ability to sit down at a piano and, without music, thump out the hit tunes of the day. I learned from him and I too can produce a recognizable version of this Jerome Kern standard. I only had to play the first five notes along with the accompanying harmonic change from G Major to A Minor (proper musicians will correct me if I am wrong) for my mother, who in other respects was left by advancing years pitiably lacking in memory, to remark that;

'That was the tune Tony played when he came home on leave from the First World War.'

A Puzzle for Paderewski

" It's a pity Alf ain't 'ere, Bert ; 'e can play the piana wonderful "

It was not difficult to decide upon a tune to play as I sat down at the piano in the dining room of deserted Talbot House before I retired for the night. The instrument was the same one as the soldiers had used during the War. An elderly lady, once a servant in the house when it belonged to a wealthy hop merchant of Poperinghe remembers hearing the piano on musical evenings when it was new. It is apparently regularly tuned but the keys have never been renewed and constant playing has worn several notes down to the wood. I wondered how many times Middle C must have been depressed for the fingers of thousands of enthusiastic amateur pianists to have worn away a sixteenth of an inch of ivory.

'And when they ask me how wonderful you are ...'

The song is parodied in *The Wipers Times*. The subject is not a beautiful girl but something on which the soldiers lavished almost as much affection – the rum jar. Supply Sergeants were always accused of stealing the rum it was their duty to dispense.

A more poignant version can be found in 'Oh What a Lovely War.'

> 'And when they ask us,
> And they're certainly going to ask us,
> The reason why we never won the the Croix de Guerre,
> They'll never believe us, no they'll never believe us,
> There was a Front but damned if we knew where.'

THEY DIDN'T BELIEVE ME !

—o—

Yet when I told them that I hadn't
touched the jar,
They didn't believe me, they didn't
believe me ;
They seem to know a sergeant's thirst,
I fear they all believe the worst,
It's the rottenest luck that there could
be ;
And when I tell them, and I'm certainly
going to tell them,
There'll be fatigues for them where'er I
be,
They'll never believe me, they'll never
believe that
The man who tapped the jar could not
be me !

Chapter 14

The Salient Revisited

On my second day in Belgium I drove off into the Salient once more in search of 'Atmosphere', with the 'Golf Notes' from Wipers Times Number One as a stepping-off point.

The 'Golf Notes' describe a sniping duel which took place between German and British riflemen just before this first issue came off the press. Such duels aroused as much interest in the Salient as boxing or football matches in more peaceful times, and there are indications that soldiers gambled on the results. The deadliness of this sort of contest is only indicated by the meticulous description of injuries sustained. In all other respects we might indeed be reading about a play-off at Royal Lytham.

With the advantage of a motor car the Salient is small. I set off down the Menin Road and four minutes later realized that I must have passed 'Hell-Fire Corner'. In 1916 the same journey would have taken about five hours. The road was impassable then and the corner itself regularly targeted for random shelling. Men, mules, wagons and guns struggled and slithered across the intervening countryside like nocturnal snails. Those brave enough travelled on the surface, sometimes crawling, always crouching, and diving for cover into corruption-filled shell holes whenever a star-shell went up or an incoming whizz-bang sounded its micro-second warning. Below ground level in the muddy communication trenches, soldiers struggled eastwards with 'A' frames, rations, rum jars, ammunition and of course rifle and pack. Meeting them and causing impossible congestion at corners and intersections would be the stretcher-bearers heading back to the aid posts and hospitals with their bloodied and broken burdens. New drafts would meet shattered companies going back for 'Rest' and zig-zagging amongst the chaos would be wounded and riderless horses and deranged beasts from abandoned Belgian farms.

For Pioneers and other working parties the journey to Hooge seems to have been divided into sections, with a comparatively secure dugout at the end of each section for shelter. These were used if there was no chance of completing a particular sortie under cover of darkness. The transit dugouts were located at 'Half Way House', 'Hell-Fire Corner' and 'The Culvert'. They were solid, pioneer-built underground shelters with sleeping accomodation, primitive anti-gas protection, casualty facilities and something of a telephone exchange. They could offer no protection from a direct hit from heavy artillery but were considered 'Pip-Squeak' and small-arms-proof. It seems these dugouts became quite congenial social centres for the nocturnal wanderers of the Salient. In most issues of the paper we read that they were renowned for whisky and warmth, medical aid and companionship. How hard it must have been to leave them when the shelling momentarily ceased or the gas all-clear sounded.

The Sherwood Foresters, it will be recalled, were the Pioneer battalion of Twenty-Four Division and for a while their Battalion Forward HQ was in a large dugout, probably the one at Hell-Fire Corner.

Here Foresters make nightly play, And in the mud hold revel high.

In one of the spurious 'Courts of Justice' reports in the paper an imaginary Plaintiff is asked by a putative Counsel:

Have you ever entered those well-known dens of vice 'The Culvert Dug-out', 'Half-Way-House' or 'Railway Wood Dug-out'?

I turned off at the Birr crossroads and drove up a narrow lane (Cambridge Road) towards Railway Wood. The ground sloped upwards gently and I could soon see a great distance in all directions; to the west was Hell-Fire Corner and the towers and ramparts of the City; on my right were the woods of Bellewarde and the rebuilt hamlet of Hooge. I

Golf Notes.

—:o:—

The Sanctuary Wood course was opened on Saturday, under delightful climatic conditions, and before a large and representative throng.

—:o:—

A match had been arranged by the enterprising Committee between the two well-known players Tom Sniper, the Wipers' professional, and Wilhelm Bos chun, that champion of Hollebeke.

—:o:—

The course, which has many natural advantages it has been planned almost entirely on the pot-bunker system so that straight driving and an accurate knowledge of all the hazards one is likely to encounter is essential, and our two experts found trouble rather more frequently than they are wont to do.

—:o:—

The first hole is not particularly interesting, and has no noteworthy feature, being of the ordinary drive and pitch variety, and was halved in 4.

—o—

The second hole, is a short one, bordering Zouave Wood, was also halved, and was noticable only for extraordinary pungent odour which assailed the nostrils near the green, and which affected the putting of both players, as they each took three putts for a short distance.

—o—

The 4th, 5th, 7th and 8th holes were halved again in the proper figures, but at the 6th Tom Sniper was hit by his opponent on the elbow and this seemed to worry him somewhat, and he consequently lost the hole.

—o—

However the Wipers pro got his own back at the 9th. He hit his second—a brainy shot—clean and hard, hitting Boschun in the neck. He claimed the hole in a dignified manner which much impressed his supporters, and the players thus turned all square.

—o—

Going to Culvert the Hollebeke representative was unfortunately stymied by a whizz-bang which cost him the hole.

Both were bunkered in the new breastwork in Cambridge Road, and a half in 7 ensued.

—o—

The 12th and 13th were won by Boschun and Sniper respectively through the other finding trouble. The 14th, known as the Fish-hook, was won by Boschun through a perfect niblick shot stopping dead. The 15th was halved in par play, but Tom Sniper took the 16th through his opponent topping his second into the stables.

—o—

The 17th saw the end of an exciting match. This hole, known as the Appendix, is a long one shotter, and blind from the tee. Boschun had gone forward to see his line, and Tom played a beauty, which caught Wilhelm full in the mouth and finished him.

—o—

parked close to a beautifully kept memorial to nine men of the Royal Engineers who were buried alive while tunnelling. Near the memorial I stumbled upon a clutch of hidden mine craters whose black depths probably still held ghastly secrets. The wind from a gathering squall whipped at my sodden trench map as I tried to orientate myself by the few features that were unchanged since the map was made in 1916. The railway was gone but I thought I could trace its line from Railway Wood down to Hell-Fire Corner. Where then was The Culvert? I turned completely round and clutched at my hat as rain and wind stormed over the hill.

A man was walking towards me across the field. He was youngish and completely unprotected from the weather. I had noticed him earlier, flying a pink kite on the hillside. The squall had grounded the kite in a series of wild gyrations and now he held it across his body with some difficulty as the fabric flapped like a wild thing in the wind. I was anticipating a greeting in Flemish or Walloon but in fact the accent was Geordie.

'I'm sorry about the railings; they're down at the workshops for repair at the moment.'

The dishevelled kite flyer who spoke like a Northumberland Fusilier or a Durham Light Infantryman was in fact an ex-Para of Falklands vintage who now worked for the British War Graves Commission in Ypres. Mistaking me for a visitor to the Engineers' memorial just behind me he was apologizing for the incomplete chain-and-post railings surrounding the little patch of Belgian landscape that is now forever designated as a British War Grave.

This brief meeting was typical of hundreds that take place every day in the Salient. In any one of the immaculately kept cemeteries there are figures with bowed heads reading names on gravestones. They pause and move on, momentarily overcome, as I was, by the enormity of the tragedy that took place right here only one lifetime ago around Ypres. Tourists visiting Belgium for reasons unconnected with the First World War become fascinated by the story and return again as historians and archaeologists, digging, photographing, researching and just talking to anyone who shares an interest in what was once known as 'The Immortal Salient'.

'I'm writing a book about *The Wipers Times*,' I said, 'and at the moment I'm trying to locate what was known as "The Culvert" dugout.'

'Let's see your map then.' My new-found guide picked up a twig and used it as a pointer. 'We are here, and a ditch ran through a culvert under the Menin Road and the old tram railway over there; they probably enlarged that and turned it into a fairly secure dugout.'

I thanked him and we talked more about the War and the perilous journey from Ypres to Hooge; how these dugouts must have been notorious as warm,

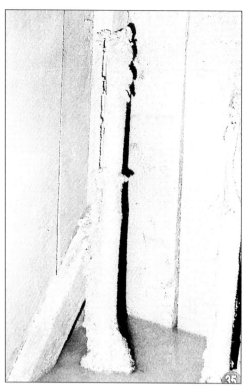

A muddy archaeologist examines the dugout interior.

A Lee-Enfield Rifle as found in the Hell–Fire Corner dugout.

'Railway Wood' (from the dugout entrance.)

A 'Boot gum thigh' found near Essex Farm.

slightly hysterical, havens of partial security with an atmosphere that incorporated a lot of the horror, humour and comradeship of the First World War.

The man from the War Graves Commission pointed down towards Hell-Fire Corner and told me that a dugout had been recently excavated there as part of the earthworks for a new roundabout. He wrote an address on the corner of my map.

'This man'll tell you all about it,' he said.

As a result of this meeting I learnt more about the permanent dugouts of the Salient. Wherever possible the Pioneers who built them used natural features for protection and burrowed deeply into the earth, probably below the water-table because pumping equipment was often found. They were candle-lit and warmed by coke-burning braziers. A gas curtain across the entrance impeded the inflow of war gases. Damp streamed down the walls and muddy water seeped between the heavy timbers of the roof. There were beds in side tunnels for casualties or men just resting, and a store of rum jars and whisky bottles to delight the eye of any tired and frightened soldier who brushed aside the gas curtain and stumbled down the last couple of steps to safety.

These photographs, which I finally tracked down in a small engineering works in the vicinity of Nottingham, show a little of the rediscovery of the Hell-Fire Corner dugout. The mud-encrusted Lee Enfield stands where it had been left in 1918, though now up to the trigger-guard in water. We can see the sturdy timbered dugout entrance along with the original skein of black telephonist's wire leading down beside the steps; the entrance, which is the area cordoned off in the foreground in picture Number 9 (bottom right) is at Hell-Fire Corner. The small wood in the background is Railway Wood and the area in between was considered one of the most life-threatening journeys in the whole Western Front; and somewhere in the vicinity they found a wader, a 'Boots gum thigh left, quantity one.'

> Can there be any emotion to equal that of lying prone in a crump-hole with a machine gun ripping across your back. Hell-Fire Corner! aptly named. The span from there to Hooge, who that has ever slithered along it in gum boots thigh will ever forget? (*Wipers Times 20 March, 1916*)

Occasionally they find boots that still have legs in them, and feet. Every visitor to the Salient has to come to terms with the reality that the whole area is a graveyard of smashed human bodies that lie only a little below the surface. Not for the dead of Ypres the regulation six feet depth of grave or the purifying fires of the crematorium. Thousands of them still remain where they fell. Just how many thousands is graphically demonstrated by

One section, of one face, of one wall, of one arch, of one aspect, of the Menin Gate memorial.

the acres of names on the Menin Gate Memorial, because those commemorated there have no known grave. All that is known about them is that they went to war and never came back. Despite heroic work by the War Graves Commission, not enough bits of any of them were ever recovered for formal identification.

The archaeologists of the Salient are almost as numerous as the bowed heads in the cemeteries. Small groups of muddied men can be seen around all the battle areas, beavering away with spade and trowel and seriously orientating battered trench maps. They are searching for any sort of tangible evidence of the War. Bones and bullets, *pickelhauben* and tin hats, rum–jars and bandoliers; the prospectors of Ypres restlessly scour the land for everything. Their motives vary. Most of them are just devoted students of the period who like to identify things. They know the difference between British barbed wire and German, a gas shell and an unexploded Minnie.

BUILDING LAND FOR
S A L E.

——

BUILD THAT HOUSE
ON
HILL 60.

BRIGHT—BREEZY—
&
INVIGORATING

COMMANDS AN EXCELLENT VIEW OF
HISTORIC TOWN OF YPRES.

FOR PARTICLARS OF SALE
APPLY:—

BOSCH & CO MENIN.

They will excitedly collect cap-badges and nose caps, a marching compass or a broken wheel from an ammunition limber of, say, the Royal Field Artillery. To them forgotten military items are treasure and human remains an occasional tragic by-product. World-wide interest in Great War artefacts is strong. A dealer friend in England tells me of a steady stream of rusting wartime hardware that makes its way to England for onward transmission to America and Australia. The problem is to dispose of the human remains in boots and helmets and to make safe the unexploded ammunition. In my friend's case anything that might once have been part of a soldier is given a respectful and sanctified burial in a local Anglican churchyard.

The whole summit of Hill 60 is designated a War Grave because of the unburied bodies which lie in the trenches and tunnels that criss-cross the area. Sheep graze among the smashed pill-boxes and the still-stunted trees, but no excavator's shovel or archaeologist's spade has ever been permitted to invade the last resting place of the tens of thousands who died there. The Wipers Times Estate Agents' invitation to 'Build that House on Hill 60.' has found no takers in the intervening eighty years and, although an invigorating breeze still moans around the summit, to my mind nothing will ever blow away the atmosphere of death.

I was blinking as I came out of the Hill 60 café and museum. Between the thunder showers the sun shone brilliantly and the spires and roof-tops of Wipers glistened in the middle distance ... well within artillery range. However, it wasn't the unaccustomed brightness that caused me to screw up my eyes, it was the memory of what I had just seen. In the museum there are banks of 'What the Butler Saw' machines, binocular viewers through which visitors can look at contemporary photographs of fighting during the First World War. Like many students of that period of British military history I was still to an extent shielded from the visual impact of trench warfare by the 1914 censorship regulations. These forbade the publication of any photographs that depicted a dead or grotesquely wounded British soldier. From my school days when I read about the War in old copies of the Illustrated London News and picked my way through endless volumes of 'The Great War in Pictures' I only ever saw soldiers with decorous wounds. They were usually bravely sitting up in hospital beds or receiving medals

SEEN FROM AN AID-POST.

There are many roads in Flanders, where
the horses slide and fall,
There are roads of mud and pavé, that
lead nowhere at all,
They are roads, that finish at our trench;
the Germans hold the rest.
But of all the roads in Flanders, there is
one, I know the best.
It's a great road, a straight road, a road
that runs between
Two rows of broken poplars, that were
young and strong and green.

—o—o—o—

You can trace it from old Poperinghe,
through Vlamertinghe and Wipers ;
(It's a focus for Hun whiz-bangs and a
paradise for snipers)
Pass the solid Ramparts, and the
muddy moat you're then in,
The road I want to sing about—the road,
that leads to Menin.
It's a great road, a straight road, a road
that runs between
Two rows of broken poplars, that were
young and strong and green.

—o—o—o—

It's a road, that's cursed by smokers; for
you dare not show a light ;
It's a road, that's shunned by daytime ;
and is mainly used by night,
But at dusk the silent troops come up,
and limbers bring their loads
Of ammunition to the guns, that guard
the Salient's roads.
It's a great road, a straight road, a road
that runs between
Two rows of broken poplars, that were
young and strong and green.

And for hours and days together, I have
listened to the sound
Of German shrapnel overhead, while I
was underground
In a damp and cheerless cellar, continually
trying
To dress the wounded warriors, while
comforting the dying
On that muddy road, that bloody road,
that road that runs between
Two rows of broken poplars, that were
young and strong and green.

R.M.O.

from the King, with minor injuries dressed in spotless white bandages. These viewing machines in the Hill 60 Museum, with their quaint old-fashioned appearance redolent of the Victorian seaside, hit you in the eye with what it really was like. A grinning half-skeleton stares at you from the wall of a shell hole. He is still wearing the helmet that failed to save him and clutches the rifle that he has fired for the last time. Most of the uniform and the body beneath it has decomposed and broken ribs and shattered pelvis are starkly visible.

Without seeing photographs, the effect of high-explosive shells on living creatures can only be imagined. My imagination is vivid, but nothing in my mind's eye had ever prepared me for the picture of a soldier who had been leading a mule in the area of the Menin Road when a shell impacted literally at his feet. The man had been cut off at the waist and his lower half was no-where to be seen. Also vaporized were the mule's front legs. The faces of man and beast were undamaged and frozen in expressions of shock, while a puddle of blood spread outwards over the muddy, tortured earth.

Suddenly a lone Mirage fighter flew overhead; 300 knots, 250 feet above ground level, the standard NATO cross-country configuration. The pilot was probably on a low-level link-route to a strike target on a range in the UK or North Germany. My one-time fighter pilot's eye recognized machine and mission instantly and I began to calculate the effects of an air strike on Hill 60. Half a dozen aircraft of the Mirage vintage could have cleared the pill boxes and trenches around the hill and opened the way for an infantry advance or helicopter landing. A combat air patrol would circle overhead waiting to nip any counter-attack in the bud while airborne forward air controllers directed fire against pockets of resistance on the ground. The job could probably have been done by even fewer of General Schwartzkopf's Gulf War 'Warthogs'. But for the 20,000 of Haig's men who died, vainly struggling up the gentle slopes of Hill 60, effective air power came fifty years too late.

Such thoughts fill the mind of a visitor to the Salient. We were all too late. For no one who climbs these hills and walks these death-infested fields, who sees the awful pictures and views the terrible mementoes of War, can understand how we, the fortunate citizens of a civilized country can ever have allowed our young men to fight and die in such ghastly circumstances. I am also not alone amongst the tens of thousands who now visit Ypres who allows no conditions in their determination to ensure that it never happens again.

Part Five

A Complete Edition

Chapter 15
Number 5, Volume 1

The *BEF Times* of 10 April, 1917 is the 15th issue of the paper. It is reproduced *in toto* and without comment so that readers may try their hands at solving some of the Riddles. The following calendar of Principal World Events simplifies a few of the allusions and one or two of the items that have already been reviewed.

11 March, 1917
Baghdad occupied by British Forces.

12 March, 1917
Start of the Russian Revolution.

14 March, 1917
Start of the German retreat from the Somme to the Hindenburg Line.

15 March, 1917
Tsar of Russia abdicates.

26 March, 1917
First Battle of Gaza begins.

6 April, 1917
USA declares war on Germany.

9 April, 1917
The Battles of Arras begin with the Battle of Vimy Ridge.

He Soon Found It

" Don't know the way? Wal, keep right on up this track till you
come to a war. Then fight!"

THE
B.E.F. TIMES.

WITH WHICH ARE INCORPORATED

The Wipers Times, The "New Church" Times,
The Kemmel Times & The Somme-Times.

No 5. Vol 1	Tuesday, April 10th, 1917.	Price 1 Franc.

THE FOSSILEUM

—o—o—o—o—

THE DUMA TROUPE OF QUICK CHANGE ARTISTS.

STARRING :—

Rodzi & Co., in their Stirring Domestic Drama,
"SPRING CLEANING."

—o—o—o—o—

Great American Film Play, Entitled :--
"TEDDY GET YOUR GUN
(SOME FILM) FEATURING THEODORE IN THE LEAD.

—o—o—o—o—

Murray's Colourmatrograph.
A TOUR THROUGH PALESTINE (Series.
NO. 3: JERUSALEM.

Publisher's Announcements.

MESSRS. STODGER AND STOUTUN.

GOD'S GOOD MAN—An Autobiography by William Hohenzollern (Author of " The Innocents' Abroad," "Misunderstood," "The Christian," etc.)

A THIEF IN THE NIGHT—By Little Willie.

THE LAST HOPE—Professor Hindenberg (Author of "Westward Ho.")

IT'S NEVER TOO LATE TO MEND—Dr. Wilson.

ERIC, OR LITTLE BY LITTLE—Dean Haig.

THE CRUISE OF THE CATCH-A-LOT— By Bill Beatty.

THE DRINK HABIT
ACQUIRED IN THREE DAYS.

If you know anyone who doesn't drink alcohol regularly, or occasionally, let me send my free book, " CONFESSIONS OF AN ALCOHOL SLAVE." It explains something important, i.e. : How to quickly become an

Expert "Bona-fide Toper."

For the first 15 years of my life I was a rabid teetotaler, since the age of 16 I have never been to bed sober. If your trouble is with reference to a friend please state in your letter whether he is willing to be cured or not. Letters treated in a confidental manner. I can cure anyone.

Address : J. SUPITUP, Havanotha Mansions.   Telegrams : " RATS."

THE
B. E. F. TIMES.

' WITH WHICH ARE INCORPORATED

The Wipers Times, The "New Church" Times, The Kemmel Times & The Somme-Times

No 5. Vol 1.   Tuesday, April 10th, 1917.   Price 1 Franc.

EDITORIAL.

SPRING has at last really come! And with it an unusual amount of hurry and bustle all round; likewise forecasts. prophecies and conjectures, all frothy and furious We have all put our watches on one hour, and are now spending our spare time throwing away our surplus kit, sharpening our pistols and swords. and having our boots soled and heeled. We are also trying to produce this number of the paper under rather more difficult circumstances than usual, and we feel sure that our gentle readers will understand that whatever may be lacking is due to circumstances over which we have no control. We have again been fortunate in obtaining a special article from the pencil, ink, copying, one, of our old friend Mr. Teech-Bomas, which we feel sure will be read with interest. This number sees the finish of our serial "Narpoo Rum," and we wish to remind our readers of our Mammoth Competition in connection with same, particulars of which we published in our Grand Xmas Double Number last December. We still have several million francs left in our treasure chest which we should like to dispose of before the "Big Push" commences, more on account of its bulk than for any other reason. It may be a long time before we can produce another number, in which case we wish to take this opportunity of bidding all our friends "au revoir," the best of luck, and thanking them all for the kind support we have always received since the day in "Wipers" long ago when we found an old printing outfit looking for a job.

THE EDITOR.

THE B. E. F. TIMES.

NEWS FROM THE RATION DUMP.

—o—o—o—

The Esquimaux have broken off diplomatic relations with Germany.

—o—o—o—

The Huns are shortening their line in the West with a view to sending a number of divisions on a punitive expedition against them

—o—o—o—

Patrols of British and French cavalry swam the Rhine last night near Cologne, and are now meeting with sharp resistance in the suburbs of Berlin.

—o—o—o—

A party of A.S.C. were seen working in the reserve line.

—o—o—o—

The Czar of Russia has antiquated.

—o—o—o—

Horatio Bottomley has accepted the Turkish throne on condition they make a separate peace.

—o—o—o—

Leave is about to re open on the Western front.

—o—o—o—

The German fleet has bombarded Wapping Old Stairs, and ruined the carpet.

—o—o—o—

40,000 Huns have surrendered. They were so thin that they walked down one of our C.T.'s in fours.

—o—o—o—

[The EDITOR takes no responsibility for the truth of the above statements.]

TEN GERMAN PIONEERS.

Ten German Pioneers went to lay a mine,
One dropped his cigarette, and then there were nine.

Nine German Pioneers singing Hymns of Hate,
One stopped a whizz-bang, and then there were eight.

Eight German Pioneers dreaming hard of Heaven,
One caught a Flying Pig, and then there were seven.

Seven German Pioneers working hard with picks,
One picked his neighbour off, and then there were six.

Six German Pioneers, glad to be alive,
One was sent to Verdun, and then there were five.

Five German Pioneers, didn't like the war,
One shouted " Kamarad," and then there were four.

Four German Pioneers tried to fell a tree,
One felled himself instead, and then there were three.

Three German Pioneers, prospects very blue,
One tried to stop a tank and then there were two.

Two German Pioneers walked into a gun,
The gunner pulled the lanyard, and then there was one.

One German Pioneer couldn't see the fun
Of being shot at any more, and so the war was done.

THE B.E.F. TIMES.

ON THE HEELS OF THE FLEEING FOE.

—o—o—o—

FROM TEECH BOMAS.

—o—o—

France, Sunday Afternoon.

This morning, many hours before dawn, I mounted my bicycle and rode through 174 of the 187 blasted villages liberated during the past couple of days by our troops. I am now in the 175th, 12 miles north-south-west of Peraume, seated in what remains of the bar parlour of its main Estaminet, eating a frugal meal, and talking to the oldest inhabitant. I have this moment tasted a mouthful of Hun ration bread, which the enemy was unable to destroy in his hurried departure. It is darkish blue-black in hue, and its taste is putrid, rancid, nauseating, foul and stinking.

The scenes I have personally witnessed to-day as I rapidly pedalled into village after village were thrilling. awe-inspiring, blood-curdling—in short the whole outfit was epic. Old men, young men, women, girls, cripples, hunchbacks, little children, large children, all in their gladdest clothes, cheered me to the echo as I flashed through the various villages, whilst the village bands played patriotic airs in the market places. Occasionally I dismounted and talked to the people. To one woman I said " What of the Hun officers ? " She gave a low shrill whistle and replied with emotion ''Bosch officier, no bon, plenty zig-zag.'' This incident, in itself trivial, sums up the situation.

On my way from the 174th to the 175th village I found myself in front of our own outposts, and amongst those of the enemy. Rapidly twisting up the ends of my moustache and turning my cap inside out, I was able to escape recognition, and observed the antics of the Hun rearguard from closer quarters than anyone has ever done before. Officers and men, Unteroffiziere, Feldwebel and Freijährige, were all gibbering with fright, and pale pink drops of sweat dripped and dropped from their mottled brows as they leapt from tree to tree.

Just before reaching this village, an exciting and almost touching incident occurred. A very tired German 17-inch shell came sizzling through the air, and burst right under my cycle. Luckily the only damage done was a slight puncture to my near off side wheel. This proves how the Bosch H E has deteriorated during the past few months.

Even now I can hear the battle raging in the near distance. I must away and leave to a later dispatch the narrative, of what I shall do and see this afternoon.

ARMA VIRUMQUE CANO.

—o—o—o—

No Prayers of Peace for me; no maiden's sigh.
Give me the Chants of War, the Viking's Song ;
Battle for me ; nor care I for how long
This war goes on.   Tell me, where bullets fly ;
Where noble men and brave may bleed and die ;
Where skilful parry foils the sword-thrust strong.
Such are the tales I love. (I may be wrong—
A warrior, and no carpet knight am I.)

—o—o—o—

The D.S.O., the M.C. grace my breast ;
My brow is bound with laurels and with lace ;
I love this war.   Perhaps you think that that
Is strange.   Well I am different from the rest
Of you poor blighters.   I live at the Base,
And use the Brain inside my mce, red hat.

C. L. P.

THE B. E. F. TIMES.

TO ALL "DOUBTING THOMASES."

Now listen ye of mournful mien, whose
   bleatings rend the air,
Who spread an air of gloom where'er
   you go,
That though of cleverness you have p'r'aps
   more than your fair share,
Yet most of us just hate your wail of woe.
   —o—o—o—
One day 'tis "this" and next day "that,"
   your bogies come at will,
Of fearful ills to come you rave and rant,
You said a year ago the war was lost—
   we're fighting still,
The job has been no easier for your cant.
   —o—o—o—
In reverse you see disaster, and a victory
   spurs you on
To still greater efforts in the realms of
   doubt,
" We'll be lured into a trap," or " we
   can ne'er hold what we've won,"
And " we'll all be starved to death " your
   constant shout.
   —o—o—o—
Tis true that mostly you are those who
   ne'er have known the joy
Of living in ten feet of mud and slime,
Or the ecstasy which thrills one, sheer
   delight without alloy,
When you're dodging crumps and
   Minnies all the time.
   —o—o—o—
So in future cut the grousing, and for
   God's sake wear a grin,
The time is surely coming in a while,
When in spite of all your croakings the
   old Huns will be " all in,"
Cut the everlasting wail and smile, man,
   SMILE !

CONCERNING APOLOGIES.
A RHYME NOT WITHOUT REASON.

" Only the Wise apologise,
   Fools always must explain."
   (EXTRACT FROM A GREAT
      MODERN POET.)
   —o—o—o—

On receipt of our verses, the Gunner
   grew pensive,
But quickly developed a counter-offensive;
And though the rounds mostly were
   duds, or fell short,
They showed themselves able to make
   some retort.
   —o—o—o—
We all know the Sappers, of course,
   never shirk
From anything looking the least bit like
   WORK ;
So pale, but determined, they swore,
   " He shall rue it ! "
And asked for two large Working Parties
   to do it.
   —o—o—o—
The Staff, though surprised, did not
   gibber or storm,
But dealt with it all on the Authorised
   Form ;
For " G " said, " Well, I know whom
   THAT refers to,"
And passed the whole matter "for
   action " to " Q " ;
While " Q " patronisingly gave it a
   smile,
Remarked, " Poor old ' G ' Branch ?"
   and wrote on it " FILE."
      P.B.L

THE B.E.F TIMES.

Ah! P.B.I., too well we know your
  woes,
And why you sometimes talk in bitter
  strains,
Of living àlways tête-à-tête with foes,
Preserving us to labour on your drains.

—o—o—o—

But pause and think, before you grasp
  your pen,
Two sides to every argument appear ;
And ere you hold us up to scorn of men,
A few poor words on our side please to
  hear.

—o—o—o—

Know then, O proud and turgid P.B.I.,
Our fingers to the bone are worn for
  THEE,
Yet still one hears thy working parties
  cry,
"We're working for the —— old
  R.E !"

—o—o—o—

Do we essay to build a modest shelter,
Just rain and windproof, to our simple
  taste ;
Lo! yet before our backs are turned
  there enter
Platoons of infantry in quite indecent
  haste.

—o—o—o—

At times for help we ask with trepidation,
A cinquantaine of fed-up troops appears,
A few hours late, amid recrimination,
And crawls off slowly, 'spite of all our
  tears.

At journey's end quite half retain their
  tools,
And most of these are sick and tired of
  war,
Digging's a pastime only fit for fools,
Let the d - - - - d R.E. go and look for
  more.

—o—o—o—

Dear P.B.I.! how gladly would we
  quit
"A" frames, and duckboards, berms, and
  C.G.I.,
Dream of pontoons and trestles, pathway
  fit
To carry our victorious P.B.I.

  THE SANGUINARY R.E.

THEIR UNION OUR
STRENGTH.

—o—o—o—

Gunners and Sappers, and P.B.I.,
Now each in turn has had his say,
And shown in poetical rivalry
That, though good at their jobs, they're
  as good in play.

—o—o—o—

At times when the nerves are a trifle
  taut,
And frayed at the edges, as well may be,
All tempers are—well! just a wee bit
  short,
Then one MUST strafe a little impatiently.

—o—o—o—

Yet their trust in each other has stood
  the test,
Through the depths to the heights which
  are drawing nigh,
Each at his job has proved " the best,'
Gunners and Sappers, and P.B.I.

THE B. E. F. TIMES.

A STORY WITHOUT A MORAL.

—o—o—o—

And it came to pass that upon a certain day the General Officer Commanding a Division said unto his A.A and Q.M.G.: " O A.A. and Q.M.G., render unto me by the first day of next month a Return showing the names of the number of men of this Division who have even refused to undergo the hardships of INOCULATION, in order that I may send forward this Return unto Corps., in accordance with C R.O. 758

And it came to pass that the A.A. and Q.M.G. said certain things unto his D.A.A. and Q.M.G. and unto his D.A.Q.M.G., the result of which was a Return of names to the number of fifty of men of the Division who had refused to be INOCULATED.

And it came to pass that the Return aforementioned was in due course sent forward unto Corps., in which place it became labelled with the mystic sign " P.A.," which, being interpreted, means " put aside."

And it came to pass that upon a much later date this same General Officer Commanding a Division said unto his A.A. and Q.M.G.: " O A.A. and Q.M.G. render unto me by the first day of next month a Return showing the names of the number of men of this Division who have done deeds such as are worthy of reward in the form of the Medal Military, in order that I may send forward this return unto Corps., in accordance with C.R.O. 869.

And it came to pass that this Return also was duly obtained, and in due course sent forward unto Corps., in which place it became labelled with the mystic sign " P.A.," which, being interpreted, means " put aside."

And it came to pass that in due course those men who had refused to be INOCULATED were duly awarded with the MILITARY MEDAL.

Oh ! great is the Corps.

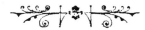

Verbatim Extracts From Intelligence Summaries.

—o—o—o—

TRENCH MORTARS.

—o—

At 1·0 p.m. the " Flying Pig " dropped a round in our front line at X 9 d 5 2. The trench was completely wrecked—the crater formed being 14 feet deep and 25 feet across It is consoling to think that over 40 rounds have been fired from this gun into the enemy trenches during the last week.

(Very consoling to the P.B.I.)

—o—o—o—

OPERATIONS.

—o—

On the 21st, in W 6 b, a party of about 10 Germans entered our lines. Our bombers, however, drove them out, in addition to killing 5 of them.

(Some bombers !)

—o—o—o—

MOVEMENTS.

—o—

At Z 5 b 21 this morning about thirty men were seen doing Expended Order Drill.

(We hope it wasn't painful.)

The following is a true extract from a return of reserve rations from a certain garrison :—

Locality—Foxhall Keep.
Map Ref.—P 67 X 19-32.
Commodity—Bully Beef.
Quantity—1 Tin.
Remarks—Not Full.

(Where's Lord Devonport ?)

THE B.E.F. TIMES.

Rubáiyát of William Hohenzollern.

Awake, old Tirpz! Bid Hindenburg
    arise,
"Der Tag" has come, I long to hear
    the cries
Of Europe! We'll proceed to raise all
    Hell,
Let's use our day from dawn. Time
    flies! Time flies!

—o—o—o—

Dreaming, it seemed to me the World
    was mine,
Waking, I think that the idea is fine ;
We'll wade right in to see what we can
    grab,
And glut ourselves with murder, rape
    and wine.

—o—o—o—

Come, fill the cup, and don a mask of
    pain
That we should have to cleanse the
    World again ;
Consider we our cause both pure and
    strong,
So first we'll try our hand in old Louvain.

—o—o—o—

Should any doubt my will, or us dispute,
Man, woman, child, don't hesitate to
    shoot ;
We'll play the policeman, and for
    Kultur's sake
My son, young Bill, will pick up all the
    loot.

—o—o—o—

How sweet is mortal sov'reignty—you
    see
How sov'reignty has made a God of me,
As I a God of it—play we the role
Thus, each one part, and that alternately.

I sometimes think that never lived so
    great
A monarch as myself—in fact of late
My greatness has appalled me and I
    bow,
I bow my humbled head upon the gate

—o—o—o—

There is no door, but that we have the
    key,
There is no depth debarred from you
    and me,
Success alone will justify our game,
So kill the land and terrorise the sea.

—o—o—o—

And if the man you burn, the child you
    kill,
Should even for one moment keep you
    still,
Think well 'tis for our sacred Kultur's
    sake,
And by a million murders steel your
    will.

—o—o—o—

Yet should success to dust and ashes
    fade,
And Justice rise from out the Hell we
    made,
We'll say that others lit the fire, and we
But fanned the flames, to mark the price
    they paid.

—o—o—o—

So Tirpz! with Hindenburg and me
    conspire,
With murder, rapine, frightfulness and
    fire,
Let's raise all Hell and, even should we
    fail,
At least we'll have "Der Tag" of our
    desire.

THE B. E. F. TIMES.

THE BULLY--BARLIN STAKES.

—o—

The Bully—Barlin Stakes took place on Friday last under the most auspicious conditions, the going being good and the average time of those who completed the course distinctly fast.

As a social event the Meeting was no less successful, a large and distinguished gathering being visible in the Paddock and on the Grand Stand, amongst whom your correspondent noticed Captain Turret and Admiral Jellicue, tastefully dressed in that inconspicuous blend of brown relieved by a soupcon of red which has become so fashionable of late. The Comptesse de Callonne looking ravishingly beautiful in a chic sandbag coat and skirt fringed with bric rubble. The Baron BYLLGEE (only capital letters can do him justice), in the Pink, many of the younger Checkes, and other notorities. Paderouski Ayetockski with his inevitable Blue and White Band played such popular items as "Buzz it and I shall hear," "You're through to Q, sir, but nobody's awake," and selections from that great tragedy "Burying Cable."

The race started punctually at 4.30 p.m., there being no false starts. Archie I and Archie II were hot favourites at the start, the betting being 4—2 on, offered freely, but with few takers. Shortly after the start, thanks to information tic-tacked back to the firm Strafit and Hate the prices and range lengthened. The Archies, however, proved as disappointing as ever to their backers, and finished a good second to Captain Tarkers "Bommy," owner up, which got off the mark like two Turkish Pashas paced by a Roumanian General. Third came the Rev. Snooker on his famous "Ironscrappes," a willing steed lacking rather in pace than pertinacity, and after that a mob of "Also rans," among whom one noticed several of the lesser lights of Bully. It is rumoured that vast sums exchanged hands over the favourite's defeat, and that the old firm of Aire, Supremacy and Suchsquish, was badly hit.

THE SUB.

He loves the Merry "Tatler," he adores
the Saucy "Sketch,"
The "Bystander" also fills him with
delight ;
But the pages that he revels in, the evil-
minded wretch,
Are the adverts of those things in pink
and white.

—:o:—

They are advertised in crêpe-de-chine,
and trimmed with silk and lace ;
The pictures fairly make him long for
leave ;
And while he gloats upon their frills, he
cannot find the grace
To read the pars of PHRYNETTE, BLANCHE
and EVE.

—:o:—

Before the war, he'd hardly heard of lace
and lingerie ;
He didn't know the meaning of chemise.
But thanks to weekly papers, this
astounding mystery
Has been solved by dainty VENN and
dear LABISE.

—:o:—

Before the war, he only knew of corsets
and of hats,
All other vogues invoked a ribald "what-
ho."
But the last decree of Fashion is a dinky
nightie, that's
Embroidered with his regimental motto.

—:o:—

It's this war, that is responsible for
teaching simple youth
All sorts of naughty Continental tricks.
And already he's decided, when it's over,
that, in truth,
He'll buy mamma a pair of cami-knicks.

R.M.O.

THE B.E.F. TIMES.

—th Infantry Brigade Intelligence Summary. No. 30,

—o—o—o—

From 12 noon, any date.
To 12 noon, date following.

—o—

1.—ATTITUDE OF THE ENEMY.

Aggressive, 12 whizbangs at 2 p.m. on POPE'S PIMPLE. POPE has now no pimple worthy of mention.

2.—ENEMY'S ARTILLERY.

The enemy fired a gas shell into X. The gas sentry at once sounded his jam tin ; this proved most effective, no further shells were fired, and the rest of the troops in the immediate vicinity was not in the least disturbed.

NOTE.—This report should be accepted with considerable reserve, it is based entirely on the statement of the sentry who, although a worthy fellow, is not remarkable for his veracity.

3.—OUR ARTILLERY.

A bombardment was carried out by our Artillery in conjunction with Trench Mortars (Heavy, Medium and Light), Machine and Lewis Guns, and Rifle Grenades, vide operation order No. 3,000. Our casualties were slight.

4.—T.M. ACTIVITY.

There has been considerable Trench Mortar activity ; our Flying Pig effectively engaged our front line trench at about M 30 6 3 9 ; the hostile Minnie 'SUSAN' vigorously retaliated on her adjacent Batt. H.Q. at N 15 d 6 20.

5.—SNIPING.

Our snipers claim to have hit M 14 b 4 3.

6.—PATROLS.

A patrol under 2nd Lieut. Jones was ordered to ascertain whether the sap at H 14 b 9 5 is occupied by the enemy. This patrol left our trenches at 10 p.m. ; after proceeding ten yards in a N E. direction an empty tin was found, on examination it proved to be labelled 'PLUM JAM.'

NOTE.—This is considered to be a clever ruse of the enemy to convey the impression that his rations include an issue of plum jam.

The patrol returned at 10·03 p.m., having secured the above valuable identification.

NOTE.—It has been suggested that the tin had contained jam issued for the consumption of our own troops, 2nd Lieut. Jones however has reason to believe otherwise.

7.—INTELLIGENCE.

Our observers report :—

3 p.m. A man wearing a shrapnel helmet, accompanied by a dog, was observed walking along the road between S 5 a 6 8 and S 5 b 9 6.

3·2 p.m. A stout man with red face and glass eye asleep by the side of road at S 5 b 9 4.

3·5 p.m. Dog (referred to above) seen to approach stout man asleep, and remain near him several seconds.

NOTE.—It is thought that possibly a relief was taking place.

3h 5m 5sec. Stout man who had been asleep was observed to rise and throw a large stone at dog (referred to above).

3h 5m 6sec. Dog disappeared at S 5 b 9 5.

3·7 p.m. Man with shrapnel helmet observed wiping with a sandbag the head of the stout man with red face and glass eye who had been asleep, but was now evidently thoroughly awake, and showing unmistakeable signs of anger.

NOTE.—It is thought that possibly dogs have been trained to rouse sleeping sentries in case of alarm.

4 p.m. Smoke was observed at S 10 b 0 0.

NOTE.—It is considered that this is a clever ruse of the enemy to convey the idea that a fire had been ignited at this spot.

8.—REPORTS FROM OTHER SOURCES.

2 p.m. Two men wearing spectacles were seen to disappear behind a hedge at K 2 b 5 7 ; our 60 Pounders searched this spot with H.E., the two men, previously seen, suddenly reappeared at K 2 b 5 9, and hastily took cover in a trench at K 2 6 3. They appeared to be strangely hampered in their movements.

NOTE.—It is thought that this hedge conceals a strong point of considerable importance to the enemy.

MIDDLING OLD LIEUT.,
BDE. INTELLIGENCE OFFICER,
—th INFANTRY BRIGADE.

THE B. E. F. TIMES.

HOW CONGRESS DECLARED WAR.

—o—o—o—

BY

OUR SPECIAL CORRESPONDENT

Tuckis Shurtin.

—o—o—o—

MR. TUCKIS SHURTIN managed, by the wonderful enterprise and skill always shown by him on these delicate operations, to hide himself behind a life-size picture of Charlie Chaplin in the White House, and was thus present at the most momentous meeting which ever took place in the history of America.

He briefly describes, in his own picturesque language, exactly what took place.

" Wal ! " said Woodrow, chewing the end of a five-cent che-root, " I'm for a show-down."

The Bull-Moose took the floor and bucked, good and plenty. " Say," he howls, " double the ante, and raise 'em sky-high for cards. I ain't in on a two-dime game. Cut it out. I'm in on a no limit, and I've got the dust. Give me half a-million boys, and I'll skin every Hun in Yurrup. Yes ! sirree ! !

Elihu P. showed a busted straight, and beat for the golden silence.

Big Bill threw in for the Bull-Moose, leaving Woodrow up against it.

" Wal ! " said he, " write me down for a two-cent boob if I don't hand it to Willie. Say, boys, I'm in the game. Boost the ante, and sky-high for cards. I'm a bold she-wolf, and it's my night to howl."

" Rah ! RAH ! RAH ! Woodrow. Oh ! Willie, beat it ! Theo's on your track, and he's hungry.

TUCKIS SHURTIN.

THEY DIDN'T BELIEVE ME !

—o—

Don't know how it happened quite,
Sure the jar came up all right ?
Just as full as it should be
Wouldn't touch it, no, not me !
Sergeants very seldom touch
Rum, at least, not very much,
Must have been the A.S.C.,
Anyway, it wasn't me !

Yet when I told them that I hadn't
    touched the jar,
They didn't believe me, they didn't
    believe me ;
They seem to know a sergeant's thirst,
I fear they all believe the worst,
It's the rottenest luck that there could
    be ;
And when I tell them, and I'm certainly
    going to tell them,
There'll be fatigues for them where'er I
    be,
They'll never believe me, they'll never
    believe that
The man who tapped the jar could not
    be me !

Stop Press News.

Rioting is again reported in Berlin. The Kaiser has gone to bed with whooping cough and ricketts.

—o—o—o—

The New German War Loan has reached the stupendous figure of 50,000 marks owing to the successful U Boat campaign.

—o—o—o—

Two juvenile food hogs were arrested yesterday. On examination it was found that their pockets were full of brandy balls.

THE B. E. F. TIMES.

OUR SPLENDID NEW SERIAL.

—o—o—o—

"NARPOO RUM."

—o—o—o—

BY THE AUTHOR OF "SHOT IN THE CULVERT."

—o—o—o—

DRAMATIS PERSONAE:

—o—

Cloridy Lyme — A Sanitary Inspector.
Madeline Carot —   A French Girl.
Intha Pink   —   A Pioneer.
General Bertram
Rudolph de Rogerum—The Earl of Loose.
Lord Reginald
de Knellthorpe —   His Son.
Q. Wemm   —   A Storekeeper.
L. Plumernapple —   A Soldier.
Herlock Shomes — The Great Detective.
Dr. Hotsam   —   His Admirer.

—o—o—o—

CHAPTER 8.

—o—o—o—

WHAT CLORIDY LYME SAW.

—o—o—o—

CLORIDY LYME straightened his aching back with a groan, and gazed around the stricken streets of Bapaume in the cold grey light of dawn with every appearance of profound distaste. "When I joined this 'ere mob I 'ad visions of red coats and flashin' bayonets ; and now I spends my time spearin' bits o' paper and orange peel on a pointed stick," mused he. Gazing upwards at the lowering sky, he saw a strange sight. A sausage was drifting by, scarcely clearing the roofs of the ruined houses. Two men hung precariously in the rigging, and a trail rope dragged over the ground. As he watched, the rope caught in a tree stump, and the

two men, hastily sliding down it, inquired of the astonished sanitary inspector their whereabouts. On hearing that they were in Bapaume, Shomes (for it was none other than he) said calmly, "Just as I thought, my dear Hotsam, my deductions are sometimes at fault but very rarely I think" Glancing sharply at the pointed stick held by Cloridy Lime, he suddenly seized it, and tore from the end a piece of paper which, after perusing, he handed to Hotsam, saying, "Just as I told you my dear fellow." Hotsam took the paper and read,

EDI
WIPERS T
SHERWOOD FORES

—o—o—o—

CHAPTER 9.

—o—

BACK AT QUALITY STREET.

—o—o—o—

"BUT my dear Hotsam, the whole thing is so absurdly simple," said Shomes curling his long wiry body up in his comfortable bunk. "What! You really have solved the problem of the missing rum ?" "There never was a problem, and the rum was never stolen." "For heavens sake explain, Shomes, I really cannot follow your abstruce reasoning." "You surely remember my good fellow, that at the time the rum was supposed to have been stolen, it was almost impossible to buy whisky in this country." "Yes I remember it very well indeed, but what has that to do with the question." "My good Hotsam, cannot you follow me now" "I really cannot, Shomes" "You met the Earl and his staff many times during those trying days, did you not ?" "Yes, I saw them nearly every day." "Did they strike you as men who had suddenly become total abstainers ?" "No, I cannot say they did." "Well, just think a little, my dear Hotsam, whisky was unobtainable then, what did they—Pass the whisky and put on the gramophone my good fellow, I think we are entitled to a tot."

THE B. E. F. TIMES.

" AU REVOIR."

—:o:—

" 'Tis sad but true," that with nearly every issue of the paper we have to reserve this column in order to say good-bye to some distinguished member of the Division.

This time it is our late C R.E , Brig.-General A. Craven.

We wish to offer him our most hearty congratulations on his hard earned and well-deserved promotion, and, at the same time, say how much we shall all miss him.

He has always been a very good friend to us all, and a staunch supporter of the paper, and we should like him to know how much the whole Division appreciates his ever ready assistance, and the considerations he has always shown both in work and play.

Good luck and God speed.

Correspondence.

To the Editor,
 " B.E.F. Times."

Sir,

Once again I feel constrained to draw your attention to the increasing rowdiness of the district. I am a peaceful citizen, and although somewhat behindhand with my rates, yet the injustice of the present conditions is apparent. Surely, when a quiet citizen wishes to cultivate his own small holding, it is not quite the thing to plant a 12-inch howitzer in the middle. I must protest, and if nothing is done in the matter, I announce my intention of voting against the present candidate at the forthcoming election.

I am, Sir,
 FED-UP.

RESULT OF COMPETITION.

FIRST PRIZE — — 10,000,000 Francs.
SECOND PRIZE — — 5,000,000 Francs.
THIRD PRIZE — — 2,500,000 Francs.

THESE PRIZES WERE WON BY the first three contestants in our MAMMOTH COMPETITION, who reclaimed the CHEQUES. Owing to a slight misunderstanding with COX & CO.. these Cheques were returned R/D.

—o—o—o—o—

IF THE LUCKY AND SKILFUL claimants will SEND IN the old Cheques, new ones WILL BE ISSUED in lieu. We hope they will meet with a better fate, but, after all, MONEY is not everything.

THE COMPETITION EDITOR.

BUSINESS ANNOUNCEMENT

Mr. POILE
(Late POILE and TROTTER.)

BEGS TO INFORM HIS NUMEROUS CLIENTS THAT OWING TO THE
SHORTAGE OF PAPER HE IS UNABLE TO SUPPLY HIS

POPULAR YELLOW COUPONS
AS HITHERTO.

THE FEW HE STILL HAS IN HAND ARE

BOOKED UP FOR THE NEXT TWO YEARS.

IN ORDER TO ENSURE SMOOTH RUNNING AFTER THIS PERIOD EXPIRES
APPLICANTS SHOULD HOPE ON, AND SEND IN THEIR

NAMES AND QUALIFICATIONS.
SOMETHING MAY HAPPEN AND THEN AGAIN IT MAY NOT,

—o—o—o—o—o—

" If at first you don't succeed,
Carry on and take no heed."

CAGE HOTELS, LIMITED.

—o—o—o—

The Proprietors can strongly recommend any of these Hotels for a SUMMER HOLIDAY to all Gentlemen (?) of

GERMAN NATIONALITY

who are in need of a real rest after the noise and nerve strain attendant on life in the trenches.

—o—o—o—

These HOTELS are pleasantly and airily situated, in pretty parts of France, with excellent views

FACING THE FRONT

—o—o—o—

Electric and Barbed Wires Throughout.
Good Shooting in the Vicinity.

Attendance Free.

—o—o—o—

' You'll find our charges very light,
Compared with those you had last night."

Emo's "Fruity Ports"

—o—o—o—

C.O.'S LOOK AT YOUR SUBALTERN'S TONGUES !

DO THEY SUFFER FROM HEADACHE AND FEEL DEPRESSED IN THE MORNING ?

DO THEY WANT TO GO OVER THE TOP IN THE EVENING ?

—o—o—o—

What they want is : —

EMO'S "FRUITY PORTS."

—o—o—o—

GET A BOTTLE TO-DAY !

—o—o—o—

" If your Subs. are out of sorts,
Give them EMO'S FRUITY PORTS."

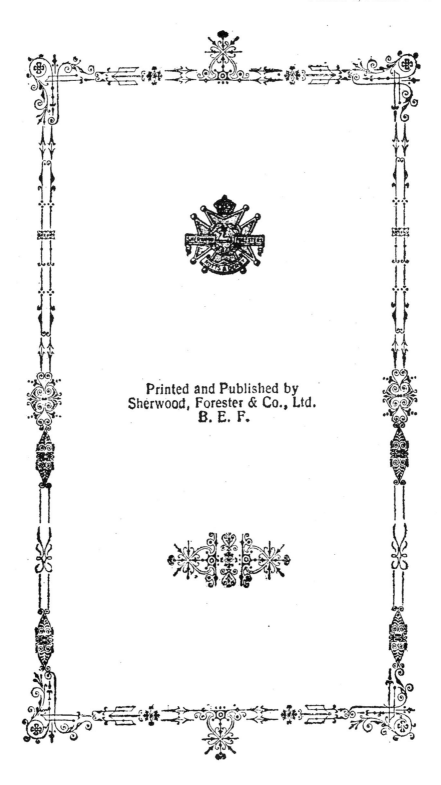

Printed and Published by
Sherwood, Forester & Co., Ltd.
B. E. F.

Chapter 16

A Diversion via Westwell

I have no experience of living every moment under threat of imminent, frightening and painful death, but I have an inkling. I can not completely comprehend the fear of showing fear that so concerned the contributors to *The Wipers Times*, but I have been near enough to that precipice to recognize it. In the Salient men lived close to death every day for four years. Can we do anything but admire them and read with renewed interest the paper that they wrote, printed, distributed and laughed at during those days.

Lieutenant Harold Price was at Ypres and in the summer of 1994 I visited his memorial at Westwell in the Cotswolds where I had been directed by a local landlord, a kind man who at least feigned interest in my obsession with Ypres and the First World War. Using my imagination and careful interpretation of sections of *The Wipers Times*, I had already pieced together a story of how Price's name might have come to be engraved upon this extraordinary war memorial.

Harold Price was in the Royal Fusiliers, an infantry regiment with battalions holding the front line in the Ypres Salient. They spent some time out of the line at 'Bulford Camp,' a training and 'Rest' establishment at Neuve Eglise. In defiance of the conditions at the time – Neuve Eglise was the home of the 'New Church' variant of *The Wipers Times* and was

SPORTS.

On Thursday, the 8th ult., the Royal Fusiliers held a very successful little meeting at Bulford Camp, and Col. Hancock and the officers were at home all the afternoon. The meeting was favoured by very fine weather and was a great success from the word go. There were certain events open to the 24th Division which drew fairly representative entries, notably the tug-of-war, in which some very interesting heats were decided, to be won finally by an excellent team of the Leinsters who well deserved their victory. Perhaps one of the most interesting events from a spectacular point of view was the Officers V.C. Race which drew about 11 entries, some of the efforts at remounting with the dummy caused a certain amount of good-natured laughter, but the winner showed excellent judgment and skill both in his heat and final. The meeting struck a note that we have more than once advocated in our columns; a more frequent occurrence of this type of friendly rivalry brings the members of the various units into closer contact with each other, and promotes a greater "Esprit de corps" in the division as a whole, not to mention the relaxation from things more serious which such occasions afford.

As a final word Col. Hancock and his officers were truly excellent hosts, and we thank them one and all for a very enjoyable day, as well as congratulating the executive on the able manner in which everything was carried out.

regularly subject to gas attack and indiscriminate shelling – the Royal Fusiliers held a Salisbury Plain style open sports day. The event was reported in the paper.

I am in need of a soldier with a long memory to enlighten me as to details of the 'Officers' VC Race.'

In my mind's eye I could see Lieutenant Price at the Sports. He would have been dressed in makeshift PT gear, perhaps a white singlet over uniform breeches and plimsols, ready for taking his part in the Tug-of-War. Hatless and with his hair slightly longer than was the military custom in peacetime, his commissioned rank would have still been quite clear. Between events he organized things; marking out a race track; directing soldiers who were building jumps or obstacles for the races. He would have kept well within sight of Colonel Hancock, his CO, to do his bidding with military promptness on any matter, from sounding the gas alert to serving whiskies in tin mugs to visiting officers from other formations. In between all this he might have won the VC Race, whatever that was, or taken the regimental prize for marksmanship.

Bang away ye 18 pounders,
Shriek ye hows in joyful strain,
Till the air with din astounders,
Leave is once more on again.

If you're waking call me early, call me early, sergeant dear;
For I'm very, very weary, and my warrant's come, I hear;
Oh! it's " blightie " for a spell, and all my troubles are behind,
And I've seven days before me
(Hope the sea will not be stormy)
Keep the war a'going, sergeant,
Train's at six, just bear in mind!

THE LEAVE WARRANT.

Week, after weary week, I work and wait
Patiently wondering, when 'twill be my lot
To find a carpet, wond'rously wrought
On mystic looms, in some enchanted state,
Gifted with Oriental power innate
To bear me hence, to other lands, I wot
(In dreams, I sit upon it, but do not
Awake in time to ring the bell of Fate)
But willingly, indeed, I would forego
This Magic Mat, for just a little bit
Of printed, primrose parchment—and to know,
That on its face my name three times was writ.
For 'tis a genie's golden key to fit
The Gate of Leave -" Chin chin, you chaps, cheer O! "

C.L.P.

POILE & TROTTER,

STATIONERS AND POULTRY
DEALERS,

—o—o—o—

ALL GOODS SUPPLIED HALF-PRICE
TO THE TRADE.

—o—o—o—

CIRCULARS PRINTED.

SEND FOR OUR ILLUSTRATED BOOKLET.

—o—o—o—

ARE YOU INTENDING

TO TRAVEL?

If so send for one of our Yellow
Coupons which will take you anywhere.

—o—o—o—

" If you're tired and need a rest,
Buy our ticket 'tis the best."

—o—o—o—

TELEGRAMS: " KEW."

Poile and Trotter, Poile and Trotter,
May I ask you if you've got a
Season ticket you can issue
To the press if so, we wish you
Would endorse and send it here,
Will you Poile and Trotter dear ?

L is for LEAVE, our goal of desire,
Ten days in Blighty away from the
mire .
Hope springs eternal, and ne'er will
expire
In the breast of the men in the trenches.

Sometime in 1915 or early 1916, having survived weeks or even months as a company commander in the forward areas of the Ypres Salient, Lieutenant Price came home to England for leave.

Leave is mentioned in every issue of *The Wipers Times*. We read of joy when leave finally came along, anger when it was postponed, and deep depression when it was over. There were many leave embargoes when manpower was stretched to the limit in the trenches; the times when so many casualties were going home dead or mortally wounded that the living could only knuckle down to another desperate week or two in their dugouts and dream of the Dover boat and home.

The 'Primrose Parchment' refers to an Officer's leave pass which was apparently printed on yellow paper and carried the bearer's name written three times.

It seems that leave passes and rail warrants were issued from the Divisional Admin Office located somewhere within the old city of Ypres and it was there that Lieutenant Price would have reported to collect the precious documentation when his turn finally came to go home on leave. The officers who staffed the leave office were called Poile and Trotter or these were some recognizable encryptions of their names.(Trial – with a London accent – and Potter, spoonerised, or possibly Pearl and Trotter with the former given a Damon Runyan intonation.) 'Telegrams Kew' identifies 'Poile and Trotter' as Q or Quartermaster branch of the Brigade headquarters.

DO NOT READ THIS!!!
UNLESS YOU HAVE A GIRL AT HOME.
—o—o—o—o—

If you have, of course. you want to send her a souvenir. WE can supply just the tasty
little thing you want   Thousands to choose from :—

GERMAN SHOULDER STRAPS : 1/· each   —   —   10/· a dozen
DITTO, BLOODSTAINED : 1/6 each   —   —   15/ a dozen
SHELL HOLES, COMPLETE : 50/· each
DUCKBOARDS—ENGLISH : 5/· each
DITTO. GERMAN : 10/· each
IRON CROSSES : 6d. a gross.

BULLETS CAREFULLY FIXED IN
OUR SPECIALITY : BIBLES (FOR MAIDEN AUNTS)
PHOTOGRAPHS (FOR FIANCEES.)
—●—o—o—o—

" To please your best girl. it is clear,
You must procure a souvenir."
—o—o—o—o—

SOUVENIR MANUFACTURING COMPANY. CAMBRAI.

The 'Souvenir' advertisement is indicative of the strong desire that soldiers always have to bring or send mementoes of war to those at home. These artefacts which are usually bloodthirsty and macabre are always hugely impractical. In the antiques and collectors' world of today such souvenirs have quite a following and are known as Trench Art. Most people are familiar with the dinner gong made from a whizz-bang shell, the lovingly polished paperweight of spent bullets, the German-bayonet fire irons. Bullets in Bibles, iron-crosses (cynically priced in the advertisement at 6d a gross), these were the sort of articles that were always present in the luggage of the fortunate few who were proceding on leave from the front. But Lieutenant Price was carrying the most unusual souvenir of all as he stepped jauntily away from Poile and Trotter's dugout in what was left of the old city of Ypres with the precious yellow leave pass in his pocket. It was a narrow brass object with shaped edges and bifurcated ends like a thigh-bone – the gothic figure 1 from a clockface. Photographs and letters confirm that it was a numeral from the clock in the bombarded tower of the Cloth Hall in Ypres, that well-ventilated home of the fantasy music halls advertised in most issues of the paper.

My imagination was running away with me. Using *The Wipers Times* and the inscription from a corroded brass clock numeral mounted on a monolithic war memorial in the Cotswold village of Westwell, I had constructed a story about the home leave of Lieutenant Price of the Royal Fusiliers in those terror-filled days early in the Great War. At an address a few miles beyond Westwell I hoped to find out how near the truth I was when I talked with surviving members of Harold Price's family.

Campagne de 1914. — Ruines d'YPRES. — Photo-Antony, Ypres.
101   *Les Halles aux draps d'YPRES après le bombardement du 22 nov. 1914.*
The Halle aux Draps after the bombardment.

CAMPAGNE DE 1914-1915
YPRES — La Rue de Lille. — The Lille street.

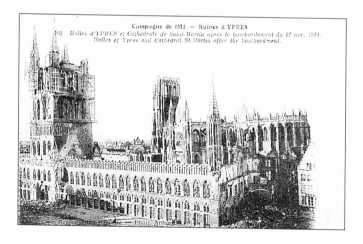

Campagne de 1914 — Ruines d'YPRES
101   *Halles d'YPRES et Cathédrale de Saint-Martin après le bombardement du 22 nov. 1914.*
Halles of Ypres and Cathedral St-Martin after the bombardment.

The inscription engraved on the clock numeral was worded thus;

To the Brave men who gave their lives for England in the Great War.

Erected by Stretta Aimee Holland in memory of her brothers.
Lt. Harold S.Price.
Royal Fusiliers
Lt. Edward John Price. R.N.

This brass memorial formed part of the clock of the Cloth Hall at Ypres

'Would I be right in suggesting that men like your uncle, Lieutenant Harold Price, were members of a generation of young men who had something of a golden future in the England of 1914?'

I was talking to Sir Guy and Lady Holland, in the magnificent surroundings of their Cotswold home, about the life and death Harold Price. In high-backed chairs around a monastic refectory table we drank coffee and recalled the intense sadness of family bereavement. With the aid of old photographs and letters, Stretta Aimée Holland's son told me all he knew of the death of his uncle and the story of the unusual memorial that his mother had erected in memory of her brothers.

Yes, they were a golden generation. The young men who went off to be subalterns in British infantry regiments in 1914 and 1915 and who were mown down and blown up in their thousands in the Ypres Salient and elsewhere in Flanders and Northern France came largely from secure, landed families. The social system that was acceptable in this country in the early part of the century ensured that these young men had a good education, that they were healthy and well fed, that they would never be without employment either in this country or in the overseas Empire. By-and-large they were personable, charming, self-confident to the point of

One cannot help recalling at this time, our Company dances, which he ran so successfully, which gave us all so much pleasure; — of the Energy he instilled into our Tug of War & other teams for the Battalion sports, — of his constant delight in hard physical work

A 'Condolence' letter from Price's Commanding Officer

Leave

Dep. : Paddington 2.15.   Arr. Home 4

.. Micklinson has just got hold of a lovely souvenir from Ypres in fact the figure I from the 'clock' face of the Cloth Hall, he has asked me to take it home for him when my leave occurs; ..

Harold Price tells his sister about the clock souvenir.

arrogance and universally obsessed with the new upper class status symbol, the motor-car.

However, the golden passport that Lieutenant Price and his generation had been born with in the last years of Victoria's reign turned suddenly into a death warrant. Social background ensured that they volunteered for active service, almost to a man; and the average life expectancy of a subaltern in the trenches was about six weeks. Some were killed in their first hour at the front; others, like Lieutenant Price, survived to bring home souvenirs on a precious seven-day leave, to divide that short break between London revelry and probably tearful visits to the country house in the Cotswolds or the Chilterns or the Quantocks or wherever … But how few of them survived the War; how many families like the Prices lost every son to the fighting.

In particular, there were some errors in my deduced story about how the clock tower numeral came to grace the Westwell war memorial. Harold Price had indeed brought it home, but it was not he who found it. It was the prize souvenir of a brother officer for whom Harold transported it to England. Both men were killed and the huge brass numeral remained at the Holland residence until after the war when it was decided to use it as part of the brothers' memorial. It was impossible to confirm if Price had been a reader of *The Wipers Times* or if he had attended the Royal Fusiliers Sports Day at Bulford camp, reported in the paper; but he was so typical of the Ypres Salient Subaltern that somehow it was not necessary to verify my assumptions. Photos and letters confirmed that he was long-haired, personable and athletic, a tug-of-war expert even. He loved motor-cars and London parties and he might have been, as Who's Who advised me Sir Guy Holland was, a member of Boodle's. The subaltern who wrote the following piece for *The Wipers Times* was a member of that famous London Club where

FRAGMENTS FROM FRANCE.

—:o:—

And it came to pass in the early fore-noon, having partaken of a frugal meal of clorinated tea and Tickler, I sallied forth and gained the chalky fastnesses of WHISKY CRATER, completely oblivious of the dangers I encountered from our own artillery and Tock Emmas! Scorn-ing the periscope, I slowly elevated my bust above the parapet.

"Jee-rusalem—surely this is not the result of excessive thorassic lubrication? No, no, a thousand times NO! It cannot be since last night the Quartermaster once more failed us, and the Army Service Corps had registered another hit."

There, before my startled gaze ap-peared the familiar form of Ginger Fritz of Doodles!

"Alas! What memories that name con-jures up! Fritz of Doodles!

But, what a change!

Quantum mutatus ab illo as we used to say in our schooldays!

Gone was the greasy evening dress, and in its place the field grey uniform.

Gone too his happy smile, and in its place a look of concentrated hate.

He stopped! He looked! He listened! Then he saw me.

With true Prussian instinct he levelled his musket and pointed it in my direction.

Like a flash an inspiration seized me! "Waiter" I cried at the top of my voice. "Waiter! A brandy and soda! A bun for the lady friend!"

At the sound of the well-known voice he started; his lethal weapon clattered to the ground, and with leaps and bounds he answered the call.

In two of the proverbial shakes he was beside me in the trench.

As I led my now smiling prisoner down the C.T. I had visions of how I would spend my week's leave. Doodles of course would be one of my first calls!

I was about to thank Fritz for the good turn he had done me, when I suddenly thought of A.O. 1965/3 . . . damm it all! I forget the rest of it—but I do remember that I can't go on leave for at least another four months,

Crafted from solid brass with a lacquer finish, this petrol lighter is modelled on the ones made during World War 1 from spent bullets. It incorporates all the original features, including a sliding storm guard to protect the flame from the wind, rope wick and large friction wheel.

apparently they employed German waiters before the war, and where the sad, happy, gallant and doomed subalterns from the front liked to spend some of their leave.

'Tickler' was a brand of Jam. The name transferred easily to an unpleasant home-made anti-personnel weapon that consisted of nails and any other scrap metal, stuffed, along with explosive and detonator, in a jam tin. The omnipresent disinfectant Chloride of Lime made the tea taste chlorinated. AO 1965/3 was one of the Orders delaying or embargoing leave.

I include the advertisement for a First World War replica lighter to remind us of the enduring nature of 'Trench Art'. The picture is from the 1993 Kleeneze direct-mail catalogue.

Sir Guy Holland was able, from his own experience, to solve the riddle of the 'VC Race.' It was a competition for men on horseback to gallop to a location where a soldier lay on the ground playing the part of a wounded man. The rider had to dismount and lift the inert body on to his horse and then race, two up, back to the start. It was, as Sir Guy stated, 'punishing work' and no doubt the competition owed its title to an occasion in British military history when a Victoria Cross had been won for some such real life act of bravery.

The Westwell war memorial was conceived and emplaced, not by public subscription, not by grateful surviving villagers, not by government or military authority, but by a private person – woman. It represents what women must have been thinking as they looked back in gradually awakening horror at the magnitude of the disaster that had befallen their Nation. The young men were gone: Harold and Edward Price, killed on active service; two other brothers dead from war-related injury. Whole classrooms, schools and universities of British men lay with them in the awesome war cemeteries of France and Belgium and the Dardanelles. In the early post-war years did anyone remember why? Did anyone question the unstoppable steamroller of war that the generals and politicians had fired up in 1914 with the dread words, 'It is our national duty …' and which no one had been able to stop until a whole generation lay dead? Was there no other solution? Did we really have to fight and fight again until there was no home in the land that hadn't lost a relative; no window in the street that didn't show the black card of bereavement?

Of course there was another way. There always is when men fight wars. And in the 1920s the pride that women had in the readiness with which their young men had laid down their lives was, in some cases, tempered by a dreadful realisation of the truth about the War. ' They told us our young men had to die for England or France or Belgium or ten yards of barbed wire and mud in the Ypres Salient; they were not telling us the truth'. Men usually never questioned the whole ghastly undertaking. At the beginning of the war they were totally brainwashed with the notion that had been sustaining the British Empire for centuries, namely that it was a sweet and decorous thing to die for one's country. By the time experience was beginning to point out that it was nothing of the kind they had obediently died in their hundreds of thousands.

Some might feel that 'brainwashing' is too strong a word to describe the process by which a young man becomes convinced that it is his duty to lay down his life fighting in a foreign land; that he should die for a cause which people, who are supposed to know best, advise him is vital for his Nation. However, the process wherby natural instincts of self-preservation and survival are suppressed and the notion of death in combat glorified was so much part of British education that those of us who have experienced it will talk, in later, wiser years of brainwashing.

I know by heart every word of the Hymn, 'O Valiant Hearts …' which means that I must have sung it a sufficient number of times before I reached the age of 10 for it to have lasted in my memory for over fifty years. If the words are so indelibly imprinted, what about the sentiments, the unashamed glorification of death in battle that I mouthed with such fervour at Morning Prayer and Evensong before I was old enough to doubt, criticise or question?

> O valiant hearts, who to your glory came,
> Through dust of conflict and through battle flame;
> Tranquil you lie, your knightly virtue proved,
> Your memory hallowed in the land you loved.
>
> Proudly you gathered, rank on rank to war,
> As who had heard God's message from afar;
> All you had hoped for, all you had you gave
> To save mankind – yourself you scorned to save.

'Greater love hath no man than this,' said the Chaplain to his pink-cheeked sub-teenage congregation, 'that a man lay down his life for his friends.'

'*Dulce et decorum est pro patria mori.*' quoted the Latin master; but, as his class of ten-year-olds struggled to translate, no one in authority added, '... and don't believe a word of it.'

In the Corps – the OTC – a compulsory régime at my school, I was trained to take pride in the profession of arms; so was my father, and so, I have no doubt, was Harold Price.

By the age of fifteen I could drill with the best of them, shoot a .303 Lee-Enfield rifle and strip and assemble a Bren gun. Tough instructors showed me how to kill a man with a bayonet or snipe at an enemy without being seen myself. The drums beat and the bugles brayed and I marched with my adolescent chest thrust out in pride, in whatever direction the sergeant ordered, until my feet in their oversized black boots would carry me no further.

'Death before Dishonour', 'Death or Glory', '*Quid non pro Patria*', '*Pro Patria Mori.*' In the 1950s, after two world wars in half a century and upwards of two million killed in battle, I was, at the age of eighteen, still convinced that war was an exciting and wonderful experience. Conscription came along and I applied for service wherever the British Military was actively engaged. My father before me – same

Hazlewell House Platoon, Cheltenham College Contingent, Officer Training Corps, 1915. More than 50 per cent of these eager young men became officers in the First World War. 70 per cent of these were casualties. None ever forgot the experience. My father (the enlarged face) became a Captain in the RFC and was decorated for gallantry within three years of this photograph.

TEMPORA MUTANTUR.

In childhood's days my wayward fancy
  ran
On battle, and a soldier brave'was I,
I led my men to action with elan,
We dashed ahead resolved to do or die.
— 0 — 0 — 0 —
Yet in my pictures scarce can I recall
What means we used to circumvent the
  wire,
Nor how we fought the direst foe of all,
If we had mud then mem'ry is a liar.
— 0 — 0 — 0 —
Green fields and sunlight, swords and
  prancing steeds,
And pistols with some score yards range
  at most,
In pleasant lands which furnished all my
  needs,
In fancy fought my foe from post to post.
— 0 — 0 — 0 —
Ah, childhood's days! No prancing
  steed have I
Who, day and night, must wade through
  seas of mud
Attired in tin hat, mac, and boots, gum,
  thigh,
I almost think my childish dreams were
  dud.
— 0 — 0 — 0 —
No flight of fancy ever found me glad
A filthy dug-out, full of rats, to see;
I cannot e'er remember being mad
Chloride of lime to sample in my tea.
— 0 — 0 — 0 —
No flying-pigs, or Minnies, had a place
In battles which my fancy freely waged,
No shrieking cans of death came out of
  space,
No stinking gas the air of war outraged.
— 0 — 0 — 0 —
Will future battles fought in childhood's
  dreams
Still hold romance and chivalry entire?
Or will the coming child draw war which
  teems
With Hun barbarities and Kultur's fire.

age, same house, same school, thirty-five years earlier – was more specific. He simply went down on his knees in the dormitory every night and prayed that the First World War would last long enough for him to be able to take part. Brainwashed? Of course we were. So were Harold Price and his doomed contemporaries of the 1914 Golden Generation who flocked to the colours almost like lemmings in the early days of the Great.

In '*Tempora Mutantur*' the poet is expressing the growing realization among the front-line troops actually fighting in the trenches that they were there under false pretences. If war was turning out to be nothing like they imagined, it seems that they were prepared to mock themselves for being 'conned'.

The young officers in the First World War had been brought up to believe that war was clean, dutiful, glorious and soon ended. When they discovered the extent to which they had been deluded by their background and education, those who survived came home bitter and disillusioned men. They did, however, have victory to sustain them and theirs was the certainty that they had carried out a horrible task with devotion and perseverance; they had 'done their bit' and it was up to the politicians to make Britain into a country fit for heroes and the world into a place where there was no more war. But how did the women feel? Those who had stayed at home and waved their men off to war, who had in some cases actually urged young men away from school and off to the Front with scornful attacks on their awakening virility and the cruel presentation of white feathers, these women were angry and embittered as well. The ladies who had been led up the garden path by propaganda and convinced that 'There was no other way' looked back at the carnage of the First World War with sadness tinged by guilt. Some women, vowing that they must, after the terrible mistakes of male-dominated politics, take a hand in the way the affairs of our country were run, led the demand for women's suffrage. Others forced their way into masculine environments such as the law, the boardroom and medicine. And others devoted some of their postwar energies to erecting superlative memorials to the men that they had lost.

As I drove home from Westwell my car radio spoke of a proposal to send British soldiers to fight – no one mentioned that they might also be killed – in Bosnia. 'It is our national duty to intervene,' the voices urged in a sadly familiar call to arms. I have no doubt that in Germany and Northern Ireland, and in the garrison towns of Britain's standing army, the same stirrings are there in the hearts of the subalterns and junior commanders. 'I hope it's our regiment that goes – please God we get out there before it's all over'; but a British Prime Minister and a British Foreign Secretary will have nothing of it.

Maybe the suggestion of anarchy mirrored in *The Wipers Times*, the awakening determination of women, the increasing tendency of the young to question orders and the power of memorials like the Wipers clock at Westwell are beginning to get through to our leaders. May God be praised.

What do you reckon you're going to do in the next war, 'Arry'?
I dunno – be somebody else's Next-of-Kin I think.